THE BIG O

The Life and Times of Olsen Filipaina
Pacific Revolution Pioneer

Patrick Skene

A catalogue record for this book is available from the National Library of New Zealand

ISBN 978-1-988516-84-4

A Mower Book
Published in 2020 by Upstart Press Ltd
Level 6, BDO Tower, 19–21 Como St, Takapuna
Auckland 0622, New Zealand

Text © Patrick Skene 2020
The moral rights of the author have been asserted.
Design and format © Upstart Press Ltd 2020

All rights reserved. No part of this publication may be reproduced or transmitted in any form or by any means, electronic or mechanical, including photocopying, recording, or any information storage and retrieval system, without permission in writing from the publisher.

Designed by Craig Violich www.cvdgraphics.nz
Printed by Everbest Printing Co. Ltd., China

Cover image: NRL Imagery

For the mothers
Sissie, Patricia, Leslie, Divya, Balamani and Margaret

'A life is not important except in the impact it has on other lives.' — Jackie Robinson

CONTENTS

Introduction: Olsen the enigma		9
1.	The centre of Polynesia	27
2.	A complete footballer and entertainer	64
3.	The one who broke through	86
4.	Free-spirited footballer	117
5.	'I don't like living here. I tolerate it.'	144
6.	The Filipaina Affair	182
7.	Kingslayer	194
8.	Deliverance	229
9.	One of the great mysteries of life	247
10.	The galloping garbo	277
Epilogue: The Pacific Revolution		301
Acknowledgments		326
Bibliography and related sources		328
About the author		336

INTRODUCTION
OLSEN THE ENIGMA

> 'Enigma was often used to describe Olsen in Australia and it's a shit word — it was code for "they couldn't figure him out".'
> — Richard Becht, author, historian, Kiwis and New Zealand Warriors media manager

It's a glorious Sydney spring night and the Wests Tigers are hosting the New Zealand Warriors in the final match of the 2017 NRL season. Both teams are 'also-rans' at the foot of the ladder — equal second last and limping to the finish line of a miserable season. The Warriors, who won just one game away from home all season, are about to lose their ninth match in a row.

Yet there is magic in the air at Leichhardt Oval, the traditional home of the Balmain Tigers who merged uneasily with the Western Suburbs Magpies at the turn of the century to create the Wests Tigers. A few times a year for the past 18 seasons, their fans come together at their old headquarters to celebrate and reminisce about their beloved 'Tiges'.

To walk to Leichhardt Oval on match day is to step back in time. Mary Street is a typical Inner West Sydney street, largely unchanged from its early days as a blue-collar heartland. Humble timber and brick, red-roofed cottages perch tightly on narrow streets and lanes. The streets are manned faithfully by fig, jacaranda and frangipani trees awaiting their call to summer bloom.

Built without any parking and with the surrounding streets blocked off by security, everyone walks to Leichhardt Oval following in the footsteps of their Tigers fan ancestors who have walked this same route since 1934.

The air is larded with the smell of boiled hot dogs, sizzling sausages and fried onions from unofficial hot dog stands, manned by spruikers and none more famous than Francis Drake, a match-day institution on Mary Street for 44 years. He's seen off countless council inspectors and competitors have come and gone, but as a hard-core Tigers fan, Drake lives for Leichhardt Oval footy days.

Every year he and many others are infected with suburban ground nostalgia. It's a yearning for smaller, intimate grounds and the simple pleasure of a tribe uniting on a grass hill. A celebration of a time when rugby league players were of us, among us. They worked in factories, on construction sites, as tradies and as 'garbos', collecting the city's trash.

Following a team provided a depth of meaning, intensity and identity. The players were ordinary men doing extraordinary things and their stories became living mythology.

Drake smiles as a familiar face walks by with a slight limp, a ghost from his early hot dog-selling days almost 40 years ago.

Tigers old boy Olsen Filipaina returns Drake's smile and nods in acknowledgement but keeps moving, keen to slip into the ground unnoticed, his first time back at Leichhardt Oval for more than a decade.

'That guy has sold a lot of hot dogs over the years,' Olsen says with a smile. He continues down Mary Street and while there are many outlandish outfits including some Tigers 'onesies', Olsen is dressed to blend in. Camouflaged in a black and white Adidas tracksuit top, crisply ironed jeans and shiny black dress shoes, he limps towards the entrance.

His aspirations to be anonymous are dashed at the front gate when fans form a gridlock around him, acknowledging an old hero, not with autographs but its digital descendant, the selfie. Olsen meets every request with a smile.

One fan proudly announces that Olsen is still his 'garbo' and that he always comes out of his house to wave as Olsen empties his bin. He was a young boy when Olsen first started his garbage run in Ryde, a community he has faithfully serviced for almost 40 years.

The mobbing fans share their Olsen stories, testing his memory with nostalgic moments. Olsen looks uncomfortable with the fanfare and attention, but he feels the love, saying: 'I don't get down here much, I try to keep to myself. I'm always amazed they still remember me.'

Eventually he enters Leichhardt Oval, a hallowed ground in rugby league. A colourful carnival awaits.

He has returned to his old stomping ground as part of Wests Tigers' 'Legends' game-day initiative in which the club honours its favourite sons from previous eras.

Another prodigal son is also in the house — the crowd swarms around Māori and Tigers legend Benji Marshall who has just announced his return to the club after four years with St George and the Broncos. Benji waves at Olsen and 'The Big O' nods in return and limps on to the corporate function.

* * * * *

As a child, I watched Olsen play at Leichhardt Oval in the early 1980s. He appeared like an intergalactic figure — arrived via a portal from another realm. With an unusual name, dark brown skin, big thighs, flashing Polynesian eyes and a beaming smile, he played an exciting style of rugby league — the silky skills of a back mixed with the power of a forward. In one of his footy cards he wore a necklace of white puka shells in a proud nod to his Pacific heritage. This we hadn't seen.

To see Olsen play the game of rugby league at Leichhardt Oval was to witness a one-man wrecking ball. It was unprecedented for a man of his size to be fast enough and have the skills to play in the backline. He was a living manifestation of force = mass x acceleration and had a unique method of leveraging his size and power to puncture watertight defences.

His suite of physical assets triggered comparisons to a young Aboriginal Arthur Beetson, who showed extraordinary skills for a big man and also first plied his trade in Sydney for the Balmain Tigers at Leichhardt Oval in the late 1960s.

Olsen's opponents in the centres and later at five-eighth would have to contend with a combination of speed and skills that was underpinned by a famous set of big thighs. His powerful-impact game would become his calling card and his thighs his most memorable feature, particularly to those he trampled over.

What made him different to the largely Anglo-Celtic players that came before him was the horsepower he was able to channel from his physical density that seasonally ranged from 95 to 105 kilograms, all piled on a short 5-foot 10-inch/177-centimetre frame.

A nightmare to both tackle and be tackled by, he personified brute force, running over or bouncing off his opponents and creating opportunities for his teammates. His game was built on exceptional strength and power, a low centre of gravity, a love of contact and playing the game with *joie de vivre.*

* * * * *

Tonight the freshly named 'Wayne Pearce' Hill is a sea of orange and black, the traditional colours of the Balmain Tigers who are resuscitated through their fans wearing thousands of old-school jerseys, the older and more faded the more respect.

The same conversations surface at every Leichhardt Oval match. A shared love of small 'boutique' grounds. How the dilapidated facilities, ancient toilets, wooden benches, rickety grandstands and grass hill are a soothing alternative to the cold, commercial product of large-stadium football. How every year could be the last of their sacred shrine. How commercial reality must eventually trump nostalgia.

Each year, Tigers fans are left in a painful state of doubt that their club will be made an offer too good to refuse and be forced to abandon its cultural heartland forever.

Yet Leichhardt Oval has survived the gallows for another year and the tribe is again united, an erratic mix of Balmain's old working-class tribe, new Pacific community fans, inner west hipsters freshly migrated to the area and the Campbelltown, Ashfield and Lidcombe fans of their merger partner — the Western Suburbs Magpies.

As a shared human experience, it's the best rugby league has to offer — classless and egalitarian, newbies and diehards sitting together on a hill pulsing with excitement and joy.

Tonight the Tigers tribe sit cheek by jowl and escape to a time when rugby league was the only game in town. The old-style scoreboard still has its numbers replaced manually by 'Big Baz'. Kids slide on cardboard toboggans like I did 40 years ago. The toilet lines are long and the beer is served in cans. As a living museum showcasing what the game once represented, rugby league will be poorer if the axe drops on Leichhardt Oval.

* * * * *

At a corporate function inside the main stand, Olsen is being honoured by his former club as part of its 'Legends' series. A motley mix of 200 Tigers faithful have assembled including smooth suit-wearing sponsors, dishevelled media men, ex-players and 'life member' fans wearing old scarves and jerseys.

The VIP guest for the night is Sir Peter Leitch, aka 'The Mad Butcher', the patron of the New Zealand Warriors who has flown in for the event and is sitting at Olsen's table. Leitch's history with Olsen runs deep and long, with Leitch first sponsoring Olsen when he was a young, unknown player at the Māngere East Hawks in South Auckland.

Olsen warms to a familiar face and exhales deeply, dropping his guard. Leitch yells out to all in attendance: 'The greatest Kiwi to ever pull on the black and white jersey!'

During the Question and Answer session, one of Olsen's comments stands out for its purity. 'All I cared about was enjoying the game and entertaining the fans,' Olsen tells the audience. 'People saved their money to watch us and the very least we could do was give them their money's worth.'

The young emcee sheepishly concedes that she hasn't seen Olsen play but says her father has great memories of his time at Balmain. Sitting next to Olsen at his table is a sponsor and media partner Alby Talarico, a rugby league fanatic and a television commentator in the Division 2 NSWRL Cup.

Now in his fifties, Talarico is a proud Italian Australian, who was born in Balmain. He remembers Olsen as a destroyer of reputations: 'On his day he had the measure of any man, but that depended on what day it was. He had his lazy days, but he destroyed the king, the prince and the heir-apparents through tough and uncompromising football.'

After dinner Olsen shakes hands warmly with a tall ex-Magpies and Tigers player, Mick Liubinskas, who alongside Tommy Raudonikis were the first players of Lithuanian heritage to play in Australia. Like Olsen, Liubinskas was an outsider with a strange name who found a home at the Tigers and joined the ranks of Balmain's multicultural pioneer players.

Rugby league's longest-serving active journalist is in the house and takes his opportunity to talk to Olsen. Having written columns under the moniker 'One Eyed Tiger' for more than 50 years for *The Weekly Times* in the heart of Tiger country, John Booth is the cultural memory of the Balmain Tigers.

Writing for a local newspaper in Olsen's home area of Ryde, Booth paid extra attention to Olsen and he always featured prominently in his 'One Eyed Tiger' pieces. Sporting an old-school pork pie 'pressman's' hat, Booth gives Olsen a big hug and they greet warmly, with Olsen noting: 'This man took very good care of me.'

Booth had a front-row seat for Olsen's career and summarises his legacy: 'I think he had a big effect and represented his people well — he was the epitome of a good Pacific Islander,' Booth explains. 'He was loved by everybody, generous, a good gentle bloke but hard on the field. He has been an ornament to the game.'

Halfway through the function Olsen is led down the grandstand steps and onto the field by the emcee for the 'Legends' Q&A session. Fans yell out their support and Olsen talks about his fond memories of playing at the ground and how happy he is that the Tigers are still having their matches at Leichhardt Oval.

After the formalities are complete, he leaves the ground and shakes hands with the Wests Tigers captain Aaron Woods who is waiting in the tunnel for the call to run onto the field. Leichhardt born and bred, Woods shakes Olsen's hand and embraces him, yelling out 'Legend'. Olsen worked with local junior Woods when he was playing in the Balmain system at the same time as Olsen's son Quin.

Olsen returns to the corporate function and Gwen Bosler, aka 'the Tiger Lady', comes to pay her respects. Bosler, who is in her mid-eighties, has followed the Tigers since 1947. She proudly declares she once put in an unsuccessful request to have her ashes spread on Leichhardt Oval. Bosler embraces Olsen and tears of joy stream down her face.

'Balmain was once a hard, working-class suburb and people lived for their football,' she says. 'It cured a lot of things for us. No matter what they threw at us during the week, we could wipe it all away on the weekend and our spirits lifted supporting humble heroes like Olsen. It helped us survive.'

Yet there was a darker side to Olsen's five seasons at Balmain. He has gone by many names over the years including 'The Big O', 'The Thighs', 'Archie Bumper', 'Galloping Garbo', 'Kingslayer' and some less than complimentary ones.

Sitting on the Leichhardt Hill I saw and heard the ugliness directed towards him and his Aboriginal teammate Larry Corowa. Vicious names. The first time I heard the words 'nigger' and 'black cunt'.

Walking with Olsen around the Leichhardt Oval Hill tonight, there is only love and affection. Fans stream down the hill to get a selfie photograph with him. Others call out 'The Big O' or comment on his thighs.

An older fan points to Olsen and bellows: 'Last of the toe-bashers', a reference to Olsen's memorable and unfashionable toe-first goal-kicking style, harnessing the power of his thighs to burst through the ball after a two-step run-up.

Olsen finally finds his destination, joining the group of New Zealand Warriors fans, some of whom have flown in from New Zealand. The news travels from ear to ear that a Kiwi legend is visiting them. After a few hugs, selfies and a hongi nose-to-nose greeting with an elderly Warriors fan, Olsen settles in to watch the action.

Olsen says, pointing back towards the crowd: 'It wasn't always nice comments coming from that hill and I am glad to see that part of the Tigers has changed.'

The off-field changes in rugby league, and in particular the reduction in racial abuse by crowds and players, has been brought about in part by changes on the field.

The New Zealand Warriors on the ground tonight are a team predominantly made up of Māori and Polynesian players. But the Wests Tigers too have a distinctly Pasifika feel — six of the starting 13 players can trace their roots to New Zealand or the islands of the Pacific. Sixteen of the 26 starting players from both teams are Māori or Pacific Islanders. The fruits of the 'Pacific Revolution'.

Twenty minutes from the end of the game, Olsen bids goodbye to the fans and limps towards the exit. When one fan asks him why he is leaving so early, one of Sydney's longest-serving 'garbos' replies with a smile, 'I've got to get up at two o clock to do the bins!'

When his body succumbed and he retired from the game, Olsen disappeared into suburban life to raise a family, but the game never forgot him. Myths don't die in rugby league. Every year commentators and fans on television, internet forums, radio and social media bring him back to life, his name ringing down the generations. A Māori friend once told me: 'Olsen's the one the uncles talk about at parties.'

* * * * *

When Olsen made his debut for the Balmain Tigers back in 1980, he was one of just four Polynesian and Māori players of the 331 players in the Sydney competition. In 2017, in the expanded National Rugby League, the Pacific community makes up 48 per cent of the 440 registered players, a total of 212 Māori, Polynesian and Melanesian ancestry players.

Although there were Pasifika outliers playing in Sydney before Olsen such as Māori Henry Tatana, the Fijian Toga brothers and Samoan Oscar Danielson, for many observers, Olsen Filipaina was the modern-day pioneer of the Pacific Revolution. His NSWRL career stats — 107 first-grade matches and 323 points in eight seasons — only tell a fraction of the story.

Olsen played in a time before NRL clubs had sophisticated player welfare programmes including cultural competence training, in-house chaplains, player welfare managers and mentoring programmes. He played under coaches who had no experience in dealing with the unique and fiercely family-centric Pacific players.

It's a different story now. By 2021, the NRL projects that at current growth rates the Pacific and Māori communities will provide the majority of the NRL's elite male player base, a figure predicted to rise to 60 per cent by 2027 according to the NRL's Nigel Vagana.

If a modern-day NRL coach does not know how to bring the best out of Māori and Pacific players, they will soon be out of a job. Cultural competence has become a requirement for any NRL coaching position.

NZRL President and former Kiwis hooker Howie Tamati says it's a non-negotiable when trying to get the best of Pacific players: 'It's really simple. You can't swear, you can't shout. You can't blast them if they won't look you in the eye. You can't disrespect elders. You have to spend time with parents and siblings and build trust. If you don't respect the sensitivities, then you won't get the best out of them.'

* * * * *

From a small base of outliers in the 1970s and 1980s, the Māori and Pacific community is now dominating the major rugby league competitions in the southern hemisphere — the NRL in Australia and the Fox Memorial Cup in New Zealand.

Today every NRL team dressing room has Pacific players and it's difficult to understate the value and excitement they have added in reshaping the game. The power and speed of Semi Radradra, the size and skill of Jason Taumalolo, Benji Marshall's revolutionary passing and 'Benji step', the brute force of Fuifui Moimoi and Sonny Bill Williams.

Powerful and adventurous, they have brought new music, food and passion to the game with other players coming along for the journey.

The Pacific communities have culturally upended the game and provided many new and complex challenges for NRL clubs who have been forced to reconcile century-old Anglo-Celtic traditions and behaviours with a new and diverse group.

This merry band of cultural disruptors have adapted to the NRL's playing structures but have not conformed to a level that would deny them their individuality, physicality, creativity and fun. They have brought with them a distinctive, instinctive playing style that has become a passionate expression of their heritage.

The Pacific Revolution at grassroots and NRL level has its beginnings in New Zealand, and for its Māori and Pasifika peoples, playing in the NRL has become a financial tide that is lifting all boats.

* * * * *

Every October is talent 'hunting season' in New Zealand. The 'source of the Nile' is the New Zealand National Rugby League Secondary Schools Championships which showcases the best and biggest raw contact sport talent in New Zealand.

The teams competing are made up of mostly Pacific Islander and Māori schoolboys. Parents, coaches and players are swamped by NRL scouts, offering high school scholarships and the best coaching and facilities in Sydney and Brisbane.

For NRL recruiters, the new mantra is 'Brown is beautiful' and for the Pacific rugby league players, Australia is the next great island of adventure for an island-hopping people.

Identification of the cream of the young Kiwi talent while still in high school and relocating the players to Australia enables NRL clubs to accelerate the talent development process and fast-track the players into the NRL structures.

The process is a lot more professional today than in earlier times when talented youth were plucked from their parents and surrounded by flimsy support structures with no thought of 'Plan B' if they didn't make it.

Sonny Bill Williams signed his Canterbury Bulldogs contract at the age of 15 on the bonnet of an old ute in front of his Mt Albert state house. From that humble beginning Williams has grown to become one of the world's great sportsmen, the king of the code-hoppers.

Inspired by stories of success like Sonny Bill's, the schoolboy hopefuls step up for the journey like restless flocks of swallows preparing for winter migration. Every year the most promising Pacific and Māori youth strut their stuff in front of cooing scouts, who in turn have their contracts ready for their parents to sign.

The 'brawn drain' is so comprehensive that according to former Kiwis coach Graham Lowe, 800 New Zealand players left to play in Australia at all levels of the game in the five years to 2017.

The 'go west' exodus of young men of Pacific and Māori families to play rugby league has an almost biblical quality and some win the lottery — a long-term NRL career on big dollars that will fundamentally reshape their family's future.

As a sell, rugby league plays well in Polynesian and Māori living rooms. For them it's a game that provides their working-class communities with a voice in the mainstream, a chance to celebrate culture, riches beyond imagination and a perfect outlet for Pacific warrior masculinity.

The Pacific Revolution has had an enormous financial impact on families, their sons exchanging their bodies and skills for foreign currency and immense family pride.

Rugby league has become their vessel of economic mobility and 'millionaire factory'. As a result, a major money remittance market has developed, with players sending money home to relatives to improve their lives in New Zealand and the Pacific Islands.

Former Kiwis player and coach John Ackland has witnessed the migration first hand and offers an insight: 'It is as much about people and families going to Australia for economic reasons as it is a rugby league story.'

The impact of the migration is being felt most in the rugby league city strongholds. Junior representative teams in Sydney, Brisbane, Auckland and Wellington are now almost all majority Pacific and Māori ancestry players.

The social fabric of rugby league is undergoing fundamental change and Australian Kangaroo Aaron Woods is part of the new generation of players who have grown up with the Polynesian community as the core group. A Balmain junior, two of the groomsmen at his wedding were Polynesians and he has always had Pacific community teammates.

Woods says: 'Whoever wants to play rugby league plays rugby league. For my generation we have always had the Poly boys. They are part of the game and what shocks me is how many of them can be as quiet as a mouse off the field but ferocious warriors on the field. They bring their music, food, tattoos and culture and they're not going away. It's their game as much as ours.'

For the rich kaleidoscope of Māori and Pasifika peoples, rugby league has become an engine of economic empowerment — a uniting canoe or waka magically transporting their people to a more prosperous future.

* * * * *

Rugby league is also allowing the Pacific community to tell their story on its own terms. The story of an ancient seafaring civilisation left anchorless after colonisation and ghettoised in Auckland after seeking a better life. They have found a sense of belonging in the sport and their community spirit, cultural energy and amazing history is now part of a global conversation.

Following the breakthrough success of Tonga and Fiji defeating New Zealand at the 2017 Rugby League World Cup, these tiny Pacific nations and their diaspora in Australia and New Zealand have coalesced into a new audience and revenue stream for the game.

Looking to the future, a significant group of Pacific NRL players are now earning enough money from their clubs to forgo the more lucrative test match fees paid by the Australian Kangaroos and New Zealand Kiwis national teams.

For some Australian-based Pacific players, the honour of representing their ancestral culture is more important than playing State of Origin, universally considered the highest form of the game.

No longer a conveyor belt of talent for the Tier-1 nations, at international level they have blossomed into a cash cow and become the new benchmark of passion. They have moved up the value chain from detritus to become central stakeholders with their own needs to be met.

The Pacific national teams are expected to mount a next-decade challenge to the Anglo domination of the international game. The revolution will be fuelled by second-generation Pacific talent schooled in the elite structure of the NRL and returning to play for their ancestral countries against their birth nation.

Sydney Morning Herald journalist Steve Mascord wrote of the Pacific Revolution, marvelling at rugby league's role as the Robin Hood of world sport: 'The Sydney club bosses and northern English overlords who've been running things for generations will have no choice but to sit back and watch on helplessly. They have been focused on G20 countries, but the real progress is being made in Pacific countries who don't have much money. Rugby league specialises in taking from the rich and giving to the poor, even when it doesn't want to. It's in the DNA.'

* * * * *

The Pacific community is now a central part of the NRL, and it is difficult to imagine a time when they were racially vilified or their style ridiculed. Thirty years ago, one man helped change that perception with a display of rugby league that announced the arrival of the Polynesian power game.

Olsen Filipaina was the first Polynesian playmaker to cross the Tasman for the televised era of rugby league. He was the first big-hitting player that also had the skills of a little man. His speed and balance gave him unique power and, combined with big thighs and a love of physical contact, he was the full package.

He could play every position on the ground but was at his best in the thick of the action. And on his day, when he had a coach who knew how to motivate Pacific players, not even the best in the world could stop him.

'Olsen was a pathfinder. The first to show what Polynesians could do,' says Sir Graham Lowe, former New Zealand, Queensland, Manly and Wigan coach. 'Olsen was the face of hope for many Polynesians who were disadvantaged by lack of opportunity. I just love the guy.'

British rugby league historian Tony Collins remembers Olsen Filipaina and his role as a ground-breaker. 'Beneath the big, game-changing personal decisions that have shaped rugby league are thousands of small decisions that also changed the game. We forget that people from working-class communities like South Auckland didn't really travel the world until recently. In England they would go to Blackpool or Scarborough by the seaside for their holidays and would only go abroad if they were in the armed forces. Rugby league gave people like Olsen a chance to travel and see the world and change the game, but he had to take the leap of faith into the unknown.'

* * * * *

New Zealand and Australian fans have varied memories of Olsen. Some saw him as a lazy trainer, rugby league's final amateur, unwilling to adapt to the weekly demands of professional sport.

Others saw him as the last of the free-spirited talents, who played for fun and would rely on his skills and intuition to create opportunities and thrill fans on match day and not leave his best game exhausted on the training ground.

The truth is somewhere in between.

For Ian Heads, rugby league author, journalist, historian and NRL Hall of Fame judge, Olsen was a dynamic new addition to the Winfield Cup: 'I don't think any of us understood Olsen. He had a sense of mystery to the fans to the media to the coaches. He dropped in at an interesting time when a bit more money came into the game.'

Heads knew there were forces at play curbing his natural exuberance: 'They tried to domesticate him, but he was a personality player who was an attraction. Any time you went to a match where Olsen was playing, he was the bloke you were going to watch. If Olsen was playing, he got the turnstiles clicking and you expected the unexpected. He was one of the innovators who threw away the shackles. You had no idea what was going to happen, and it worked for the fans but not for the coaches.'

For Parramatta's Mick Cronin, Olsen was always in their plans when they played Balmain: 'We always did well against Balmain and looked forward to playing them, but we certainly didn't look forward to playing Olsen. He was their danger man and his unpredictability meant you always had a special plan for him. If you couldn't control him, he would make trouble and there is a hell of a lot of players I would rather face than him.'

Olsen's Balmain teammate and captain, Kangaroo Wayne Pearce says Olsen was a mystery: 'Olsen was a hot and cold player, an enigma. On his day he would destroy defences or make game-changing tackles and as captain I would go to him when we were in trouble. On other days he wasn't as effective, and we couldn't work out why. But when he was on, we were always a good chance of winning.'

* * * * *

Olsen's time playing in Sydney is charted differently from a New Zealand lens.

Author, journalist and Kiwis and Warriors media manager Richard Becht has seen it all in New Zealand rugby league. He started covering the game for the *Auckland Star* at the age of 18 in 1973 and the sport has never left his blood.

In addition to reporting on the game as a journalist for 45 years, Becht has authored nine rugby league books including those on Sir Graham Lowe, Gary Freeman, Dean Bell, Tawera Nikau, Stacey Jones and Ruben Wiki. For Becht, Olsen's legacy will be etched in stone for as long as the game is played.

Becht first acknowledges Olsen's role as a Pacific community pioneer: 'He was a trailblazer for the Polynesians. He carried the torch and really came bursting through. Not just as a tough ball carrier but as a skilful playmaker and a destructive creator-provider. I was privileged to see him play a lot and saw the impact he had on the Pacific community.

'Enigma was often used to describe Olsen in Australia and it's a shit word — it was code for "they couldn't figure him out",' says Becht. 'They looked at him in a different light. He had a quality they couldn't fit into their system. They just didn't know how to use him, and he didn't conform to their norm, wasn't one size fits all.'

Kiwis and Norths captain and New Zealand 'Player of the Century' Mark Graham enjoyed playing alongside Olsen: 'On his day there was no better player. If the clubs in Sydney had treated Olsen the way New Zealand did, he could have beaten sides all by himself and he still terrorised them in Sydney despite all the crap. He was a joy to be around and so gifted, he was a sensation at just about everything he tried. We used to joke that Olsen was so good that he could make love standing on a hammock.'

For former All Black Eroni Clarke, Olsen was the chosen one: 'We talk about how we as Pacific people navigated the oceans of the Pacific by just using stars. Olsen was like those stars for us; he dared to open the pathway.'

For Clarke, a man of Samoan ancestry, Olsen's career had a spiritual dimension: 'Olsen gave us permission to dream, express our talent and individuality without conforming and he gifted us a map to navigate through. He dared to try things and was a ray of hope — he gave us fuel to be resilient. He made me proud of who I am and he broke through the ceiling. His achievements were our achievements.'

Olsen's resilience in facing his struggles in Sydney was appreciated by his community says Clarke: 'I thank Olsen because he bore the brunt of the guys who did not want to let us in. We knew the challenges he faced and when he faced them and came out the other side to play that level of football — when I saw that I knew I could get through my challenges.'

Olsen's Kiwis and North Sydney teammate Clayton Friend is clear on Olsen's legacy and the obligations it created: 'We saw what Olsen was going through and he came out the other side. It was our job to finish what he started,' says Friend.

'I'm so lucky I got to play next to Olsen Filipaina and my job was simple. Give him the ball. He was the only player I played with or against that I could honestly say could win a game by himself.'

* * * * *

Although some Australians viewed Olsen as an unsolvable mystery, there was nothing mysterious about him for the bruised and downtrodden Pasifika communities of New Zealand. For them Olsen Filipaina was an articulation of their truth — what it was to be a Pasifika man. Entertaining, tough and humble.

Their ancient Polynesian stories were crumbling and devalued in their new western world and Olsen's transplanted South Auckland Pasifika people needed a new story.

Olsen stepped up and became their first hero. Through his example, their identity would not be erased but celebrated, their buoyant playing style encouraged not suffocated.

The road he chose was one of resilience and non-violence and taking it all with a smile, regardless of the internal damage. He built the foundation brick by brick and although coaches tried to 'cure' him of his true and natural exuberance, he would not be bowed.

Olsen left the enveloping warmth of the Polynesian capital of South Auckland and dropped into an intolerant Australian monoculture that for 80 years had been exposed to one set of ideas and people, hardwired by intergenerational experience.

He battled hateful discrimination from players and fans and showed up and played at grounds that on some days were a treacherous swamp of racists, spewing their vulgar babble about him and his people.

By his very presence Olsen was a disruptor — a vanguard, and to understand his story is to understand rugby league's Pacific Revolution.

1
THE CENTRE OF POLYNESIA

'Successful people don't do it alone. Where they come from matters. They're products of particular places and environments.'

— Malcolm Gladwell, *Outliers: the story of success*

Every rugby league player has their beloved green space — a sacred place where they developed their skills and toughness and made their rite of passage with the local kids.

Before rugby league captured his heart, Olsen Filipaina played bullrush at Sutton Park located directly behind his family home in Māngere East in South Auckland.

Bullrush/Kingasini/British Bulldog has been played for more than a century in New Zealand and is embedded in the national psyche. It was played by both genders in backyards, parks, prisons, beaches, churches, ice rinks and in front of marae.

For New Zealanders it was a simple, egalitarian game — elemental and unstructured. No coaches, hand–eye coordination, complex rules, referees, balls or whistles and everybody, both jocks and nerds, was guaranteed to win and lose.

The game is so culturally embedded in New Zealand that it spawned a celebratory book praising its virtues. In *Bullrush!*, author David Slack interviewed a wide range of old bullrush players from All

Black Josh Kronfeld, who said bullrush was crucial for his All Blacks career, to Prime Minister Jacinda Ardern whose ducking and weaving skills, developed in bullrush, served her well in avoiding media scrums.

Author and journalist Richard Becht says its impact went beyond the playground: 'It's fair to draw the conclusion that it helped prepare kids for collision sports like rugby league and rugby union. After all, it was effectively a tackling game without the ball. There would be a share of bruises and blood and some tears, but the tough kids loved it.'

The bullrush version Olsen and the Māori and Pacific boys of South Auckland played was a distant relative of the *Macquarie Dictionary* definition, with players not gently tagging each other but having to run a gauntlet of murderous tacklers using evasive sidesteps or brute steamrolling power.

Sutton Park also doubled as Olsen's primary school playground, and every school break, 20 to 30 kids would sprint from class to commence hostilities. One would volunteer as the tackler and accompanied by shrieks, laughter and the curdling screams of 'Bullrush', the kids would charge at each other until the bell called them back to class, tired, exhilarated and having let off steam.

If Sutton Park transformed into a survival of the fittest Okavango for bullrush, Olsen was its Lion King and his big hits and bullocking charges left many kids broken in the sick bay.

Nine times out of ten Olsen was the last kid to be tackled and they would all call out his name. He would oblige with a grin and set off towards them, ploughing into the wall of students, causing concussions, bruised lips, scratches, scraped knees and occasionally bone fractures.

Like his rugby league teammates in the future, his wiser friends would follow in the wake of his bullrush runs, knowing gaps would be created in the chaos as he steamrolled and swatted tacklers. For Olsen it was like going into battle, and he counted the hours until he could next play it.

His mother would despair at his ripped shirts and grass stains but could not keep him away from Sutton Park, his magical place at school and weekends. Smart rugby league and union clubs recruited kids out of the bullrush games and a number came to watch Olsen and his friends play.

Olsen made lifelong friends through bullrush and would often head back into the class the hero of the day, which boosted his confidence, respect and mana.

On weekends when he played against the bigger boys from other schools, he learnt that he did indeed have a gift that the others didn't have. Big thighs, a craving for heavy contact and a unique mix of speed, footwork and power.

* * * * *

The joint shaping forces of the Filipaina family were two great cultural phenomena of twentieth-century New Zealand — the urbanisation of Māori, and Pacific Island immigration.

Olsen's mother, Sissie, was a Māori of the Ngāpuhi tribe, the daughter of a shearer. Olsen's Māori grandfather was renowned as the best shearer in the district and was loved and widely respected as a humble peacemaker.

In Northland and other parts of New Zealand, Māori men and women flocked to working in the shearing sheds as a lifestyle that fitted perfectly to preserve the extended family structure of Māori. They worked as a collective group rather than individuals and the group nature of the profession enabled Māori to maintain their communal life.

Māori shearers had prestige and mana throughout New Zealand's shearing history, first with hand shears and evolving to modern electric shears. Leading New Zealand shearing contractor Lee Matson contends that Māori shearers are the best in the world. 'They're very, very good at it. A lot of them, their fathers and grandfathers all shore sheep and they enjoy the camaraderie of the team thing.'

It is also a serious sport and working shearers are super-fit athletes. Māori dominate New Zealand's annual Golden Shears competitions and today they comprise 90 per cent of competitors according to Sport Shearing New Zealand.

* * * * *

Olsen's father, Aloese, was a Samoan immigrant worker and boxer, whose father was a builder. He was the eldest brother in his family in Samoa and had been sent to New Zealand as a 10-year-old on a school scholarship.

A few years after arriving at Whenuapai Airport in Auckland to stay with a New Zealand family and go to school in Grey Lynn, Aloese 'disappeared' up to Northland to cut scrub and clear the land with a roving group of male Samoans. He joined a migration pattern of Pacific Islanders who set up working colonies across rural New Zealand and married into the local populations.

Once the family in Samoa lost touch with Aloese they appointed his younger brother Tausaga as the new family '*matai*' or chief and he still performs the duties from his home in Sydney.

'He went missing and we thought he was dead,' says Tausaga Filipaina. 'There was no internet or mobiles and the New Zealand police knew nothing. We had to move on as a family and it was very sad — somebody had to step up to perform the ceremonies and I was next in line.'

In Northland, the ancestral home of Ngāpuhi, Aloese met Sissie Lemon and the two fell in love, married and started a family.

Their son Olsen Orekewa Filipaina was born under a cabbage tree on 23 April 1957, behind a farm shack on a dirt road in Awarua, Kaikohe, deep in the rolling green hills of Northland. When Olsen came into the world, he already had a brother, Joe, and would be followed by four more — Alfred, Jerry, Philip and Ray

* * * * *

Northland occupies the northern tip of the North Island of New Zealand and holds a special place in the foundation of both Māori and

Pākehā (European) culture, a joint historical rollercoaster covering war and peace, hatred and love.

This warmer area of the country was settled early by voyagers who sailed some 4000 kilometres from eastern Polynesia, and it was also among the first European settlements. Northland is the site of New Zealand's first capital, first pub, first shipyard, first hanging, first treaty and first civil war.

Ngāpuhi, who have lived in Northland for an estimated 800 years, are the largest, most famous and infamous Māori iwi or tribe. History records an extraordinary group of warriors, traders and diplomats that at various times brought the Māori nation, the British Army and the New Zealand colony to its knees.

For Ngāpuhi, intertribal war was an ancient sport and exercise for their men. Hostilities were conducted in an eerily similar fashion to a rugby league season. It was governed by a strict code of honour. A schedule was drawn up in advance including the agreed battle sites and times. Battles were to be conducted in broad daylight with no ambushes and prisoners were exchanged.

War was also a seasonal affair, as warriors from both sides could not be spared from working in the kūmara (sweet potato) fields for more than a few weeks, before returning to their wives and families. Hostilities were often limited to the two best men of each tribe in one-on-one combat with traditional weapons, like a couple of five-eighths or props squaring up in a rugby league match.

It's little wonder rugby league is so popular among Ngāpuhi Māori, and today Northland is a rugby league heartland including their own rebel breakaway league — Tai Tokerau Rugby League.

The community is joyfully proud of Panguru's Adam Blair, the latest Ngāpuhi captain of the New Zealand Kiwis, but he was not the first Ngāpuhi to put on the captain's armband.

That honour belongs to Olsen Filipaina. Other captains with Ngāpuhi blood include greats of the modern era Ruben Wiki, Stacey Jones and Jesse Bromwich.

Ngāpuhi stars in the NRL include the New Zealand Warriors Tohu Harris and young guns James Fisher-Harris and Corey Harawira-Naera.

* * * * *

It was the Ngāpuhi leaders in 1835 who, representing an independent nation, negotiated terms with the three great Pacific colonising powers — France, Great Britain and the United States. Ngāpuhi selected Great Britain as their guest and partner, allowing them to use their land as a base to explore the Pacific.

It was Ngāpuhi leaders who first signed the Treaty of Waitangi in Northland's Bay of Islands with Great Britain in 1840 and who declared war on the British for breaching the treaty, triggering the Northern Wars in 1845.

Of all the Indigenous nations who were colonised by Europeans, Ngāpuhi were among the shrewdest and most adaptable, closing technology gaps and often beating the British at their own game.

* * * * *

The Northern Wars were made up of five separate battles between the British forces and a Ngāpuhi guerrilla army. Led by Te Ruki Kawiti, a 70-year-old grey-haired Ngāpuhi chief from Olsen's hometown of Kaikohe, the army declared war on the British and defeated them in four out of the five battles, including slaughtering 114 British soldiers at the Battle of Ōhaeawai.

Kawiti, nicknamed 'The Duke' by the British, was a master strategist who employed innovative tactics, including trench warfare. Hopelessly outmatched in technology and numbers, he lured the British into his masterpiece forts at Ōhaeawai and Ruapekapeka to defeat them convincingly.

Kawiti's men were proficient in the use of muskets and he had obtained his armoury of weapons trading flax and produce with the fledgling government at Port Jackson, which would later become Sydney.

In Sydney, Kawiti had witnessed the Eora Aboriginal people pushed to the margins and felt only a show of force would prevent the same fate befalling Ngāpuhi.

At the end of the Northern Wars, Ngāpuhi returned to their lands undefeated. James Belich, the pre-eminent historian of the Northern Wars, concluded: 'In one war the wrong side is still said to have won.'

* * * * *

The fighting spirit of Ngāpuhi was in full bloom a century later when the 'Gum Diggers' (so called for the Northland kauri gum diggers) terrorised the Germans in the Second World War. The Gum Diggers were part of the famous and distinguished 28th (Māori) Battalion who were a fearsome force that included many farmers, cowboys, shearers and stockmen. They received more individual bravery decorations than any other New Zealand battalion and took on the Afrika Korps with unrivalled ferocity.

There is no higher praise than from your opponents and German Field Marshal Erwin Rommel's chief of staff, General Siegfried Westphal, is reported to have said, 'Give me a Māori battalion, and I will conquer the world.'

Olsen's mother came from fighting people.

* * * * *

Whānau, or family and extended family, is everything in Ngāpuhi country. Land was shared and harvesting from the land and bush was a family affair, each having their favoured fishing sites and eel weirs, kūmara patches, berry trees and hunting places to feed their family and trade with other whānau.

The kaumātua or elders were revered for their knowledge and wisdom and had a key role in nurturing and teaching culture to the young. The centre of Ngāpuhi and all Māori existence was mana — respect and authority.

Olsen's mother Sissie Filipaina was part of a deep tradition of wāhine toa ('warrior women') — proud and resilient Māori women who participated centrally in Māori culture including as matakite, or seers.

She could swim, fish and hunt better than any of the boys and could always guarantee a feed for her family. And she would never accept an insult without a fiery response with words or fists.

Her family was swollen with pride when she graduated from Northland Agricultural College and Olsen's cousin Ben Lemon remembers a 'lovely-natured woman' who could also be a 'livewire' that was staunch, fiery and loyal.

Yet Olsen grew up knowing little about the greatness of his Ngāpuhi ancestors. In 1960, when he was just three years old, his mother and father left their farm in Awarua, packed the family car with their belongings and drove south along the brand-new Auckland Northern Motorway in search of work and opportunity.

There was an economic miracle taking place in the major cities of New Zealand, and the Filipainas, along with tens of thousands of Māori, wanted a slice of the action. The Māori felt it was their birthright to be part of the riches being made through industrialisation on their land. After all, they were equal partners with Pākehā, according to the Treaty of Waitangi.

Mass migration from country to city stripped many Māori families of the cream of their youth, and for some Ngāpuhi, the move was the first disconnection from their land in several hundred years.

For the Filipaina family, Auckland was a place of magical beauty — a subtropical, fertile paradise ringed by over 50 volcanoes and cradled by the South Pacific Ocean and the Tasman Sea. It was a city of blinding optimism.

It was also, increasingly, the arrival point for thousands of Polynesian migrants from Samoa, Tonga and other Pacific Island nations. Intermarriages between Māori and Pacific Islanders thrived in this new cultural potpourri as other couples joined Aloese and Sissie in creating a new blended Pacific generation.

* * * * *

For the new Polynesian migrants, the transition to Auckland's cold winters was tough. Many yearned for the tropical paradise they had left behind. In addition to their traditional lavalava clothing they brought with them Fa'a Samoa and Anga Fakatonga — the Samoan and Tongan codes of living.

Much more than food, song and dance, these new migrants brought with them a 3000-year-old proven cultural operating system in which family needs are always placed above those of the individual.

The men were unchallenged monarchs and the children's sworn duty was to assist their parents. Money was saved and sent to their home islands to improve the lives of their families. In their new and unfamiliar South Auckland home, disparate families bound together tightly to survive in their new land.

Similar to the Māori 'migrants' when they first moved into Auckland with their big families, the Polynesian newcomers experienced friction in their dealings with the forerunner of Housing New Zealand. In Samoa, their standard house was a fale — a traditional cyclone-proof, open home with no walls in which all family members slept together in one room. Orientation over privacy. The small three-bedroom houses provided to the Pacific migrants by Housing New Zealand quickly filled with extended Polynesian family, leading to accusations of overcrowding.

Education, too, was not designed or culturally friendly to the new Māori and Polynesian migrants. In 1960, one year after the Filipainas settled in Auckland, the New Zealand Government released 'The Hunn Report' which identified that the incoming Māori had lower levels of education and skills and were being forced into blue-collar, low-skill jobs like road maintenance, construction, factory work and meat processing and freezing works.

Despite these findings, the Hunn Report concluded that the Māori people were to be encouraged to move from the remote country areas into the towns and cities where they experienced the trap of exclusion, alienation and marginalisation.

In Hunn's world, only the 'fittest elements' of Māori culture would survive 'the onset of civilisation' and create a new blended culture. Communal Māori culture would give way to the European model focused on the individual, creating a new breed of 'brown Pākehā' or 'plastic Māori'. The chief battleground of this cultural war was the school, noted by Hunn as 'the nursery of integration'.

The Eurocentric school syllabus, which, for example, taught students that New Zealand was discovered by Abel Tasman, rather than the great Polynesian navigator Kupe, created great cultural confusion in the home for Māori and Pacific students.

The cultural war was fought on many fronts. Olsen and his brothers were told that their mother's people, Ngāpuhi, were lazy criminals, uneducated cannibals and murderers.

They were advised to keep quiet about their Māori heritage and focus on their Samoan side. Although Sissie spoke fluent Māori and Aloese also spoke it well, having learnt it in the fields of Northland, English was commonly spoken at home.

'Mum and Dad sort of had a discussion, for want of a better term, around speaking Māori and Samoan,' recalls Olsen's brother Alf. 'My dad wanted to teach us Samoan, and the grandparents on my mother's side wanted to teach us Māori, but they had a discussion and it was decided we would learn only English.'

To assist with their integration, the freshly minted Auckland Māori and Pacific migrants were 'pepper-potted' — scattered throughout the city by the housing authorities, blending into the Pākehā suburbs and preventing a concentrated enclave from forming.

Still, discriminatory landlords refused to rent to new Māori and Pacific families due to their reputation for overcrowding and big extended families, forcing authorities to create public housing estates in the outer suburbs.

Auckland was a city in transition. New greenfield suburbs began to eat up the farmlands on its urban fringe, while a new working-class army of Māori and Pacific labour muscle built the suburban dream. Working gangs built bridges, roads, houses and laid power and telephone cables to house the new shiny, happy Aucklanders.

The growth was dizzying. Across the city, politicians cut ribbons to open new housing estates. After living in some temporary housing organised by the Māori Housing Board, the Filipaina family joined other Māori and Pacific families in one of these new suburbs, Māngere East.

'Where we lived, on Tennessee Avenue, there were hardly any houses and a lot of it was farmland and market gardens,' says Olsen. 'It was still mostly white people back in the day, then came the Māori, then the Samoans and Tongans and then the gangs. It was always on the move and blending in new ways.'

Few could have predicted that the acres of Chinese market gardens that became the suburb of Māngere East would produce some truly world-class athletes — Jonah Lomu and Frank Bunce in rugby union, boxing heavyweights David Tua and Joseph Parker, UFC legend Mark Hunt and rugby league heavyweights Jason Taumalolo, Roger Tuivasa-Sheck and Olsen Filipaina.

* * * * *

After settling into Māngere East, Olsen's mother Sissie found employment as a machine operator at Fisher and Paykel and his father Aloese as a fitter and turner at Pacific Steelworks. They worked hard alongside their Pacific and Māori brothers and sisters to build a better life for their families.

And waiting with open arms for this new brown working class was the game of rugby league.

* * * * *

To understand the why of rugby league, the epicentre of the story is the tough industrial north of England. One summer's night in 1895, 22 Northern English rugby union clubs met at The George Hotel in Huddersfield and agreed to break away from the southern English Rugby Football Union to create the Northern Union, eventually renamed rugby league.

The split was based on the unmet needs of mill, mine, factory and wharf workers, who played rugby union on weekends in front of big crowds and wanted fair compensation for wages lost through playing time or injuries.

These 'broken time' payments were sneered at by the southern England-based rugby union authorities who were making good money from gate receipts but were not fairly servicing their northern working-class players.

The Northerners were the best players in rugby union and generated the biggest crowds, much larger than the southern clubs. They asked for their fair share but were ignored, and as a result they broke away and started their own game.

Rugby league, originally the sport of white, working-class outcasts, spread south across the equator through trade union and other working-class networks and was embraced by working-class communities in Australia and New Zealand.

The first official rugby league match in Auckland was played in July 1909, and from the outset Auckland was New Zealand's hotbed of the 13-man code.

Sir Dove-Myer Robinson, the Mayor of Auckland from 1959 to 1965 and from 1968 to 1980, was an avid rugby league fan. He never played the game due to his tiny frame and glasses but was passionate about it, supporting it wherever he could. As a Jewish migrant from England, he believed Auckland was 'the finest city in the world . . . a place of salvation'.

'Whatever the city might be to New Zealand,' he said in 1971 with an eye to the future, 'it's the centre of Polynesia with the largest Polynesian population in the Pacific. Its people are Pacific people. And it is to the Pacific that Auckland's future might belong.'

Like Robinson, the new Pacific residents of Auckland found a welcoming home in rugby league. For Māori, Samoan and Tongan men, the rugby league club was a place of relaxation, a support network of cross-cultural friendships and employment opportunities. A place to pull out the guitar and sing songs and escape the harsh reality of the working week. A place to be themselves.

In Auckland, rugby league had been the game of the white working-class men of the factories, the wharves, the freezing works, building sites and breweries, which provided a fertile recruiting ground when the Māori and Polynesians began to work alongside them.

'For those urban Māori born and raised in the city it wasn't long before they were attracted to rugby league,' explained Hemana Waaka, a veteran sports broadcaster in a documentary on Auckland rugby league. 'There are many Māori playing rugby league in Auckland. Why? Because of the excitement and satisfaction it offers to players and supporters.'

Dual Tongan and Kiwi international Duane Mann says the attraction for the game was instant for new Polynesian migrants who embraced a unique platform to express themselves. 'Polynesian players are suited to the game because of the contact and there's flair in both attack and defence,' explains Mann.

'The essence of being in a team and the culture within clubs itself exists. There's a distinctive rugby league culture, a psyche. It is grass roots and blue collar and that's the attraction for salt of the earth people.'

The new Samoan and Tongan migrants in South Auckland were invisible in New Zealand mainstream life. They were a strong and proud people and yearned for an outlet to 'show their stuff'. Rugby league gave expression to that strength and allowed them to enter the conversation.

* * * * *

In 1964, when Olsen was seven years old, the Beatles world tour, led by John Lennon and Paul McCartney, hit Auckland like a meteor, sending the city into a fever. For the citizens of Māngere, though, an event of far greater importance and impact broke new ground for the community.

The Māngere East Rugby League Club took its first breath, sending out a surprising 14 teams to play in its inaugural year in the Auckland League.

Foundation President Jack Neal was overwhelmed with the response to the call-out for players and said in the local press: 'It was beyond our wildest dreams. We thought six to seven teams would be a good result. It proved that Māngere East was ready for and wanted a rugby league club.'

Māngere-raised David Lange, who served as New Zealand Prime Minister from 1984 to 1989, was one early supporter, acknowledging the game's role in building Māngere's civic identity.

'Māngere East was developing a character of its own and stopped being a dormitory for Ōtāhuhu and Papatoetoe,' Lange wrote in the club's 40th anniversary publication. 'Four-bedroom houses proliferated and migration from the countryside was overtaken by arrivals from the Pacific. The place became alive with young people.'

Lange openly admired the club's journey and purpose: 'Through the ups and downs the club has kept its character. Countless young people have been nurtured in comradeship and fitness. Local youngsters have gone on to become greats of rugby league. The Club is a major community asset.'

When the Māngere East club appeared, Olsen signed on immediately. 'My mates told me that I should come and play for Māngere East because you get a hamburger and Fanta after the game.'

Proudly wearing his Māngere East jersey, he found an outlet for his energy, power and natural hand–eye coordination. He was smitten with rugby league.

'Olsen was already a big Islander boy and they couldn't tackle him from the earliest ages,' says Gary Kemble, a Kiwis teammate who also played alongside him in South Auckland junior representative teams. 'You knew then he was a top-quality player — he had hand–eye skills and physique and we were all in awe. Add to that his temperament. He never got angry, was always calm and relaxed. He was great to be around.'

Dane O'Hara, a 36-test Kiwis legend, played alongside Olsen from a young age in South Auckland all the way to the Kiwis and remembers an extreme talent: 'Olsen just knew from the earliest age. He was one of the most unselfish players and even when they bottled him up, he created opportunities for others.'

For O'Hara it was more than just flair: 'He had a genius for the game from the start. When running hard at the line, he somehow knew where the gaps were. When he chipped over the top, he had already factored in everything, where the fullback was, where to land it. It was an artist practising his artform, separate to everyone else on the field. What a pleasure and an honour it was to play with him at all levels.'

'My first memory of Olsen was being 10 years old and playing at Sutton Park,' says Philip Beasley, who played alongside Olsen as an Auckland Under 12 representative. 'Everyone wanted to be on his team for league or bullrush. We called him "thunder thighs". No one could tackle him. It was brutal and he embarrassed a lot of bigger kids.'

* * * * *

Māngere East Rugby League Club continued to grow and finally found a permanent home when they were allocated Massey Park in 1972. Olsen remembers walking barefoot on ice in the coldest of winters to training at Massey Park when he was 12.

It's an ironically named park, deep in working-class territory and honouring Walter Massey who owned the original farm in Māngere and was a former New Zealand prime minister, Freemason and renowned anti-Catholic.

Massey was famous for using 'Massey's Cossacks' — a squad of brutal strike-busting special constables, mostly farmers and farm workers, to break up workers' strikes in 1913. He was loathed by the urban working class of his time, precisely the community that surround and use the park today.

* * * * *

In 1973, a year after their move to Massey Park, Māngere East welcomed

Sir Peter Leitch and his alter ego 'The Mad Butcher' into the club as their main sponsor. This chance occurrence would change Olsen's life.

Leitch grew up in a working-class suburb of Wellington, the son of a Scottish coal miner, and he left school at 15 to work as a gravedigger before training to be a butcher. He opened his first butcher shop in Māngere and famously went on to build a national chain of stores dotted around New Zealand, becoming a celebrity as the face of the 'Mad Butcher' commercials.

Leitch got to know the Pacific and Māori communities over time through his involvement with the club: 'I made a lot of good friends at the Māngere East club. I'm a working-class man and they were good people, not pretentious or from silver spoon families.' Leitch was knighted in 2010 for services to business and philanthropy.

Olsen and Sir Peter Leitch have one of the great and enduring rugby league friendships, the best type in rugby league that brings people from all walks together. However, Olsen's first memories of Peter weren't rosy.

Olsen remembers: 'We used to go into his Māngere shop to buy some meat and Peter would say, "Hey! Here's big Mama, what can I do for you today",' referring to his mother Sissie's then hefty frame.

'I used to think: who does this guy think he is calling my mum that? I remember thinking, "I'll get you when I'm big for saying that to my mum",' Olsen laughs. 'But I never did!'

Over time Leitch would give Olsen cheeky comments which Olsen remembers with a smile: 'He would start having a joking go at me but after a while he started giving me free small sausages and I changed my tune. I would go in there when I was hungry and he'd give me all sorts of stuff. In the end I told him he could call me or my mum whatever he liked.'

Leitch's involvement evolved from supplying meat raffle prizes, to becoming the major sponsor of the club. He saw something different in Olsen: 'He was a natural from the very start. Nothing could bother him and some days it was like he was floating above the other kids — in a world of his own.'

Leitch helped out Olsen's family with whatever they needed for his league career — boots, petrol money, food and accommodation for representative games.

For the 'Mad Butcher' it was Olsen's humility that was his most special characteristic: 'I've helped over 200 players over the years and Olsen is the only one who has never asked for anything, no tickets, nothing. Not one time. His mother raised him to be a humble boy with a beautiful personality.'

One Māngere East prize night, a young and shy Olsen took the microphone and presented Leitch with a trophy in return to thank him for his support. Olsen had visited the trophy shop and had the trophy made from his own money. 'What kid does that? I've still got that trophy in my house,' says Leitch.

* * * * *

Saturday, 26 June 1971 was the day Olsen began to believe in New Zealand rugby league.

As a 14-year-old he witnessed a rugby league miracle at Carlaw Park with almost 14,000 other fans, when the heavy underdog Kiwis destroyed the Australians 24–3, a team that was captained by Immortal Graeme Langlands and included superstars Bob Fulton, Bob McCarthy and John Sattler.

'We got free tickets from the club and watching them play live was like a dream come true,' recalls Olsen. 'I wanted to be out on the field with them but being so young I knew I had to wait my turn.'

Led by Polynesian captain Roy Christian, the Māori Orchard brothers and the super boot of big Māori prop Henry Tatana, this gang of amateur Kiwis would be the last team to defeat Australia at Carlaw Park until 1985. But it gave Olsen belief: 'I saw as a youngster with my own eyes that the Aussies were beatable, even with our part-time guys. It got me thinking.'

* * * * *

Olsen's nickname in high school at Ōtāhuhu College was 'Horse' because he ran so upright and could generate serious horsepower in his bullrush charges. His talent was noticed early by both the club and school system and by 1972, at the age of 15, he was selected as the captain of the New Zealand Secondary Schools rugby league team.

That he was identified as leadership material so early shows the mana he had developed even at schoolboy level. In a world based purely on enjoying the game and expressing your creativity, young Olsen was the king.

The photo of the 1972 Kiwis Schoolboys team in the *New Zealand Rugby League Annual* betrays little evidence of Olsen's thoughts, only a little wild-haired teenage boy sitting in the front row with the hint of a smile — the captain of his country.

Olsen remembers his pride at the appointment: 'I was really proud of that and I didn't expect my name to be called out. I was pinching myself that it was real. My mum taught me to take everything in my stride, but it really was an honour. I took it seriously as well because there were boys older than me in the team. In my captain's speeches it was the first time that I had expressed myself verbally.'

Olsen's hero in high school was a rugby union player, the original 'Mr Big Thighs' — Samoan-Cook Islander Sir Bryan 'Bee Gee' Williams who broke into the All Blacks in the 1970s and was the first Pacific community mainstream hero in New Zealand.

Olsen says: 'I learnt my sidestep from watching "Bee Gee" play on television. At halftime I would go straight outside and work on his moves. I was using that same sidestep and swerve the next match for Māngere East and it worked. He was different to the other guys.'

He saw himself in Bryan Williams: 'The whole community was buzzing that there was a Polynesian with a new style of attack and for me it was so exciting.'

* * * * *

Maternal love was a core feature of Olsen Filipaina's upbringing. His mother Sissie harboured a deep and protective love of her children and was not a woman to be messed with.

Sissie drilled values and principles into her boys on a daily basis. Being self-centred, selfish or lazy was not good. Too much self-confidence and arrogance would be their downfall. And, above all, show humility and respect to elders and their tūpuna before them.

She ran an open house characterised by the Māori concepts of aroha and manaakitanga — the daily practice of compassion, respect, kindness and hospitality. The house doors were never locked and guests were treated as royalty.

'Sissie nicknamed me "Bones" and was on a mission to fatten me up,' says Olsen's childhood friend Philip Beasley. 'After playing footy we all used to go to the house, the Filipainas and the Beasleys and others, and there she would be at the door with a smile and she would say, "Come in, son." Then she would put four dozen eggs in a roasting dish and lots of toast and we would eat the whole lot.'

If people abused Sissie's hospitality, though, her voice would deepen and her face harden.

Those that crossed the line would incur the wrath of utu, the Māori principle of reciprocity defined by New Zealand anthropologist Joan Metge as 'anything received should be requited with an appropriate return'.

Sissie would breathe fire and declare utu when one of her boys was wronged. During one match at Ellerslie in Auckland, when Olsen was being mercilessly abused by one of the opposition fans, Sissie was sitting close by and told the fan to be quiet.

When the abusive fan condescendingly dismissed her, Sissie confronted him and knocked him down with a right hook in front of hundreds of people.

Olsen recalls watching the scene unfold while on the field: 'I saw my mother move towards the guy and we just knew what was going to happen.'

Neville Kesha, a New Zealand international referee famous for his on-field disagreements with Wally Lewis, remembers Sissie well. If

Olsen was being penalised or targeted, she would let the referees know during and after the game.

'Once her blood was up, she was into you,' says Kesha. 'After one Māngere East game, we were having a few quiet beers when Sissie stormed into the club and chased one of my touch judges around the table. For a big woman she could really move.'

Kiwis teammate Howie Tamati remembers Sissie's verbal presence at test matches: 'Playing at Carlaw Park you were very close to the crowd, but it didn't matter how much noise there was, you could always tell exactly where Sissie was. Every time Olsen got tackled hard or penalised you could hear her!'

Sissie's wrath extended beyond the football ground. Olsen remembers going with his mother down to see future Prime Minister David Lange at his electoral office in Māngere and Sissie giving him a fiery lecture about local issues.

Olsen recalls a mother who changed personality when her boys were playing sport: 'Mum was very protective at any match involving one of her boys. In summer when we didn't play any sports, she was a completely different person. Big, passionate and happy-go-lucky.'

Olsen's teammate Philip Beasley remembers Sissie coming into her own after a Māngere East loss: 'Sissie would come into the change rooms afterwards and say, "Big Mama Cass is here. It's not the end of the bloody world," and she would go to each player and talk to them until she got a smile. What an amazing and unique woman she was.'

Sissie enjoyed buying meat for the family at the Māngere butcher shop owned by Sir Peter Leitch. 'Whatever the situation, the more you gave her the more she gave you back,' he says of Sissie. 'Good or bad, take your pick.'

Leitch remembers Sissie as a legend of the club and Auckland rugby league. A woman that was tough as nails. He recounts with a smile a story of the Māngere East Australian tour to play sister club Ryde Eastwood Hawks in Sydney. As part of the post-match celebrations, one of the Ryde Eastwood players, their drinking champion, challenged the Kiwis to put their best man up for a drinking contest.

The challenge was met with silence until Sissie stepped forward. Leitch says: 'Their guy laughed out loud, but we were delighted to put Sissie up against him. We knew. After four or five hours he fell apart and slowly sank into his chair. Anyone that was there could never forget it and she drank right through the night, laughing and celebrating. She was hard.'

* * * * *

Aloese, meanwhile, was an intimidating father, prone to unpredictable violence. Drunk and often having squandered his money gambling, he would return home and beat Sissie.

'Every community in New Zealand had a "Jake the Muss",' explained actor Temuera Morrison, who played the terrifying Māori father, street fighter and wife beater in the award-winning New Zealand film *Once Were Warriors*. For the Filipaina family's patch of Māngere East, Aloese Filipaina was their Jake 'The Muss'.

Sissie's smile and generous hospitality masked the dark secret of the house — while providing safe harbour for many, she had no refuge from a terrifying internal force. Olsen and brother Alf don't remember when it started, but they both have memories of huddling in fear, terrified at the noises coming from the bedroom.

By day, Aloese was an unassuming hard worker who rarely spoke. He held a steady day job and he could also be charming and fun at family gatherings. But alcohol and gambling were his twin demons and the kids were always wary when he was drunk. He could switch moods at any time, resulting in a family living in fear.

'We all got walloped by my father,' says Olsen. Some of the Filipaina family believe Aloese had unresolved anger that he projected onto his sons and wife. Anger at being abandoned, at being sent to Auckland on his own as a young boy and due to his loss of status in South Auckland.

Others say that his discipline was a core part of the Fa'a Samoa living philosophy in which men are absolute family monarchs and brutal disciplinarians.

Like many Samoan fathers, Aloese enforced the tough love code of Fa'a Samoa on his sons. He couldn't control what happened outside the house in Auckland, the stresses and indignities of migrant life. But he could control his own boys. The control would be reinforced through beatings.

Once, when Olsen was a teenager, he ran away from home — unable to cope with the violence any longer. He lived away from his parents for the first time, got inked with some street tattoos and rolled with the local gangs. Eventually, his brothers were sent out to fetch him, convincing him to return home.

What followed was the most horrifying event of his life. Aloese, enraged at the mutinous breach of his household authority, locked himself in a room with Olsen and proceeded to beat him to a pulp. 'Today,' Aloese told his son Olsen, 'is the day I'm going to kill you.'

The violence and murderous rage were so brutal that Olsen's older brother Joe kicked the door down and bravely rescued his younger brother. 'My father was possessed by the devil that night and Joe saved my life,' says Olsen. 'I will always be grateful to Joe, but I never forgave my father. I couldn't believe he would try to kill me.'

Olsen wasn't alone in dealing with a tough and brutal Polynesian father. There is a Samoan saying, 'Ua usiusi-fa'ava'asavili', which translates as 'To obey like a canoe before the wind'. For those sons who didn't obey, it could be a miserable existence.

Olsen's Kiwis teammate Fred Ah Kuoi offers an explanation based on identity confusion: 'Samoan fathers carried a lot of anger and frustration. Now they have left Samoa, their kids don't know who they are. Are they Palagi or Samoan? Our fathers know that the roots of culture hold you steadfast or you become a lost tribe. They try to recreate Samoa here and sometimes it doesn't work. It's all they know and all their dads and granddads knew.'

Dual league-union international Israel Folau shared his experience with his father in an interview with the PlayersVoice website: 'I was intimidated by my dad. He was strict in the way most Polynesian fathers are and I was scared and shy in the way most Polynesian sons are. Polynesian kids are taught from a young age to respect their elders to the point of not talking to them, even if they really want to say something. And you are never to look them in the eye.'

Father–son relationships in Polynesian families are complex. In a Sky NZ documentary titled *The Anger Within*, All Black Jonah Lomu spoke of brutal fistfights with his Tongan father and domestic violence in their Māngere home.

Lomu said: 'When Dad got angry and wanted to bash us, she [his mother] would get in the way and she would get beaten up quite badly. That is tough to take. It built up a lot of things inside of me.' Lomu would make peace with his father and forgive him before he passed away.

In MMA legend Mark Hunt's book *Born to Fight*, he details his Māngere East upbringing under his brutal Samoan father. All the neighbours were scared of Hunt's father, and he ran a regime of terror, making his own children beat each other and beating them himself with a washing machine hose.

Hunt wrote about the impact of his father's transition from Samoa to New Zealand where the promised land of milk and honey evaporated: 'We were kings there, but not down here. The old man was God in that house with a wrath that could equal any ancient vengeful deity. The only authority figure that meant anything was the old man's fists.'

Their life in South Auckland was an endless struggle, with Hunt reflecting on the deprivation: 'If there were any board games or holidays or trips to the movies or the rugby or the museum, or anything that parents and little kids do together, then I don't remember them. All I remember about that house is a shitload of beatings and what felt like endless days of hunger. We were hungry as street dogs.'

Oscar Kightley, a Samoan-born comedian, actor, writer and director, has viewed the Polynesian father syndrome from all angles. 'When we came to New Zealand we learnt shame for the first time,' he says. 'A lot of people expressed that shame in different negative ways, some with violence, others with alcoholism. In Samoa it is simple — the man is supposed to provide and if he can't, it's deeply shameful. They had hard-core upbringings in the Islands. We got bad hidings, but our dads got worse.'

It's little wonder that some Polynesian males are sometimes referred to as 'lifelong mummy's boys', a consequence of an inextinguishable obligation to the nurturers — the mums, grandmothers, aunties and sisters who gave them refuge and comfort from the strict discipline of their fathers.

Sir Peter Leitch agrees that in his experience most Polynesian players have an inseverable link to the women in their life: 'I won't name him but there is one Auckland Warrior who still sleeps in the same room as his grandmother. No one teases him — it's seen as a good thing.'

* * * * *

For many disconnected Polynesian youth, marginalised on the fringes in South Auckland, gang culture replaced tribal traditions. Gangs pooled angry young men together, creating new tribal units and providing a release to prove their manhood.

The suburbs of Ōtara and Māngere became dangerous places where territorial gangs roamed the impoverished housing estates mimicking African American inner-city gang life. Polynesian brotherhood took a backseat when the Sons of Samoa and Tongan Lynch Mob would clash on the streets, big men clubbing each other for bragging rights.

A shared love of rugby league brought some gang members into the orbit of the Filipaina family.

'Back then if you were in a gang it was a very serious thing,' says Olsen. 'Once you're in, you're all in. You're "patched" and you can't get out. We all knew who they were. We had them 200 metres down the road. They were doing it to build confidence, strength in numbers and get a new whānau. A lot were from bad situations, but my parents drank with them and played darts with them so we were sweet. Ours was a rough area, like a ghetto. Very, very hard and lots of very tough men, but none scarier than my father.'

From the outside, South Auckland in the 1970s was synonymous with government benefits, crime, poverty, drugs and danger. From the inside, resilient communities were developing, but their youth faced an identity crisis.

On the return trips to Samoa, some that had lost their language and culture felt inadequate and disconnected. They were caught between two worlds. On the Samoan side they were branded as not an authentic Samoan — 'fia Palagi' ('wanting to be European') — and on the other side they were derided as 'not real New Zealanders', an ancient and proud community ridiculed as 'coconuts' or 'FOBs' (Fresh off the Boat).

The yearning for identity gave birth to a new blended Polynesian urban culture. New Pacific families were created as many went outside whānau, Fa'a Samoa and Anga Fakatonga to marry and start new mixed-community families from eight Pacific sub-communities — Māori, Samoan, Tongan, Fijian, Niuean, Cook Islands and Tokelauan and with the broader Pākehā/Palagi community.

Intermarriage was producing afakasi (mixed ancestry) children automatically bound to a broader Polynesian identity. This new cultural phenomenon was based on shared location, mixed gene pools, ancient kinship and a common enemy — discrimination and racism.

And the newly formed and blended community had a name — Pasifika.

* * * * *

For Pasifika communities, the violence in the home was compounded by terror inflicted by the state. On 12 December 1975, Olsen's first year out of high school, a conservative government led by Prime Minister Robert 'Piggy' Muldoon swept to power.

With New Zealand experiencing an economic downturn, Muldoon pandered to his conservative base by promising to toughen up on crime and 'crack down' on a convenient scapegoat, the Polynesian migrants.

His government's first tool of community repression and removal was the now infamous police 'Dawn Raids' to catch visa overstayers.

From previously being encouraged to join New Zealand's miracle economy, Polynesians were suddenly targeted for arrest and deportation. For Muldoon's conservative supporters known as 'Rob's Mob', their beloved leader was faithfully executing a key election promise built around a racist campaign linking Polynesians with crime, taking jobs, violence and overcrowding.

To conservative voters and politicians, the Pacific migrants had outlived their usefulness and were to be removed like a noxious weed. Police stormed into houses with sniffer dogs, dragging overstayers out of their beds and bundling them into cells at Mt Eden prison with hardened criminals. Some community members went 'on the run', putting great stress on family networks.

The raids traumatised and outraged the Polynesian community who were officially made to feel like outsiders. The racial bias was there for all to see. It was later confirmed that Pacific overstayers totalled only one third of the Auckland total — the majority were British, South African and Australian migrants who were not targeted.

In the second phase of the strategy, the police tactics evolved from the dramatic Dawn Raids to randomly checking the identification of Pacific-looking people on the streets. The checks bluntly targeted brown men and grouped Polynesians and Māori together as one.

Aloese Filipaina had already experienced a prelude to the Dawn Raids in the early 1960s. 'My father was an original Samoan overstayer,' recalls his son Alf. 'They chased him out the back of our old home up north, well before the Dawn Raids, and he lived in fear until they stopped. In contrast, my father-in-law was English, and he was an overstayer and he happily lived through the Dawn Raids. Not even a phone call.'

Olsen tried to concentrate on rugby league but still could not escape the police attention. 'No matter what you did, how well you behaved, it was a matter of time before you got talked to — the questions kept coming. Where are you off to? How far are you going? What are you doing out so late? I thought to myself — what have we done to deserve this?'

Oscar Kightley, who later directed a play called *Dawn Raids*, believes the policy drove a wedge through New Zealand society. 'The Dawn Raids struck fear into Pacific Islander households, and families hid in terror of separation. Muldoon came into power spreading fear and we were the bogeymen that everyone was taught to be scared of. It was a painful time to be a Pacific Islander and it made us feel like we weren't New Zealanders. We were outsiders.'

In effect, the raids and label of 'overstayers' had an unintended consequence of cementing Pacific and Māori relations, creating an even deeper Pasifika fraternity.

And in Olsen Filipaina, a rising star for Māngere East Rugby League Club, this new Pasifika community would soon have its first sporting hero.

* * * * *

During his early high school years at Ōtāhuhu College, Olsen Filipaina played rugby union for the First XV on Saturdays and rugby league for Māngere East on Sundays. He was not an academically inclined student. 'The only subject I passed in all that time was science,' he told the *Sydney Morning Herald*, 'and that was because it was multiple choice.'

While Olsen was not known for his academic prowess, he became popular through his rugby union performances. Ōtāhuhu College First XV teammate Tua Saseve remembers him as a natural: 'Olsen was one year below me in school, but he was a standout talent and had already been identified as a future star in rugby league.'

For Saseve, Olsen was something different: 'Olsen lived for playing. Every school break he would be out playing touch with his classmates. And he carried himself in a way that he never got into fights. He was a class act even back then.'

Olsen's leadership extended from the playing fields to the school yard when he was made a prefect of the school: 'I was honoured but really it was because I was one of the biggest and they wouldn't listen to the Pākehā prefects,' Olsen says. 'I would take the kids' smokes and give them a big lecture and then smoke them myself. Back then everybody smoked; it was like you were crazy if you didn't.'

* * * * *

In Olsen's final year of high school, he finally achieved his dream of playing at Carlaw Park when Ōtāhuhu College defeated Mt Albert in the newly introduced secondary schools rugby league competition.

The memories of that day will never leave Olsen: 'We were the underdogs but when I finally got on that ground, when I finally got to play on Carlaw Park, there was no way I was going to lose.'

Ōtāhuhu College were crowned champions and Olsen remembers a spiritual moment as he walked off the ground: 'I remember thinking this is my home. This is the ground that I can make a mark for me and my family. This is my ground.'

* * * * *

The war between rugby union and rugby league in New Zealand had been raging long before Olsen stepped onto the battlefield. From 1909, the very first year of organised rugby league in New Zealand, rugby union administrators have engaged in childish tactics to thwart the 'other game'.

In 1927 the *Auckland Rugby League Gazette* reported its frustrations with its 'elder brother' rugby union's stranglehold on school sport: 'Those enthusiasts who have undertaken to establish League among the younger generations are having a pretty rough time at the hands of some of the headmasters'.

Rugby union was the golden child of the British upper-class school system, and it became the chosen sport of the New Zealand National Party and its rural and middle-class constituents. The political battle lines were cleanly drawn with rugby league's natural alignment with the working-class Labour Party and its attendant trade unions.

From the outset, the New Zealand rugby union establishment used its significant political influence to collude with local councils and deny the rebel code access to parks and big stadiums.

In Auckland, where rugby league was at its strongest, the Auckland Rugby Union was forced into introducing rebel rule changes — known as 'The Auckland Rules' — to improve the speed, running and dynamism of the game and to counter its new exciting competitor.

Rugby union's global disdain for rugby league's existence was on full display when the British Lions rugby union team toured New Zealand to play the All Blacks in 1930.

When the Lions Tour Manager James Baxter was asked why rugby league was so popular in Auckland he famously replied: 'Every town must have its sewer.'

Replicating the English experience of containing the growth of rugby league at all costs, New Zealand rugby union's main strategy was to dominate school sport.

To enforce its monopoly in schools, the New Zealand Rugby Union had on its side a vast unpaid army of foot soldiers, from principals to schoolteachers.

In lockstep, they waged a passive-aggressive campaign to keep rugby league out of schools and ensure the best physical talent was forced into the All Blacks pathways and talent funnel.

The prejudice that existed towards rugby league was primarily one of class. Howie Tamati, Olsen's Kiwis teammate and President of New Zealand Rugby League, remembers rugby league players being seen as 'unclean' by the rugby union establishment.

'If you played even one game of league and wanted to play union again, you had to beg your way back in to be reinstated by a local rugby union board,' says Tamati.

'You had to go through a cleansing process, like you had been contaminated. I will never forget we were once having a game of touch footy when a father of one of the kids came over and dragged his son away by the ear, muttering that he couldn't be tainted by league. It was a class thing — a form of racism, prejudice and bigotry.'

There were other factors that left rugby league under siege in New Zealand, including not having the benefit and validation of the 'muscular Christianity' movement that flourished in Australia in the early twentieth century.

'Quite simply, Australia had the Catholic Church behind rugby league and we didn't,' says Tamati. 'It was huge in Catholic schools in Sydney and Brisbane, a big factor in its growth that not many people talk about.'

Despite a century of obstruction, Tamati believes rugby league will always hold its own in the code war: 'League survives in New Zealand because it is a game for the people.' In his opinion, 'educated farmers have always dominated rugby union and although it looks diversified, you peel it all back and it's still the same'.

* * * * *

One man that experienced a unique view of the New Zealand code war is John Hart who served as the All Blacks head coach from 1996 to 1999 and crossed the tracks to serve as Executive Director of Football at the Auckland Warriors from 2006 to 2011.

Hart did his best to traverse the 'sharp divide' between league and union, noting the fault lies squarely with the 'arrogance of rugby union'. He has lived through the 'Code Wars' and has no doubt as to the motive: 'Prior to rugby union going professional in 1995, there was always the great unspoken fear that the pro game would swallow the amateur game, and union would do whatever it took to prevent people playing league.'

Former Kiwis coach Sir Graham Lowe heard many stories from his players about the league–union apartheid. He says: 'There was a class system problem in the old days. If you played rugby league you were an outcast at school. Some of my players had to clean toilets if they didn't play rugby union on a Saturday.'

Mark Graham, Olsen's Kiwis captain and voted New Zealand Player of the Century, notes a strange time: 'Being a rugby league player in New Zealand was like being a leper.'

Clayton Friend, Olsen Filipaina's halfback in the famous 1985 test series, had a frustrating high school experience: 'They got me into the principal's office and told me I have to play rugby on Saturday. I said no and he pulled out the strap and threatened me with it and I jumped out the window and ran back home. I was exhausted and my mother was furious. She stormed into the school, dragged the principal out and tore strips off him. I was so proud.'

Cook Island Māori Stan Napa was a talented footballer who won a Brisbane Rugby League premiership with the Norths Devils and had four games with North Sydney in the NSWRL before a knee injury ended his career. His league genes live on through his son Dylan Napa who plays for Canterbury Bankstown and Queensland State of Origin teams.

Stan Napa was a schoolmate and friend of Olsen's at Ōtāhuhu College and remembers the pressure from rugby union. He recalls sitting at the back of the class with Olsen and the other 'league rebels'. 'They wanted us to focus purely on First XV rugby union, but we loved league and wouldn't let it go. They seemed to take greater delight in caning the league guys, bending us over the ping pong table and whacking us.'

For Kiwis legend Darrell Williams, the war between rugby league and union was waged with unfair tactics.

'I've got a black spot in my heart for rugby union,' says Williams, the first Kiwi or Pasifika player to win a Winfield Cup premiership, which he achieved with Manly Warringah in the 1986 NSWRL competition. Of Samoan ancestry, Williams was a promising talent in West Auckland when the local rugby union officials came around on a recruitment drive.

Williams remembers: 'They took a bunch of us young guys to a building in Massey and gave us a huge spiel on rugby union. Then they showed us a 30-second video of the vicious fist and head-butt fight between Newtown's Steve Bowden and Manly's Mark Broadhurst. They said to us, that's what rugby league is all about. Don't play it.'

In the old days, Williams says rugby league was blocked on many levels: 'Amco Cup games were shown at one o'clock in the morning and we would all be bleary-eyed the next day. In the Sunday papers there would be one little column on league, five pages in. Even when I played for the Kiwis under Graham Lowe, we couldn't publicly socialise with the All Blacks. They were so cruel against people who were playing a game they loved. I can't forgive them.'

* * * * *

Little has changed in the modern era according to veteran NRL player agent Dixon McIver. A proud Māori, McIver played for the London Broncos in the English Super League and returned to New Zealand to set up a player agency specialising in progressing teenage talent into the Warriors and Australian NRL clubs. He notes: 'Rugby union is still putting the same pressure on kids that they always have and there is no one that can stop them.'

For McIver, the school principals and sports masters are the villains: 'Can you believe I've got kids I am working with now who are told to go to another school if they don't play rugby union.'

The social impact of rugby union's pressure on Māori and Pasifika families is real for McIver: 'The parents are upset, the kids are upset. It's an infringement of human rights — a clear legal case. These schools just care about squeezing whatever they can out of the boys, winning their First XV competitions, and don't care whether the kids kick on or not after school.'

* * * * *

Rugby league was not played in New Zealand high schools until 1973 — a direct result of the efforts of rugby union to retard the growth of its 'mongrel cousin'. Yet under pressure and popular demand, a number of schools were forced to open their doors to the 13-man game.

Ōtāhuhu College, a rugby union school, decreed that students could play either union or league, but not both. Officials from the school drove to Olsen's family home in Māngere East to secure his, and more importantly his parents', commitment to rugby union. They could sense, perhaps, that Olsen was an All Black in waiting.

'Olsen was an absolute standout in rugby union,' says Joe Stanley, a legendary All Blacks international and captain who played 27 tests. Stanley played alongside Olsen in junior rugby union representative teams and at 16 was selected with Olsen in a New Zealand schoolboys Allstars team picked from all of the schools in New Zealand.

'He was known for being a big skilful guy,' Stanley says. 'Off the field I loved being around him and on field I would follow in his wake and feed off the devastation and carnage.'

Stanley would never forget playing union with Olsen: 'When the All Black players would watch league games together, Olsen is one of the players we all agreed would have been a certain All Black. It would have been a tough decision for him not to continue because he was so naturally good at it.'

As it turns out, it wasn't Olsen's decision to make. Under Samoan and Māori traditions, the parents make all major decisions on behalf of their children.

When Olsen was 16, his parents Sissie and Aloese were presented with an ultimatum by Ōtāhuhu College rugby officials in the living room of their home in Tennessee Avenue.

If Olsen wanted to continue to be eligible for Auckland Rugby Union representative teams, he would have to exclusively choose union over league.

For Aloese, rugby union was a game for the Palagi, a rich man's game and a strictly amateur sport where you couldn't earn money. If any money was earned, in his experience it certainly wasn't reaching the Polynesian community. He had a preference for the speed, toughness and excitement of league, and he watched all of Olsen's games, garnering respect in the community for being Olsen's father.

Olsen remembers the suspense of having the school rugby union coaching staff at his house and his father coming into his room to tell him that he had selected rugby league.

For Olsen there was a clear reason underpinning the decision: 'Peter Leitch had a lot to do with it. If I had gone to union, we would have let him down and he did a lot for our family. He donated meat for funerals, birthdays, weddings and always covered my footy costs. We got nothing from union, and it was my father's way of thanking him.'

Rugby union was also shamefully tied to race politics. For decades the All Blacks had selected all-white or predominantly white players for tours of apartheid South Africa in an effort to appease their racist hosts.

Rugby league, on the other hand, was a game developing close bonds with the Māori and Pacific communities.

Aloese, a proud Samoan, could see what league offered his people as well as the tangible assistance and love that Olsen had received from Māngere East Rugby League Club.

If they wanted a decision, rugby league it was.

'And that was that. I was a leaguie. I just did what I was told,' says Olsen. 'The funny thing is that we rugby league players were painted as the mercenaries who could never return to rugby union for accepting money.'

For Olsen and his league peers, the reality could not have been more different: 'But none of us were earning money from playing. Little bits came in to help with travel or boots, but we were mostly paid in meat or beer. The rugby union guys earnt way more than we did and walked into good jobs. We used to have a great laugh about that — we're the pros but we're all poor!'

* * * * *

And so began the rise of Olsen Filipaina rugby league footballer, and his ascendance coincided with the start of a golden era for rugby league in Auckland. In 1974, the committee of the Māngere East club signed a sister-club relationship with the Ryde Eastwood Hawks from Sydney.

Māngere East officially adopted the 'Hawks' nickname, and an annual 'Hands Across the Sea' match between the two clubs was established.

Māngere East Hawks, which had been stripped of its illegal poker machines by the police in 1975, were strapped for cash and Olsen was paid beer and travel money for his efforts. To make ends meet, he entered the workforce doing odd jobs making trailers, driving forklifts and manning a garbage collection truck.

* * * * *

Nineteen seventy-six was a breakout year for the free-spirited Māngere East Hawks who became the new entertainers of Auckland Rugby League, scoring a record 98 tries across Senior and Premier grades. They also won the Hands Across the Sea trophy against the Ryde Eastwood Hawks for a second year running.

Olsen, at 19 years of age, won his first of four consecutive Māngere East player of the season awards and was the only Māngere East Hawk to be selected for the Auckland representative team.

Olsen's future Kiwi mentor Sir Graham Lowe was coaching the Ōtāhuhu Leopards in 1976 and remembers first seeing Olsen: 'I wasn't alone in being excited about this new kid with big thighs and big hair. We were all excited about his explosive power combined with great skills, style and grace,' says Lowe. 'More than that, he brought his own enjoyment to Auckland rugby league and it was refreshing.'

Olsen brought another unique quality — a permanent smile while he was playing: 'That smile of his, most photos have him smiling but some people took it as evidence of not concentrating or taking it seriously,' says Lowe. 'That smile disguised what a threat he was — it was a deadly smile. A smile of a man doing what he was born to do.'

In 1976, the Fox Memorial Cup was on the move. New Zealand journalist Richard Becht recalls the competition moving to the next level: 'When Olsen first arrived on the scene, the Fox Memorial Cup represented the heartbeat of the game in Auckland — and Carlaw Park was the stage on which it could thrive. And thrive it did. Lights had been erected just the year before and would prove a boon by opening the way for weeknight games as well as extended Saturday and Sunday fixtures.'

* * * * *

Out of the primordial brown soup of South, West and inner-city Auckland came the embryo of a Pacific rugby league revolution. In 1976, Olsen was Māngere East's leading try-scorer, while future Kiwi internationals Samoan Fred Ah Kuoi and Tongan Kurt Sorensen played starring roles for Richmond Rovers and Mt Wellington. Richmond's Toa Fepuleai, a Māori-Samoan flyer, won the Tetley Trophy for top try-scorer of the season.

The Polynesian addition to the talent pool also translated to international success in the cross-Tasman Amco Cup, when Auckland defeated Brisbane's Redcliffe 30–5 at Lang Park in Brisbane.

Auckland were subsequently knocked out by eventual champions Balmain, but by then it was already clear that something special was brewing in the working-class, mixed-race Pasifika ghettos of New Zealand's capital city.

Richard Becht was a journalist for the *Sunday Star* at the time and remembers Olsen being on the front line in the changing of the guard: 'It was in this era when there was an influx of Polynesian people into Auckland and into rugby league. They loved the game and were built for it. It took little time for Olsen to explode on the scene with his lethal mix of pace, power, aggression and wonderful ball skills.'

'You knew something big was happening back then in the mid-70s when the Pacific community arrived in our game,' says Sir Graham Lowe.

Lowe found it refreshing and what rugby league in New Zealand sorely needed: 'Like any change, there is a few hiccups,' says Lowe. 'But if you're not careful and don't reinvent yourself you become stale. They brought the flair.'

In addition to the skills and power, the new Pasifika players brought a previously missing ingredient. 'Rugby league was an intense, hard game in New Zealand and the Pacific players brought with them a magic serum,' contends Lowe.

'One of the most important things that Olsen and guys like Fred Ah Kuoi brought to our game is that they reminded everyone that it's a game, not life and death. That was a very important new element.'

The impact of the Pacific players was felt equally off the field. In rugby league clubhouses, in supermarkets, in churches, Lowe remembers a people filled with cultural energy that loved to sing and dance — that had a 'spring in their step'.

'They impacted the Pākehā community and brought out some special qualities in us working-class white boys,' added Lowe: 'We generally didn't have confidence to dance and sing in front of people but even the shyest Pacific guy would step up. They brought in new music to rugby league and both communities were getting to know each other through our game.'

Lowe felt the first heat and light of a phenomenon: 'They brought in some magic and it was a surprise to nobody in New Zealand when they started making NRL teams in Sydney — they seemed made for it, like it was their revolution, their time to shine.'

* * * * *

According to Olsen, the Pacific Revolution began during those pick-up games in the parks of South Auckland, where sidesteps and fends were honed against bigger boys and feats of physical strength were performed at great personal risk.

'Anyone watching us play bullrush at Sutton Park,' Olsen says, 'could have told you that Polynesians were coming in rugby league.'

2

A COMPLETE FOOTBALLER AND ENTERTAINER

'Olsen Filipaina is the most sensational and startling footballer we have seen for years.'
— George Rainey, Auckland and NZRL Rugby League Chairman 1972–92

Playing alongside men as a teenager had hardened Olsen Filipaina. At 19 years of age, he had been through an initiation period at Māngere East Hawks and was now comfortable mixing it in Auckland's Fox Memorial Cup — the toughest club competition in New Zealand rugby league.

'He was full of energy and never seemed to tire,' recalls Byers Beazley, a Māngere East clubman who would often pick up young Olsen and drive him to games. 'He loved that he could contribute to making grown men happy.'

It was a new world of rough language, cigarettes, gang tattoos and unbridled masculinity. Olsen's teammates were seriously hard working-class men.

'I was still a school kid and they definitely took me into a man's world,' Olsen later remembered. 'Teammates like Alan Popata, who was a hard-core gangster, he was a man you didn't mess with. One time he was coaching a team and couldn't get them to start training. He went over to his car and got a shotgun and sure enough they were doing their drills quick smart.'

What set Olsen apart was his playing style. He was physical and confrontational in a new and unique way. He would pull off powerful hits and run at defences with great velocity courtesy of the biggest set of thighs in the league, attached to a 100-kilogram frame.

For a big man, Olsen had speed over the first 20 metres and just before he would crash into defenders, he would do a signature stutter-skip to increase impact.

'That little skip step was straight from bullrush, like a power punch, before you bump into them or run over the top of them,' Olsen says. 'Then I would use my thigh strength to keep powering forward. I loved being physical.'

There was another reason that Olsen stood out. Rugby league players of the previous era were overwhelmingly white and clean-cut with standard short back and sides haircuts. Olsen would stand out in the centres, waiting for the ball to entertain the crowds; and he presented a new prototype to the Carlaw Park faithful.

With his socks pulled down to his ankles, thick 'kauri tree' thighs, big fuzzy hair, a permanent grin and a big moustache, he became an immediate fan favourite, a seemingly untameable force.

He could drink until the early hours of the morning and still be the man of the match, further contributing to his legend and mana. If league was a religion, he was indeed Auckland's chosen one.

Olsen had been always a permanent fixture in representative league teams. He captained the New Zealand Schoolboys, was selected for the Junior Kiwis and in 1976 broke into the strong Auckland team for the Australasian Amco Cup tournament.

But if 1976 was his breakthrough year, 1977 was the season in which Olsen Filipaina was recognised as the rising star of New Zealand rugby league. It was the season in which he became a full international and the season in which he had his first real taste of success.

His meteoric rise peaked when Olsen was selected for his beloved New Zealand Kiwis to play in the World Cup. 'When they read out my name it was like getting hit with a brick, I couldn't believe it,' Olsen says. 'I had put in hard work and so many people had helped me to get there. Kiwi internationals just didn't get picked from a little club like Māngere East. It was a dream.'

* * * * *

The Kiwis' first match of the World Cup against Australia was a reality jolt. On Sunday, 29 May 1977 at Auckland's Carlaw Park, the Kiwis were defeated 27–12 by a rampaging Kangaroos side.

Olsen was picked as a centre in his debut match, and tasked with marking Michael Cronin, a legendary point-scoring centre who played club football for the Parramatta Eels. Cronin would later be nominated by Olsen as the player he admired the most and that gave him the most trouble across his career.

The defeat, Olsen later recalled, highlighted the gulf in quality between amateurs and professionals. 'I couldn't believe how fast it was. It was like a blur playing against guys you'd only heard about. All of a sudden, I was tackling Mick Cronin, Tommy Raudonikis, Graham Eadie, John Peard. It was the first time I'd played against such talent.'

Despite the convincing victory, Cronin remembers Olsen as a standout young talent. 'He always gave us a tough time even from the first time I lined up against him in his first test.

'Even then, my early memory was his size and low centre of gravity. When you saw him get the ball and move towards you, it was going to be rough as he was hard to handle. If you went low you were wasting your time, so I had to try and go high and try to annoy and wrestle with him.'

It would be a disappointing World Cup for New Zealand, who would also lose to Great Britain before registering an eight-point victory over France. But for Olsen, who missed the final match against France, it marked the beginning of a golden decade in which he would go on to play 29 tests and 50 overall matches for his country.

On a personal note the match had been positive — he had made his parents proud and played alongside his hero, Dennis Williams, a flamboyant Samoan-Māori five-eighth. 'He was on a mission to do great things,' says Williams. 'Wherever he played he was an asset. I tried to take him under my wing and give him direction.'

* * * * *

For the Māngere East Hawks, Olsen's selection for the Kiwis was a milestone moment in the club's history. A player produced by their humble club had pulled on the black and white Kiwis jumper for the first time.

After he had made his test debut, family, friends and fans gathered at a function at the Māngere East League Club to celebrate Olsen's achievement. At the function Olsen took the microphone and, in a rare public speaking moment, paid tribute to those who had helped him along the way.

'Olsen got up and started talking about this bloke who helped him out, this great guy who had done so much for him,' recalls club patron Sir Peter Leitch. 'He said he wanted to repay this man by giving him his first Kiwi jersey. Everyone was murmuring and looking around wondering who this person could be. Well, you could have bowled me over with a feather when he called out my name. When he gave me that jersey there were tears in my eyes.'

In the years to come, more Māngere East players would follow in Olsen's footsteps and play for the Kiwis. The walls of the clubhouse would be decorated over time with headshots of those club players who wore the black and white of New Zealand: brothers Joe, Iva and Tea Ropati, George Mann, Lesley Vainikolo, Jerry Seuseu, Alaimatagi 'Ali' Lauiti'iti, Frank-Paul Nu'uausala, Shane Cooper, Sam Moa.

Olsen, the man crowned as Māngere East's 'greatest player', still takes pride of place. 'We've had 11 Kiwis play for the club, but Olsen sets the benchmark, he was the first,' explains Tasha Tasmania, the Māngere East Hawks chairperson.

'He is a man unto himself. You can't compare him to any other league player — we still haven't seen anyone to match him.

'Back in 1977 it was a very small and tight-knit community and we were so proud of his legacy,' Tasmania adds.

'He set the platform for other Māngere East players and we are especially proud of the determination of that proud Māori/PI man for breaking down the barriers and sacrificing himself for the young ones to follow.'

As well as being selected to make his debut for New Zealand, Olsen was a key member of the giant-killing Auckland representative side that, over three gloomy nights in June 1977, defeated the might of Australia, Great Britain and France.

Three days after making his test debut for New Zealand, Olsen lined up in a midweek game for Auckland against the Kangaroos at Carlaw Park. Alongside him were a motley crew of 'long-grass' amateur footballers, thrown together from the club sides of Auckland's Fox Memorial Cup.

Captained by legend Dennis Williams and including future New Zealand Player of the Century Mark Graham, the Auckland representative team were a random group of part-timers including a garbage man, printer, salesman, mechanics, freezing workers, an insurance agent, ditch diggers and two policemen.

Olsen, a 'garbo' at the time, crossed for the first try of the night, evading several Kangaroos tacklers to score between the posts. There was a sense of excitement in the air as 9000 Aucklanders witnessed their team beat the Australians 19–15 in one of the very first matches to be held under floodlights at Carlaw Park.

The players, all of whom were accustomed to beer money as their payment, had the pot sweetened by a promised $500 cash win bonus by one of the team sponsors. One report in the *Auckland Star* subsequently claimed that the Auckland team 'had 500 good reasons for hanging on to beat Australia'.

The second match in Auckland's historic 'Grand Slam' took place against Great Britain on the following Tuesday night. The Sunday prior,

Great Britain had comprehensively beaten New Zealand in the World Cup match — the Kiwis fielding seven Auckland players, including Olsen, lost 30–12. And yet Auckland salvaged Kiwi pride by slugging out a four-point victory over Great Britain in the Carlaw Park mud.

'Again, Auckland produced what the Kiwis have no idea of doing — imaginative, positive play and with it, a sticking, courageous defence,' reported Richard Becht in the *New Zealand Rugby League Annual*. 'It was too much for the Kangaroos and the British faltered to the same approach losing 14–10. Auckland had succeeded where New Zealand couldn't.'

The following Tuesday, Auckland completed the 'Grand Slam' treble in a rousing 17–0 victory over France. It was a historic achievement, never to be repeated. Of the 19 players who played for Auckland in the three historic matches, 14 would play for New Zealand for a total of 245 caps, five were named Kiwis captains and three would be inducted into New Zealand Rugby League's 'Legends of League' Hall of Fame.

Eight of them — Olsen, Gary Kemble, Mark Graham, Fred Ah Kuoi, Kurt and Dane Sorensen, Stan Napa and Dane O'Hara — would make the leap from amateur to the professional game and play internationally in Australia or England. This Auckland giant-killing team of 1977 provided the nucleus of New Zealand's rising golden generation.

On the night of the final victory over France, however, the celebrations were muted. 'We had two beers and all went home,' says Olsen. 'All of us were up early for work the next day and just glad not to be injured and miss work. We didn't really understand how big it was back then and it has gotten bigger over time.'

* * * * *

Of the 19 players in Auckland's 'Grand Slam'-winning squad, Olsen Filipaina was the youngest and the most exciting prospect. Reporters hung on his every move.

After returning to play for Māngere East in the Fox Memorial Cup, he single-handedly destroyed Maritime, a team of tough-as-nails wharfies. The match report in the *Sunday News* was headlined: 'Big Olly mows Maritime down'.

The *Auckland Star*, reporting on an Olsen-inspired Māngere East victory over the Richmond Bulldogs, called him 'the star attraction of the Auckland Rugby League'.

For all of Olsen's youthful talent, however, Māngere East were not the best side in Auckland. That title belonged to Ōtāhuhu Leopards, coached by Sir Graham Lowe, who defeated Richmond Bulldogs in the 1977 Grand Final — one of three trophies won by the club that season.

Despite Ōtāhuhu's dominance, Olsen tormented the Leopards' defence in their matches against Māngere East. Graham Lowe knew he was watching a once-in-a-generation superstar. 'We tried to poach Olsen for Ōtāhuhu because he was absolutely unstoppable, but he was seriously loyal,' he recalls. 'If we had him, we were guaranteed a dynasty.'

Olsen's brilliance in 1977 was widely recognised by his peers. 'A bumping, bruising, crashing centre, standing 5ft 9in and weighing just on 15 stone, he was a constant thrill every time he touched the ball,' reported the *New Zealand Rugby League Annual* on one of his matches against Ōtāhuhu.

'Ōtāhuhu had a much-vaunted defence but Filipaina proved the tackle-hungry Ōtāhuhu players were mere mortals when he had the chance to run against them in the champions of champions. His hip-bumping style — and he is a superbly balanced runner — made him the most difficult man to stop in Auckland. At the age of 20 there is a lot more excitement still to come from Filipaina.'

After one dominant match the *Auckland Star* carried a match report titled: 'Filipaina in unstoppable mood' on a game in which he tore the heavily favoured Richmond Bulldogs apart:

'Yesterday 20-year-old Olsen Filipaina almost singlehandedly eliminated last year's grand finalist Richmond from the Roope-Rooster Cup 42–21.

'Filipaina sealed the victory in the space of seven minutes when he scored two tries, the first coming from a 50m burst in which he bumped, fended and bounced off a series of defenders. Richmond could never figure how to stop Filipaina in full flight. In the end it seemed the only safe way would be to throw a net around him.'

* * * * *

By 1978 Olsen had earned the nickname 'Archie Bumper' — a play-on-words reference to the American sitcom character Archie Bunker. It paid tribute to his 'pinball' bumping style, which saw defenders bounce off when trying to tackle him.

Olsen had perfected a unique way to break defences and by charging and bending down at the point of contact he could blend hips, shoulders and thighs into a powerful unified wall of flesh with devastating results.

Future Kiwis teammate Howie Tamati will never forget his first exchange with Olsen, playing against him in a representative game for Central against Auckland in a trial match.

Tamati remembers his moment of first contact: 'I was the hooker in the middle of the park and he charged straight at me and I caught his thighs and went over onto my back. I'd never been hit with that sort of power ever in rugby league. It was like a train had hit me.'

One standout memory for Tamati is cursing his Central teammate for kicking the ball straight to Olsen. He remembers screaming at the perpetrator: 'Don't kick it to him!'

From a young age, breaking the line was Olsen's strength and it continued into senior football. He could break defences but also defend, attack, kick bombs, chips and 'grubbers' and create opportunities on all sides for teammates.

His reputation was beginning to spread beyond Auckland to Australia. On Wednesday, 24 May 1978, Olsen was the star player in Auckland's 36-point Amco Cup thrashing of Riverina, a representative side from south-west New South Wales.

The match took place at his future home ground, Leichhardt Oval in Sydney, and for the first time, Australians began to take notice of New Zealand's dynamic young centre, who won a $750 colour television for his efforts.

'Filipaina was brilliant and unanimously won Man of the Match,' reported commentator Ray Warren in the *Big League* magazine. 'He is built very strongly, possesses a great turn of speed and his acceleration is blistering.'

* * * * *

Olsen's dynamic form meant he was one of the first selected for the New Zealand Kiwis' 1978 tour of Australia to take on the Kangaroos in a three-test series. Immediately he became the subject of intrigue among Australian reporters.

In the week before the first test in Sydney, Olsen agreed to be interviewed by *Rugby League Week* reporter Brad Boxall, telling him: 'I don't like publicity . . . especially interviews', and that he was unimpressed by Sydney. 'I haven't liked what I've seen so far,' he said. 'I wouldn't like to live here at all.'

Boxall was intimidated by Olsen and after completing what he termed 'the shortest interview of my life', Olsen told him that there were more important things in life than rugby league. Disillusioned, Boxall 'shuffled off to the pub to cry into my beer':

'I thought of all the hopefuls who would go without a year's pay to play first grade in Sydney and gladly die for a chance to wear the green and gold. What if all those lads thought the same as Filipaina, a player who caught the imagination of NSW fans with a slashing Amco cup display for Auckland against Riverina. Go to the tests and watch him play and you'll see why it would be such a crime if he was allowed to float away from the game in a few years. He's strong enough to bust a tackle and fast enough to beat it and isn't averse to scoring the odd try or three. Tommy Bishop, coach of those Illawarra whiz kids, reckons he's the best centre he has seen since Fulton. Others merely say Filipaina's brilliant.'

Many years later, Olsen recalls the interview with Boxall with a smile. 'I never liked doing media, I just wanted to play,' he explains. 'Halfway through the interview his jaw dropped from happy to sour. I thought, "What's wrong with this bloke?"'

For Olsen rugby league in Australia was too serious: 'A lot of Aussies got offended by what I said about not caring. I was right, though. There is more to life than rugby league and problems happen if you don't have other things in your life. Fans and players took it personally that I didn't care if I played in Sydney or that rugby league wasn't my be-all and end-all.'

Olsen also refused to kowtow to the notion that Sydney was the centre of the universe: 'As far as Sydney goes — I just didn't care for the place. People were rude and made racist comments and acted as if I didn't understand what they were saying. Kings Cross was scary and the whole city was too fast — everyone in a hurry to go nowhere.'

With his reluctance to be excited about an opportunity that was the dream of millions of boys in Australia, the Sydney press latched on to the idea of 'Olsen the Enigma' — a theme that would be repurposed and follow him throughout his career.

* * * * *

On a positive note, Olsen impressed journalists with the entertainment focus of his playing style.

'Every era in rugby league history has its great players, the champions whose names live on long after they hang up their boots,' enthused E.E. Christensen of *The Sun* newspaper.

Listing historical crowd-pleasers such as Dally Messenger, Harold Horder, Dave Brown, Brian Bevan, Reg Gasnier and Larry Corowa, Christensen concluded: 'New Zealand has come up with a young fellow who has that same magical effect on crowds. The Kiwi "Corowa" is Olsen Filipaina, the 21-year-old centre here on the tour of Australia.'

* * * * *

In the 1978 test series, Olsen lived up to the hype, despite being part of an outgunned New Zealand side. In the first test, held on Saturday, 24 June at the SCG, New Zealand were hammered by 22 points, but Olsen was 'easily his side's best player with an eye-catching performance', according to the *Sydney Morning Herald*.

Things went from bad to worse for New Zealand in the second test at Brisbane's Lang Park, but again reporters pointed to Olsen as the shining light in the Kiwis' 29-point loss.

'New Zealand,' reported the *Sydney Morning Herald*, 'were ponderous, predictable and clumsy. They seemed intent on turning the ball back inside towards the forwards leaving its best attacking weapon, Olsen Filipaina, with little chance to display his talent.

'From the Kiwi team yesterday, probably only centre Olsen Filipaina would be certain to make a Sydney first-grade team. Filipaina gave the Australian defence their only scare in the first half when he slashed through.'

After a third consecutive test loss, this time 33–16 at the SCG, Olsen and his beaten teammates were looking forward to the flight home across the Tasman. It had been a dispiriting tour — the Kiwis had scored just two tries and conceded 95 points — but according to Kiwis prop forward Lyndsay Proctor, Olsen only enhanced his mana.

'He was the only one that came out of that series with his reputation intact,' says Proctor. 'The Aussie fans seemed to love him in those three tests with his line breaks. He was another person when he pulled on the Kiwi jumper. On his day he could show anyone up. No one was immune.'

Proctor noticed Olsen's growing maturity: 'On that tour he was my babysitter and he bailed me out quite a few times. One time we went out on a boat on Sydney Harbour and we landed down in Rushcutters Bay and I was so drunk I made a fool of myself and ended up on the floor. And it was Olsen, on his first tour, who made sure I got back to the motel and into my bed. I'll always be mates with a guy like that.'

* * * * *

Olsen, now a 21-year-old wrecking ball, put the disappointment of the 1978 Australia tour behind him and back in South Auckland led his Māngere East Hawks to their first Fox Memorial Cup Grand Final.

In the process, his golden seam of form won him a slew of awards including the Māngere East Player of the Year, Auckland Rugby League Player of the Year, and New Zealand Rugby League Player of the Year. It was a clean sweep that confirmed his brilliance beyond all doubt.

'In 1978, Olsen continued to dominate as the absolute superstar of the rugby league scene and was the most talked about player of any code in New Zealand,' wrote journalist Bill Hansby in the Māngere East 40th anniversary publication. 'His sheer brilliance was unmatched.'

The 1978 Grand Final of the Fox Memorial Cup was the biggest event in the brief history of the Māngere East housing estate. The suburb swelled with pride for its team. Fans decorated shop windows with banners and pennants, and bumper stickers were proudly displayed on cars. Busloads of Māngere East supporters, including hundreds of schoolboys in their playing uniforms, descended on Carlaw Park to witness the club's first grand final.

Sadly for the Māngere faithful, their boys were beaten 29 points to 12 by a well-drilled Ōtāhuhu side who came prepared with a single-minded plan.

'We had watched Olsen destroy every team that year — New Zealand had never seen a footballer this exciting,' says Ōtāhuhu coach Sir Graham Lowe. 'Our game plan was simple — to stop Olsen and every time he got the ball we had four men assigned to him. Nobody can beat four men.'

For Olsen it was a rollercoaster season of mixed emotions. He was playing the best football of his life and receiving awards and adulation wherever he went.

Winning the Steve Watene Memorial trophy for New Zealand Player of the Year was a particular highlight. It was one of his 'proudest nights' as he was wrapped in a traditional Māori korowai cloak at a ceremony proudly attended by his mother. Sissie, like most Māori, was well aware of Steve Watene's pioneering role as the first Māori captain of the Kiwis in 1936 and who led the giant-killing 1937 NZ Māori side to a 16–5 upset victory over the Kangaroos.

Olsen remembers feeling overwhelmed when Watene family members placed the korowai on his shoulders, a special honour he likened to 'wearing the golden fleece.'

* * * * *

What few people realised, though, was that amid all the glory, Olsen had been devastated and fuelled by the loss of one of his closest friends, Johnny Touson, who had died in a tragic industrial accident.

'The whole year was a tribute to Johnny. At that stage he was more of a brother than my other brothers,' says Olsen. 'I was very close to his family. He knew nothing about rugby league so he didn't care about my achievements or the hype. I needed a friend outside league and he made a huge difference in my life. It felt so unfair and I remember walking the streets crying. I dedicated 1978 to him.'

* * * * *

Were it not for an arcane transfer ban by the International Rugby League Board, which forced players to sit out for 12 months after moving countries, Olsen Filipaina might have been playing club football in Sydney in 1978.

Following his lone-hand heroics on the Kiwis test tour in June, the *Sydney Morning Herald* reported that four clubs were interested in signing him: Balmain and South Sydney, Easts in Brisbane, and a 'bush' club in Illawarra.

John Coffey, a doyen of New Zealand rugby league reporters, can recall the offers coming in from Sydney and English clubs. 'And he deserved them!' wrote Coffey in the *New Zealand Rugby League Annual*. 'He really was the Kiwis' best player in that 1978 series. The standout. He just didn't want to leave his mother and family. The Sydney clubs thought all should be beholden to them, but Olsen was different.'

And so Olsen remained in Auckland, working at a commercial printing business and playing for Māngere East Hawks on weekends. As Olsen's stature grew in the Auckland league, his mana increased within the Māngere East Hawks and South Auckland.

He had single-handedly raised the profile of the unfashionable Māngere East Hawks, a small club with a short history who had risen out of nowhere to challenge the blue-bloods of the Fox Memorial Cup — the Ōtāhuhu Leopards and the Richmond Rovers.

Before Olsen, Māngere East rarely played in the main game at the showpiece Carlaw Park, but that changed in 1978 when they were increasingly scheduled as the main game.

'The older players would pay me a lot of respect which humbled me,' says Olsen. 'In many ways I was still a kid, but they treated me like a hero. I didn't want to be the captain, but I could lead in other ways. I was always about recognising the other players as well and it was always embarrassing for me to walk out of awards nights with the flags, trophies and pennants. I never enjoyed it. What I did love was prize-giving — giving away awards to the kids. Your mana should always be shared with the rest of the village.'

* * * * *

One evening in August 1978, Olsen spotted 'a beautiful young woman' making a phone call at a phone booth inside the Māngere East League Club after a prize-giving function. He tapped her on the shoulder and introduced himself.

'I'm Leslie,' she responded, shaking his hand and sizing him up with a smile.

Leslie Anne Taylor, an 18-year-old Māori woman of Ngāti Maniapoto affiliation, had not been raised on rugby league and had no idea who he was. Still, she agreed to accompany him to a party at his mother's house that night, where they hit it off immediately and started seeing each other.

Olsen says: 'She was a glamour and I thought I'd have no luck here. Shock and horror, she said yes.'

Like his recently departed best friend Johnny Touson, Leslie appreciated Olsen not for his football prowess but for who he was as a man. She became his key person outside the rugby league bubble. 'I didn't even like rugby league and had been brought up on union,' says Leslie.

'I had no idea how big he was until I went to Carlaw Park and I heard the crowd screaming for him.'

For Leslie, the attention continued off the field: 'Going shopping was a major drama — if people came up to talk to him, it wasn't in him to walk away from them, so I would leave him there, do my shopping and come back.'

For Olsen, it was crucial to have a new person in his life who could fill the void left by his friend Johnny's death. 'Leslie had no idea I was a well-known player so I could be myself and get away from the hype. It was refreshing to talk about other things and she used to read the paper but not the sport section. She is smart and beautiful and I got lucky.'

* * * * *

As Olsen's star rose, so did his people's. His Māori and Polynesian communities were connecting into the global human rights and anti-apartheid movements and ready to make their own move for their rights. The Māori renaissance had an unlikely source — a feisty Māori woman named Tuaiwa 'Eva' Rickard.

Rickard, 52 years old in 1978, shot to prominence as a land rights campaigner. Raised in Raglan, two hours south of Auckland, Rickard was part of the Tainui Awhiro people who had lent the New Zealand Government some land for defence purposes during the Second World War. Instead of returning the land to the traditional owners after the war, the government had sold part of the land, including some Tainui Awhiro burial grounds, to be developed into a golf course.

The land theft was arrogant and plainly wrong. In 1978, led by

Rickard, the traditional owners staged a protest, occupying the ninth hole of the golf course.

Television cameras captured footage of Rickard and 16 others being arrested for trespassing on the Raglan Golf Club fairway, and the sight of the wiry Māori elder being manhandled by police shot her to national fame.

She was the star of a high-profile court case in which she was eloquently able to prosecute her people's case in a bitter battle with the Crown.

Channelling the leaders of great underdog victories in Māori history like Te Ruki Kawiti, Rickard beat the Pākehā at their own game. She flooded the various governments with letters and paperwork, protested peacefully and became media savvy, giving heartfelt interviews that connected emotionally with New Zealanders. Her campaign of non-violent civil disobedience led to the return of the land to Tainui.

'She had the strong Māori will, tenacity and commitment. She was a Māori mother on the national stage,' says Leslie, who watched the televised news reports in awe with Olsen. 'Winning through aroha and the strength to stand her ground. She was tiny but honest with big mana. We were all inspired by her and it was a real turning point. She gave us strength.'

New Zealand, once a sleepy, monocultural backwater, was injected with disrupting energy by the emerging Māori political consciousness and the new blended Pasifika culture.

In this milieu, Olsen felt right at home enveloped in the familiar bosom of South Auckland. He worked different jobs including seasonal work at Hellaby's meat freezing works, developing his upper body strength carrying stacks of carcasses and loading them onto pallets. He played rugby league in brutal grudge matches between different freezing works and remembers them as 'mean games'.

Olsen's friends and life revolved around rugby league, Leslie and his family, who were starting to move ahead. Younger brother Alf had become a policeman, elder brother Joe was a truck driver, Jerry was in labour hire and Philip worked at Coca Cola. Following the

Samoan and Māori tradition, all of the brothers gave their salaries to their parents who in turn paid them an allowance. Aloese's gambling addiction would take care of any surpluses.

As Olsen's personal sponsor, Sir Peter Leitch was frustrated in trying to help Olsen with money but was unable to breach the cultural obligation: 'That part of the culture is so strong it's unbreakable,' says Leitch.

'We knew where Olsen's money was going. I tried so hard to give Olsen money directly, but he would always give it to his father. Instead of giving him cash, I once made a cheque out to him and sure enough two days later he was back to ask me to change the name on the cheque to his father's name. He was so loyal to his dad.'

Olsen and his brothers lived at home and helped his mother Sissie out with chores, enabling Sissie to run a true open house for family members on both the Māori and Samoan sides.

Olsen remembers a high turnover and mix of family members at the house: 'It was a safehouse. I would come out some mornings and in the garage were all of the aunties and uncles and cousins on the Māori side. And on the couches were uncles and cousins from the Samoan side. I remember going out to wake people up to give them some kai and having no idea who they were and I was always surrendering my room to relatives.'

He enjoyed an idyllic time with Leslie as they began to build a life together. Leslie remembers joyous days in the fields, picking strawberries together across South Auckland for the Chinese market gardeners, before the land became too valuable and was converted into new housing.

His joy in his new relationship was tempered by that with his father, and Olsen lived in fear of his father's mood swings. Aloese's gambling habit was destroying the family finances yet he still showed care by attending all of Olsen's games for the Māngere East Hawks.

Olsen remembers being knocked cold by an illegal tackle in one match at Massey Park and when he regained consciousness, the first thing he heard was a horse-racing commentator. It was coming from his father's transistor radio in his pocket because Aloese had run onto the field to check if Olsen was okay. After Olsen came to, Aloese threatened the offending Samoan opposition player into a whimpering apology.

* * * * *

Olsen was content continuing to play his football in Auckland, telling the *Sydney Morning Herald* in early 1979 that he was looking forward to a 'quiet year' in his beloved Fox Memorial Cup. The Auckland competition was the heartbeat of New Zealand rugby league and clubs had risen and fallen since its inception in 1910.

Then journalist Richard Becht remembers the dynastic change in the late 1970s: 'Ponsonby and Ellerslie had been the glamour sides in the early 70s but the complexion began to change. Indeed, the year Olsen arrived in 1976, Mount Wellington, boasting the gifted young Sorensen brothers Dane and Kurt, took out the Fox grand final from Glenora. Ōtāhuhu and Richmond were also strong and soon enough Māngere East challenged on the back of Olsen's brilliance.'

Champion Ōtāhuhu coach Sir Graham Lowe has coached in every professional league in the world excluding France and his feelings on where the Fox Memorial Cup rated in the late 1970s are unequivocal: 'It was as good a comp as you could get,' says Lowe. 'The standards, the big crowds at Carlaw Park, it was special. It was a breeding ground for stars.'

For Lowe, the off-field interactions offered a template for young men to see older men at their best: 'It was a great thing for a young guy to be sitting in the stands at Carlaw Park and see absolute wars, it was on for young and old and as tough as any rugby league ever. Then that same young guy could see those opponents in the dressing rooms and pubs getting along together as great mates.'

He is saddened by the barriers that blocked the Fox Memorial Cup's best players from showcasing themselves in Australia and England, leaving New Zealand rugby league players operating in a parallel dimension: 'Guys like Olsen and Fred Ah Kuoi were fortunate to get out and play professionally. There were hundreds of great players before them that never got a chance, restrained by ridiculous transfer fees.'

* * * * *

Having reluctantly taken over the goal-kicking duties for Māngere East for the new 1979 season, Olsen went on a rampage, scoring more than 300 points across club, representative and international matches. His first 100 points came in the opening six games of the season. He scored 25 tries and kicked 93 goals for Māngere East, winning the Tetley Trophy for most points in a season and the Painter Trophy for most goals.

'Olsen hit the scene in 1977 with a thud, but in 1978 and 1979 he became an extraordinarily remarkable player,' suggests Richard Becht, then a league writer for the *Sunday Star*. 'Māngere East were a small club and he put them on the map. He was the gem, the impetus and he drew people to Carlaw Park like nothing on earth.'

One reporter declared that 'Olsen Filipaina is about as dangerous as foolin' around with your local traffic cop's missus', while journalist Bill Hansby wrote: 'We've never really seen another rugby league player like Olsen Filipaina. He was a complete footballer and entertainer who got the Carlaw Park crowds cheering on their feet.'

Some compared Olsen to Bryan Williams, the legendary rugby union international. 'Filipaina, only 22, has already established himself as a great player in the code — one who if he were playing union would have the sort of national following Bryan Williams does in the All Blacks,' reported the *New Zealand Listener*.

* * * * *

In 1979 Olsen was in full 'entertainer' mode, a recipient of footballing genius at the peak of his powers, and most importantly he was enjoying his rugby league.

He says of the time: 'I lived to entertain the crowds at Carlaw Park. They were a tough crowd, not impressed easily, and I knew how miserable some of their lives were during the week. I knew how homesick some of them were and it was an honour to brighten their lives with some good footy.'

Olsen was selected again for the 1979 Kiwis side and played at centre for all three test matches against the touring Great Britain side. They lost the first test 16–8 in a close, brutal match and lost the second 22–7 with Olsen the only try-scorer. John Coffey, writing for *The Press*, said: 'A typical Olsen Filipaina try, when he bulldozed his way through and over three opponents.'

He also starred for Auckland in representative football and coach Don Hammond said of Olsen's impact: 'In Auckland, Olsen makes the crowd rise every time he has the ball. He is the only player for many years to be able to do that and he has played some phenomenal football.'

Yet rugby league in New Zealand, forever in the shadow of rugby union, was unable to provide the appropriate platform for Olsen and the emerging golden generation of players.

'He had been killing it in Auckland and had outgrown our league,' says Ellerslie Eagles prop Lyndsay Proctor, who sat beside Olsen on a flight home from Sydney after Auckland lost its Amco Cup clash to Cronulla at Leichhardt Oval in July 1979.

Leichhardt Oval, the home of Balmain Tigers, had become a familiar ground for Olsen through his Amco Cup games for Auckland, most of which were played there. And it was Balmain, a foundation NSWRL club which had not won a premiership in a decade, that emerged as the frontrunners for his signature.

'I doubt whether he has even scratched the surface of his potential,' Keith Gittoes, the Balmain club secretary, told the *Sydney Morning Herald*, '. . . it is doubtful whether he has ever been fit!'

The competitive, win-at-all-costs nature of professional rugby league in Sydney created some concern among the Filipaina clan and friends.

'To be honest a lot of us were worried,' says Sir Peter Leitch, Olsen's personal sponsor. 'He was a nice boy and wasn't one of the big rough, tough Kiwi forwards that had gone before him to Sydney like the Sorensens, Henry Tatana and Oscar Danielson. The Aussies then had no idea how to handle the softer side of Polynesians. It was all macho, tough guy, no emotions.'

Sissie and Aloese, meanwhile, wanted their son to grasp the opportunity. At almost 23, it was Olsen's last chance to join the professional system and his parents thought he was stagnating in his comfort zone. But while Sissie wanted Olsen to play for mana, Aloese's primary concern was the bigger money his son would soon be sending back home to feed his gambling addiction.

It was the second big decision of Olsen's life, and like the decision to choose rugby league over union, it was made in the living room at their house in Tennessee Avenue.

'I remember Mum saying, "No, no, you have to go",' says Alf Filipaina, Olsen's brother. 'She said, "You'll be getting paid good money and you need to do it for the Pacific people."'

Olsen's younger brother Alf himself thought that as the Auckland League's best playmaker, Olsen was being 'increasingly unfairly targeted by hitmen using cheap shots', and his brother needed a new challenge.

'Although Olsen was very proud, he took it as it comes,' remembers elder brother Joe Filipaina.

'Wherever it was played, it was just another game to him and for Olsen, ultimately it was whatever his mother decided. In Sydney, Olsen could make a name for himself and Polynesians. For the pain he was going through playing rugby league, at least in Sydney there was a pot of gold at the end of the rainbow.'

Until this point Olsen had only played as an amateur and his contracts were all done on a handshake. As a junior he played for Fanta and a hamburger; as a senior for a case of beer.

But man cannot live on beer alone and on the insistence of his mother Sissie, Olsen finally accepted an offer to join Balmain for the 1980 season.

It was a smart piece of recruitment from the Balmain Tigers Head of Football, Keith Gittoes. Not only had he impressed Sissie by meeting them the Māori 'eye to eye' way, flying into Auckland and coming to the house, but he had also negotiated terms directly with the New Zealand Rugby League so that Olsen would not have to sit out for a 12-month transfer ban and could continue playing for the Kiwis.

Media across Australia and New Zealand trumpeted the news. Some believed it was the biggest signing of the off-season. The two-year deal also included a $3000 scholarship for Māngere East to support a young promising footballer.

When Olsen broke the news to the Māngere East faithful at the clubhouse, though, it was a bittersweet moment for supporters and players alike. 'Olsen couldn't speak,' recalls Sir Peter Leitch. 'We were excited for him, but he felt he was letting us down. He broke down and cried in what should have been his happiest moment.'

According to Richard Becht, Olsen and his range of electrifying skills were central to the Auckland Rugby League's financial model.

'Chairman George Rainey always made sure that Māngere were the main event game because Olsen brought people in and they happily paid their money,' says Becht.

'He would attract big crowds with his bump, fend, power running, crunching defence and offloads. He played with so much joy on his face and there was joy in everything he did. He was able to express his skills with amazing regularity and to the Auckland Rugby League's financial benefit.'

Now, as the Auckland rugby league community prepared for the 1980 season without its star player, one headline in the *8 O'Clock* newspaper summed up the sense of loss: 'Wanted — a super star to enthral the crowds. Who will replace Olsen?'

3

THE ONE WHO BROKE THROUGH

'I know you've taken it in the teeth out there, but the first guy through the wall — he always gets bloody, always.'

— John Henry, *Moneyball*

On the morning of 4 January 1980, Olsen Filipaina kissed his mother goodbye, shook his father's hand and boarded a flight to Sydney.

Olsen was hoping to slip quietly out of Auckland, but his family and the Māngere East Hawks club members came out in force to farewell him. Olsen describes the scene: 'It was the old and young that got me. Both my Samoan and my Māori grandmothers were there and there were seven- and eight-year-olds from the club who started crying and their parents were saying, "It's all right, he'll be back."'

The situation gave Olsen pause: 'One minute everyone was laughing and once it was time to go, all of a sudden everyone was crying.'

He had agonised over the decision to leave his family and now had second thoughts on whether to get on the plane. His mother Sissie squared him up and Olsen recalls her saying calmly: 'You have to go now. We all love you.'

Olsen's partner Leslie avoided the emotional scene. She pleaded with Olsen the night before and tried to get him to stay. Looking back, she says: 'I was going to miss him a lot and he wasn't ready for the separation. I feel selfish about it now, but it was too much for me to go to the airport. It would have been too emotional to do a personal send-off in front of people. I stayed at home and cried.'

For the three-hour flight to Sydney, Olsen sat uncomfortably in his seat, eyes squeezed shut, knuckles white from gripping the arm rests. He was utterly terrified.

It was not his first flight — he had previously been on football trips to Sydney and Brisbane. But those had all been in the company of teammates, with the promise of a quick return. Now, he was all alone, flying into a city he did not like, with an unknown future waiting for him.

What's more, 37 days before his departure, on 28 November 1979, Air New Zealand Flight 901, on a sightseeing flight, crashed into Mt Erebus in Antarctica — killing all 257 passengers and crew. The national tragedy, featuring charred wreckage scattered against a white landscape, beamed into living rooms around New Zealand, triggered in Olsen a lifelong fear of flying.

A lazy off-season had caused Olsen to gain a few pounds, and to his size he had added a large 'afro' haircut, rendering him almost unrecognisable to Phil Dries, his pick-up man at Sydney Airport.

Dries, a board member of Ryde Eastwood Hawks — Māngere East's sister club — finally approached Olsen and the pair drove back to his house in North Ryde for what was planned to be a two-week stint.

In the end, Olsen would stay with the Dries family for two and a half years. Phil, his wife Margaret, and their children Michael and Lisa, would become his adoptive 'Aussie family', helping him deal with the separation from family back home in New Zealand.

The culture shock was immediate. 'I'll never forget the fifth of January 1980 — my first day training with the Balmain Tigers,' says Olsen. 'It was the height of summer and they made us do the 10-kilometre Leichhardt Bay Run which was torture. It broke me. All we did was play touch football and ball work in New Zealand; no one trains that hard. In Australia you have to be a long-distance runner as well as a footballer.'

On the first run Olsen felt an outsider: 'While we were running, a friend of Larry Corowa's drove his car up to us and all the boys jumped in and there was no room for me. They drove back to the Tigers and I had to finish the run and they all splashed themselves with water to make it look like they were sweating. I had the biggest throw-up ever, three or four times, and I never forgot that.'

The morning after his first Bay Run, Filipaina sat on the steps of Balmain Leagues Club, physically devastated, homesick and ready to quit. He pleaded with Balmain management to be released from his contract. 'I said, "Look, I want to go home; no one trains this hard to play league." Their mouths dropped to the floor and they replied, "But we've already paid you your money!"'

In desperation, Olsen offered to pay the club back their airline ticket money, but Balmain refused to accept it. As a last resort he rang his mother Sissie to plead his case. She told him that he couldn't come home and would have to stick it out.

* * * * *

Rugby league in Sydney was a totally different proposition to Auckland. In Sydney the game was a colossus, dominating rugby union and all other winter sports on every metric — media, participation, glamour and money.

Rugby league's code and ethos appealed to Sydneysiders and aligned with Australian values. It was played across cities and country towns and it was the sport of the fair go. Players were bona fide residents of the area their team represented. The game had tribalism, loyalty, emotion and passion as its foundation. It also had a considerable middle-class following which made it attractive to sponsors.

Unlike in Auckland and Brisbane, where poker machines were banned, Sydney rugby league clubs had been fattened up by the profits of gambling. The 'pokies' money transformed tin-shed clubhouses into wealthy leagues clubs and allowed football departments to spend freely on recruiting the best players. Tobacco sponsorship and television money followed, changing the game from a working-class pursuit to a commercial enterprise.

By the time Olsen landed in 1980, Sydney rugby league was at a crossroads. It deliberately elevated itself above the other major leagues in Brisbane, England and Auckland whose players were considered provincial, foreign and of little use.

Players like Queenslander Aboriginal Arthur Beetson and New Zealanders Henry Tatana and Oscar Danielson had bludgeoned their way to credibility, often with their fists, but they were all treated as outsiders. Sydney was the big show.

Sydney rugby league, claims journalist Andrew Webster, was 'the city's lifeblood' in the early 1980s. Yet it was also gratuitously violent, totally insular and poorly managed. The sport, wrote Webster, was 'staggering about like the drunkest guy at the party' and crowds were plummeting. The game was stale.

'In New Zealand you had to entertain people in order to get them through the gates,' explains Sir Graham Lowe, who moved from Auckland to coach in Brisbane in 1979. 'In Sydney, because of poker machines, they didn't have to worry so much about getting people through the gate. They didn't seem to need the people who go to the game and any money they got from the gate was a bonus. It meant clubs were less entrepreneurial and lazy.'

While Olsen was preparing for his first year in Sydney, up north in Brisbane Ōtāhuhu captain Mark Graham and coach Graham Lowe had both just completed their first year for Brisbane Norths.

Graham told *Rugby League Week*: 'To tell the truth I really don't like Sydney as a place, although it's the best football competition in the world.'

For the 1980 season Mark Graham was joined in Brisbane by Olsen's old schoolmate Stan Napa, a rampaging Cook Islands Māori, and both looked forward to reuniting under their old Ōtāhuhu coach Graham Lowe.

In retrospect, Olsen once explained, it might have been better for him to join the Kiwi trio in Brisbane rather than slug it out alone in Sydney.

* * * * *

Olsen was not the first Polynesian or Māori to play in Sydney. In fact, Māori were a crucial stakeholder at the very genesis of Australian rugby league in 1908.

When Australians talk of rugby league's history, the contribution of their Māori brothers in the early and fragile part of the game's development is rarely mentioned — gently airbrushed out of the conversation. The Māori and Pacific communities are treated as recent interlopers who should be grateful for the opportunity. The historical record tells another story.

'We Māori were partners at the very founding of the game in Australia,' explains Howie Tamati, former Kiwis hooker and President of the New Zealand Rugby League. 'We are a concrete part of the foundation. Not many people know it, but the proceeds from the "All Māoris" tours of Australia in 1908 and 1909 were crucial in saving the game of rugby league in its moment of crisis.'

Those rebel Māori rugby union players, who sailed into Sydney Harbour in 1908 under a cloak of secrecy, had told authorities back home in New Zealand they were embarking on a rugby union tour.

Instead, they defected to the brand-new game, playing 12 games of rugby league in Sydney, Newcastle and Brisbane, and returning in 1909 for a second tour to play another 10 games.

Along the way the Māori team provided a significant financial windfall for the fledgling NSWRL, and in 1909 they left behind their centre, Peter Moko, who joined Glebe and became the first Māori/Pacific imported player to appear in the Sydney competition.

He would be followed by other pioneers: Punga Pakere, also known as 'Glen Barclay', who played for North Sydney in 1910; Huatahi Turoa Brown Paki, nicknamed 'Brownie Paki', who played 15 games for St George in 1922; the Fijian Toga brothers who joined St George in 1968;

Samoan-born Oscar Danielson, who joined Newtown in 1970; and tough Māori Henry Tatana who joined the Canterbury Bankstown Bulldogs in 1972.

By the time Olsen arrived in Sydney, there were just three other Polynesian/Māori players plying their trade: Cronulla's Kurt and Dane Sorensen, of Tongan-Danish heritage who had previously played against Olsen in Auckland; while Balmain had Lloyd Martin, an Auckland-born Māori halfback who had been with the club for two seasons.

Martin had been playing rugby league in Australia since arriving as an unknown aspiring 17-year-old in 1973. He was light-skinned and with his moustache and name could pass as another Anglo-Celtic player. Like the Sorensen brothers, he escaped a lot of attention and wasn't the 'superstar' of another league coming over to try his luck, bearing the weight of expectations and cynics.

Martin had been seasoned in the Sydney professional system since a teenager and had not played senior football in the Fox Memorial Cup whereas Olsen had been airdropped from the amateurs into a pro league at 23. Lloyd wasn't deemed a foreigner, yet Olsen was.

Cronulla's Kurt Sorensen notes the difference between him and Olsen: 'I had three things going for me,' says Sorensen, 'white skin, an English-sounding name and I would fight if someone had a go at me. Olsen had none of those going for him. He was an immediate target with his skin colour, name, his look and he chose not to fight.'

* * * * *

The Balmain Tigers in 1980 were a club of outsiders, a diverse mix of rugby league misfits — Queenslanders, country boys, 'blackfellas', Europeans, Māori and now a Polynesian.

They were the 'Star Wars Bar' of the NSWRL including Māori-Samoan Olsen Filipaina, Aboriginals Percy Knight, David Grant and Larry Corowa, Māori Lloyd Martin, Harley-Davidson-riding long-haired country boy Kerry Hemsley, Queenslanders Rod Morris and Greg Oliphant, Italian Frank Marino, Serbian John Bilbija, golden local boy Wayne Pearce and country boy accountant Neil Whittaker who would go on to be the CEO of the NSWRL.

At the apex of this team was Dennis Tutty, one of the great rebel-heroes of rugby league and a rookie first-grade coach. Tutty, who had retired from Balmain as a player in 1977, famously took the NSWRL to court for restraint of trade — manning a personal crusade for players' rights to freely move between clubs, a right today called free agency.

A Balmain junior and a man of great principle, Tutty had gone on strike for two years in 1969 and 1970 after Balmain refused to grant him clearance to join another club.

During that time his marriage broke down, he developed ulcers, was forced to sell his car and spent all his savings to cover lost earnings. He also missed out on the 1969 Balmain Tigers grand final victory that he would have certainly played in if fit.

Ultimately, Tutty would be remembered as a hero and pioneer after the courts ruled in his favour and the archaic and restrictive transfer system in rugby league was deemed a restraint of trade and dismantled.

Decades later, in 2018, a commemorative plaque bearing Tutty's name was unveiled at Leichhardt Oval — a historic act of penance by the club that had almost destroyed his life.

At the ceremony Ian Prendergast, the president of the Rugby League Players Association, spoke of Tutty's momentous fight. 'He took his stance at a time when he didn't have the support of a players' association, his fellow players or the team he was trying to get to,' said Prendergast. 'He drove it himself and it had a huge impact on him personally, professionally and financially.'

In 1980, Tutty was in his debut year as a first-grade coach. His challenge was to blend a group of players with disparate personalities and cultural backgrounds into a team ready to grind out a year in the toughest rugby league competition in the world.

His main selection criteria, he later explained, was toughness. 'I just went for tough blokes. It's not a game for the faint hearted. Olsen had toughness written all over him. He didn't look like he was going to do the tough stuff because he was one of those quiet unassuming players, but he did the yards for me.'

Tutty knew Auckland well — he had visited the city several times in off-seasons to work in factories and freezing works, deliberately gaining weight on 'big Māori feeds' and getting to know more about the Polynesian communities.

Olsen was fortunate to have a coach like Dennis Tutty to ease him into Sydney life. From Leslie's vantage point he was a blessing: 'He didn't realise it, but Dennis was the most culturally sensitive coach at the time. He was a polite gentleman and mixed with everyone at the club. He didn't treat anybody different.'

'Dennis helped me to settle in to Sydney and he taught me how they played,' says Olsen. 'He knew about Māori and Polynesians and he let me play my game. He gave me lots of praise, and areas to improve in games and training and did it without giving orders. When he yelled, you always understood why and could wear it.'

There was a sense of expectation that Tutty's Tigers could be premiership contenders. 'This could be the year of the outsider and, for mine, watch out for Balmain this year,' wrote Reg Gasnier in *Rugby League Week*.

'I know it's far too early to be talking about premiership winners, but if there ever was a team with a chance of knocking off the more favoured sides it's the Tigers. There are a couple of reasons: they have Dennis Tutty as coach and a bloke called Olsen Filipaina in the centres. Tutty is a fitness fanatic and because of this I'll guarantee the Tigers won't be run off their feet. Filipaina impressed greatly when he was here in 1978 with the New Zealanders. He is a very strong man and will add a tremendous amount of penetration to the centres.'

In pre-season hit-outs against Broken Hill, North Sydney and St George, a still-overweight Olsen showed early signs of promise and Balmain did not lose a game.

But before the trial match against St George, television cameras zoomed in on him dressed only in Speedos, pacing around the dressing room in nervous agitation.

'Balmain's star import, Kiwi centre Olsen Filipaina, suffers badly from camera shyness,' reported the *Daily Mirror* the following day.

'A TV crew tried to film him in the dressing room at Leichhardt on Friday, shortly before the Balmain–St George game. The big fella shielded his face and politely told the cameraman to push off. They refused. Filipaina quickly moved to another part of the dressing room, hotly pursued by the TV crew. He locked himself in the loo, ignoring all appeals to come out. Only when he was assured the cameras had gone would he open the door.'

'I was puzzled why the cameras were in there when guys were walking around half naked,' says Olsen. 'Nobody had told me this was going to happen and I wasn't up for it. I'd never experienced it and didn't like it at all.'

Aboriginal teammate Percy Knight was also not big on the media spotlight: 'I was with Olsen a few times hiding in the toilets from the media,' Knight recalls: 'We were shy and didn't want to bignote ourselves, we just wanted to play footy and entertain the fans.'

After qualifying for the grand final of the pre-season Craven Cup, Balmain began the season poorly. A 27-point loss to Parramatta in Round 1 was followed by a 26-point loss to South Sydney and a 14-point loss to Newtown.

'One minute we're on top of the world and the next we're looking for a friend,' wrote veteran Tiger Allan McMahon in a midweek column. 'We desperately need a win. We all feel sorry for Filipaina. He is a super player and joined us thinking we were a top outfit. He's doing his best and making some good breaks but we're not supporting him.'

Tutty took action in two key areas. First, he promoted McMahon into the captain's role. Next, he brought Percy Knight, a skilful Aboriginal halfback, into the five-eighth position to spice up the attack. It worked a treat. In Round 4, Balmain registered its first win of the season, beating Cronulla 27–10.

'With Percy controlling the attack today we were able to make plenty of runs,' Olsen told reporters after the game. For him, it felt like the start of something special. He had played well against his fellow Kiwis, Kurt and Dane Sorensen, and could finally celebrate a first-grade victory with his new teammates.

The feeling of euphoria and the release of tension, he later remembered, 'was like letting the air out of a balloon. It was a big night out that night at the club.'

* * * * *

On the morning of his twenty-third birthday, Olsen Filipaina ate a slice of a green, football field-shaped cake decorated with little posts and a rugby league ball.

Wearing a traditional Samoan lavalava, surrounded by the Dries family and his partner, Leslie, he wiped away tears. 'He said it was the first birthday cake he had ever received,' recalls his 'Aussie mum' Margaret Dries.

After three months of living in the big city, Olsen was beginning to settle. Phil Dries had secured him a regular job as a garbage collector for Ryde Council, which meant 2 am starts every morning but also extra money to send home to his family in Auckland.

His position in the Balmain Tigers' starting side seemed assured, and a solid friendship was building with his centre partner, Wayne Wigham. Four days after Olsen's birthday, the Tigers won a second consecutive game against Penrith, with Wigham crossing over for two tries.

The Bay Run and fitness work were still a challenge, but for the first time in his life he had developed a six-pack stomach. And Leslie was here to stay, but not immediately with Olsen.

Leslie had decided to give Olsen some space and was staying with a Māori friend two streets away. She was keen to make her transition as smooth as possible: 'Olsen had developed a wonderful family life at the Dries house. He would come and stay with me sometimes, but he was on a good thing there and settling nicely.'

'When I got there he had lost all his weight and was down to 95 kilograms, a lightweight compared to what he was in Auckland,' Leslie recalls.

'I was there to support him, so we developed a plan for match day. Olsen would sleep until 11.30 am because he was exhausted from a week on the garbage bins. I would have everything ready — shorts, socks, Speedos and singlet. For some reason he wouldn't let me clean his boots — he was superstitious about that.'

Leslie's support was just as valuable after the games: 'Olsen would be stiff like a statue after games and would be limping and bruised.'

She remembers a lot of pain alleviation sessions in the early morning: 'Olsen wouldn't be able to move at 2 am after a match and he didn't want to miss a garbage shift because he could be easily replaced. I would have to massage him, dig in the elbows and walk on his back to get him going. Some days he was in real pain, but he would never miss the bins.'

* * * * *

Mid season Olsen returned to New Zealand to play for the Kiwis in a two-test series against the Kangaroos, both games held at Carlaw Park. Olsen was the standout Kiwis player in both matches but they lost 27-6 and 15-6.

For Olsen, test football against the Kangaroos was exciting but frustrating: 'We played much better than in 1978 but the Aussies were still too good. We were getting closer but I knew we had to be patient, keep believing and have a crack at them in another two years.'

* * * * *

Olsen returned to Balmain after the tour and was beginning to make an impression on the Sydney competition. In Round 12, in a return match against Parramatta, Olsen hit legendary hard-man Arthur Beetson with a tackle he would remember for years to come.

'I remember being crunched by him in a match one day when I was playing at Parramatta and having to get my neck manipulated for three weeks afterwards,' wrote Beetson in his autobiography.

'The tackle he hit me with was made right on the line, when I thought I was set to score. There were few players who could stop me that close to the try line — but running into Olsen was like being hit by a Mack truck.'

Olsen remembers clearly first seeing Artie on the field: 'It was weird but straight away we needed to sort out who was the hardest. I looked and he fronted me with the same look, a look of "we need to sort this out now". We were defending our line and he ran straight at me. We got it out of our system and outside that, we hardly clashed.'

In Round 16, Olsen scored three tries in a 41-point demolition of Penrith. For the club, however, it was a difficult season in which they lost 15 games, won just seven, and finished third to bottom on the ladder.

The only consolation was the fact that the Tigers had made the grand final of both the pre-season tournament and the midweek Amco Cup, rebadged in 1980 as the Tooth Cup.

In *Big League*, Peter Peters wrote a feature on the top 10 centres for the year and Olsen was ranked at 6 out of the 63 players who had played in the centre position for NSWRL clubs.

Peters also wrote a report card on Olsen's season:

'New Zealand's best centre who has settled in well with the Tigers after a slow start to the season. Very professional in his approach and plays to his strength all the time. Next to Cronin is probably the hardest centre to ground in the 12 teams. Uses a bump more than a step to beat his opposition and does it most effectively. Has a sharp turn of speed over a short distance and while not a consistent defender, is safe. Has scant respect for any opposition and usually reserves his best for the top-liners. Swallows up close-to-the-line tries.'

Watching Olsen develop was one of the highlights of a difficult debut year for coach Dennis Tutty. 'Olsen put in the whole time. I always found him a quiet bloke, a good man who loved having a bit of fun. You wouldn't meet a nicer bloke.

'The season got harder and harder for me,' says Tutty. 'I had a couple of players working against me, which was a shame because we weren't that far off the money.'

Hearing rumours that Balmain were looking to replace him with Frank Stanton, the incumbent coach of New South Wales and Australia, Tutty stood down and moved north to continue his coaching career in the bush with Forster.

* * * * *

The arrival of the Tigers' new coach Frank Stanton, nicknamed 'Cranky Franky' for his disciplinarian approach, was a great interruption for Olsen. Although Tutty had been a fitness fanatic, he had made allowances for naturally gifted individuals like Olsen.

Stanton, on the other hand, was a Manly Warringah blue-blood who ran a one-size-fits-all regime.

'Five minutes into his first speech, I thought: I don't like this guy,' Olsen recalls of his first interaction with Stanton. 'It seemed to be his way or nothing.'

The Tigers had also been negotiating with Olsen's future Kiwis coach Graham Lowe, who had pulled off a miracle win for Norths in the Brisbane competition in 1980.

Frank Stanton was also coaching in Brisbane, one year into a three-year contract with Redcliffe, who had placed fifth in 1980. Lowe had beaten and outcoached Stanton in all three Norths–Redcliffe matches, but the Tigers went with Stanton due to his Sydney pedigree.

We will sadly never know the outcomes for Olsen if the Balmain Tigers had chosen the culturally competent Lowe to be their coach for the 1981 season.

* * * * *

Balmain's Aboriginal five-eighth, Percy Knight, was captain for 12 games in 1981 but remembers Stanton as a dour, regimented coach who struggled to connect with his players.

'Frank brought a Manly "silvertail" culture to a working-class club. It was a bad fit and his results were terrible,' explains Knight. 'Balmain was the first majority black backline. Lloyd Martin, a Māori, would pass the ball to me, an Aboriginal. I would flick it out to Polynesian Olsen who would charge forward and be supported by quicksilver Aboriginal Larry Corowa. When we were on fire and took some risks, the fans loved it.

'Not so much Frank, though,' says Knight. 'It was Frank's job to get the best out of Olsen and he had no idea how to, except to punish him by putting him in reserves or humiliate him with words.'

Frank Stanton admits he did bring a Manly culture to Balmain but insists that it was a good thing. Now retired on the Tweed Coast, just south of the NSW–Queensland border, Stanton recalls: 'I understood Balmain culture to be that they never gave in. I played at Manly, grew up there and my expectations were what I was used to at Manly, which was winning. We were all in it together and we all had to work hard.'

When the Tigers lost two of their opening three games under Stanton, Olsen was dropped to reserve grade, a strange purgatory of 'has beens', journeymen, fading legends and 'still to be's' — and no place for New Zealand's once-in-a-generation playmaker.

Next match, the Tigers were thrashed 52–13 by Canterbury, but still Olsen languished in the reserves. In Round 8 he returned to the bench, and in Round 9 found himself picked as a five-eighth for the first time since he had arrived in Australia.

He lined up for the first time alongside Percy Knight in the halves in the greatest challenge available — an away game against the defending premiers Parramatta at a hostile Cumberland Oval.

It was a bad day for Balmain and for Olsen. Parramatta scored six tries to one and Olsen was involved in his first on-field fight in Sydney with Parramatta's hooker Paul Taylor.

Olsen remembers the fight with a grimace: 'It was a short scuffle and we were holding each other, wrestling around with some short punches. It was embarrassing for me as he was the shortest guy on the field.'

What Olsen feared more than Taylor was his mother finding out about the fight and he was relieved to get through his post-match phone call with Sissie without her mentioning the incident.

Before leaving Auckland, Sissie had made him promise that he would never get into a fight. His father had also given him a lecture about not bringing shame to the family name.

Filipaina explains why he never lashed out or retaliated at racial abuse or cheap shots: 'If I had punched someone and got sent off, people don't care why. It would shame my parents and family name and as one of the first Polynesians, I didn't want to give us a "troublemaker" stereotype. If you called me "nigger" or "black bastard", I would take your number and if I don't get you this game, I'll wait the whole season and I'll get you in the end. Call me whatever you want but I would tell them, "I'm not going away".'

Turning the other cheek was difficult for Olsen. He says: 'When you are kicked, or punched or insulted, the normal instinct is to let them have one. I knew how to handle myself from living in a tough suburb, but I really didn't want the headlines or to get a reputation as a brawler. It's hard to explain, but I couldn't let my mum down. That's who I reported in to.'

Olsen's reputation as a big hitter sometimes helped calm things down: 'Some guys in particular would always be into you with racial stuff or cheap shots, but I was able to get revenge by putting big hits on people that did and said things to me. I would remember them and knew that at some stage of the match, I could put them in pain legally. If not this match, then the next one. Some of them kept going, but it stopped a lot of them.'

Olsen wasn't the only Polynesian to take this stance for his people. Across the code lines, All Black Sir Michael Jones adopted a similar non-violent approach to any thuggery and racism. He told ESPN of his response to any underhand tactics: 'I found a way to send a message to them that I didn't need to throw a punch back, but I could smash you hard in the tackle, aim for your ribs in the ruck or rub your face in the ground. They'd get the message that way. I'd never take a backwards step, but all legally and in the rules of the game.'

Jones says he has enormous respect for the stance Olsen took in an era riddled with cheap-shot merchants: 'I appreciated the cleanness of Olsen's game and he highlighted and proved that we didn't need to get involved with negative stuff. You could do it all within the rules of the game.'

As a fellow Polynesian pioneer, for Jones, the stakes were high: 'Olsen and I understood we were role models to a generation of kids who saw violence on the streets and for some in their own homes. We demonstrated that you could control your wrath and show self-control. Olsen would send this message straight to our youth.'

* * * * *

There are other historical precedents of sporting pioneers absorbing physical attacks and racial abuse to push their people forward. On 15 April 1947, Jackie Robinson shocked America by smashing through the colour barrier to become the first African American to play Major League Baseball for a US team. His brave decision kickstarted a revolution that ended with desegregation of sports in schools and all US government institutions.

Robinson had experienced the sting of racism in the US Army in 1944 when he was court-martialled for sitting at the front of the bus. When Robinson decided to make the leap from the Kansas City Royals in the Negro Leagues to the Brooklyn Dodgers in the Major Leagues he knew he was entering a hostile white man's world.

The Brooklyn Dodgers' manager, Branch Ricky, launched the Jackie Robinson 'noble experiment' which gripped American baseball fans, who watched every move of the league's new first baseman. A condition of Branch Rickey agreeing to sign Robinson was that Robinson was not to respond to the provocation from white players waiting for him in stadiums across America.

Jackie Robinson played himself in the 1950 biographical film *The*

Jackie Robinson Story which portrayed the famous scene in which Jackie made a promise much like Olsen's, to not retaliate and create a negative stereotype.

Jackie Robinson: 'Mr Rickey, do you want a ball player who's afraid to fight back?'

Manager Branch Rickey: 'I want a ball player with the guts enough not to fight back. Do you have the guts enough to play the game no matter what happens? If someone punches you in the cheek, what do you do?

Jackie Robinson: Mr Rickey, I've got two cheeks.'

It was the Philadelphia Phillies, led by their Alabaman manager Ben Chapman, who were the most relentless in taunting Robinson, with Chapman reportedly greeting Robinson at the batting plate: 'Hey boy, come shine my shoes. Hey boy, how come you ain't pickin' cotton?'

Like Sydney for Olsen, for Robinson, Philadelphia was no city of brotherly love.

In Robinson's memoirs, he wrote of almost snapping under the pressure: 'For one wild and rage crazed minute I thought to hell with Mr Rickey's noble experiment. It's clear it won't succeed. I thought what a glorious cleansing thing it would be to let go. To hell with the image of the patient, black freak. I could throw down my bat, stride over to that Phillies dugout, grab one of those white sons of bitches and smash his teeth in with my despised black fist.'

For the privilege of playing professional baseball, Robinson was kicked by opposing players, pitchers aimed at his head and opposing base runners slid with their spikes up, gashing his legs.

The stakes were high. If Robinson could succeed in the previously all-white Major Leagues, institutions like the military, police, colleges, schools and other sports had a role model to use to begin their programmes integrating African Americans. Robinson had to succeed and was a lightning rod for those who wanted to keep the status quo.

When he went on the road with the Brooklyn Dodgers, spectators and players would rain abuse on him and Robinson received death threats, stayed in separate hotels to his teammates and ate meals on his own.

Jimmy Cannon of the *New York Post* described Robinson as 'the loneliest man I've ever seen in sports'.

Jackie Robinson's sacrifice had a wide societal impact. Martin Luther King Jr suggested Robinson was 'a freedom rider before freedom riders'.

Alton Waldron was the first African American congressman from Queens, New York. Robinson's impact was clear for him: 'Everybody talked better, breathed deeper, walked taller, stepped with more glide in their stride and dip in the hip because Jackie Robinson had come to baseball.'

Other political pioneers took their inspiration from Robinson. Douglas Wilder, the first elected African American governor, described the importance of the players to follow: 'The first is really no good unless there's a second to the extent that the first can open the door and the second creates the trend. Those doors can't be permitted to even appear to shut or to close. The foot first, the arms and elbows second and the total body next in the door to keep it open for others to come through.'

And they did. Not only in baseball but other sports. Basketball race pioneers Nat 'Sweetwater' Clifton and Bill Russell both credited their careers to Jackie Robinson. Jackie opened up opportunities across the United States for African Americans — the fruits of turning the other cheek to the threats and abuse. He had a sense of purpose and dignity and would not be denied.

Jackie Robinson represented the beginning of change and inspired the next generation of African Americans as did rugby league and union race pioneers like Olsen Filipaina, Arthur Beetson, Larry Corowa, Lucius Banks, George Bennett, Jimmy Cumberbatch, Roy Francis, Martin Offiah, Clive Sullivan, Sir Bryan Williams and Sir Michael Jones.

Robinson's story shows the true magical powers of pioneers 'taking a bullet' for those that followed. African American baseball legend Willie Mays was energised by Jackie to believe he had a chance to play in the Major Leagues and said: 'When Jackie came in he could do everything — he could run, he could hit. He was very special. I said to myself, "If Jackie can make it, I have a chance to make it in the Major leagues."'

* * * * *

As Olsen walked off the field after his fight with Paul Taylor at Cumberland Oval, he was hit in the head by a full can of KB beer and racially abused by a large contingent of Parramatta fans. They called him a 'black bastard', 'coon' and 'nigger' and told him to 'go back into his cage'.

The volume of words stung Olsen and had a deep impact on Leslie, sitting in the crowd. She will never forget what she heard that day: 'As soon as I heard the N word I was shocked. Where were we living? I mouthed them back and as you can imagine that only made it worse.'

Driving home from Cumberland Oval that afternoon, Olsen felt a part of him breaking. He felt like a ghost of himself, going through the motions.

'For some reason people don't understand that racism is different,' Olsen later explained. 'Call me short or fat or dumb or ugly — I can deal with that. But insult my colour or my people and you are insulting my parents, my friends, my children, my grandparents and all those that came before them.

'If you were to insult a white person's mother, they would go crazy on you. But that's exactly how I felt in a lot of matches when I was racially abused, often while pushing my head into the ground. I understand things happen in the heat of battle, but not that many times from that many people. At least one person saying sorry would have been nice.'

Olsen was amazed at the ability of Aboriginal teammate Larry Corowa to seemingly absorb the racism. Olsen says: 'Larry was used to it, but it had never happened to me before in Auckland. Some fans didn't know about Polynesians so sometimes I copped the same slurs as the Aboriginal players. I could have passed for one except for my big thighs!'

* * * * *

The science is in on the impact of racism and it's compelling. Elizabeth Brondolo, a psychologist at St John's University, New York, conducted research on a programme counselling New York's traffic police who were routinely verbally abused and most of whom were African American. Brondolo says: 'When they were called "a fat pig" or told to "get a job", our team could treat them with standard behaviour therapy tools like relaxation and skits, which usually worked. But the racial insults involved so much despair that we couldn't do the same kind of intervention.'

A strong body of research shows that racial insults do more damage than other types of insults. Brondolo has studied the psychological and physical toll of racism and found the short-term impact is stress, anxiety and depression and over longer periods high blood pressure, cardiovascular disease and in some cases post-traumatic stress disorder (PTSD).

* * * * *

Māori Tony Kemp was the next Pacific playmaker to follow Olsen to play professionally in Australia and for him the abuse was no different. He did not face any racism in New Zealand where the European players treated Pacific and Māori players as equals. Australia was a different environment.

'I got called a "black cunt" a lot in my time at Newcastle which started in 1988, the year Olsen left. It came from the opposition players and crowds and sometimes from my own teammates which led to some actual fistfights. It was disgusting and I have refused to go to a number of Newcastle Knights events because of the scars.'

Kemp knew what was coming to him before he arrived and was disturbed by the Australians' treatment of Olsen. 'We really got offended when word filtered back what Olsen was going through. He is a softly spoken gentleman with a big infectious smile and so positive and we were honoured just to be around him. There would not be a person in New Zealand who would say a bad word about him. What cowards they were to put him through that experience.'

* * * * *

It wasn't just the racism that Olsen found difficult to swallow. Some teammates had it in for him and for the first time in his career he experienced treachery from the inner sanctum.

It was a shock for Olsen when reserve-grade teammates at Balmain deliberately tried to injure him at opposed ball work sessions between first grade and reserves. At one session they finally got their man when his sternum was cracked by a deliberate elbow.

'We were supposed to be playing "hold" not tackle, but every time I got the ball I had all these reserve-grade players hitting me as hard as they could and one got me,' Olsen says. 'Frank didn't care. I had to play the next Saturday and it was incredibly painful. I had to tape a big sponge on my chest every match for a month. It was dog eat dog and I couldn't believe what some Aussies would do to get in the team.'

On reflection Olsen can now understand their behaviour as a product of a larger system: 'When I look back at how desperate Aussies were to play it makes sense. Players got a bonus for being in the first grade and there was a big drop in pay if you were sent to reserves. It created pressure and trying to injure guys was their way of trying to get back in the team. I was an easy target and if I fought back, I would be fined and branded a whinger. So I sucked it up.'

The lack of respect from some teammates at Balmain meant that sometimes he didn't want to turn up to training. Olsen remembers having cans of beer tipped on him at an after-match function. He still feels disgusted at his own teammates talking behind his back. Olsen says: 'When that stuff is going on, the joy of playing together is not there; it ruined league for me.'

Leslie recalls an uncharitable atmosphere at times for Olsen in the Balmain Tigers clubhouse: 'Some of the players gave Olsen a hard time. They thought he was getting paid a lot more than a lot of them were and they were jealous and had the shits with him. There was a lot of really petty jealousy and undermining. It's always easiest to pick on the outsider.'

They were disorienting times and Olsen says it came from all sides, his otherness playing into a fear of change: 'Opposition players would play harder against me, more viciously and aggressively like they were protecting something — like something new was happening and they didn't like it.'

* * * * *

Olsen's only on-field fight was matched by a lone incident off the field. He would be approached in bars and pubs, particularly by drunks who would challenge him to fights or attempt to provoke him. Olsen had an opening line for the would-be heroes trying to make a name for themselves: 'You'll have to throw the first punch so make it good.'

Only one person crossed the line and Olsen was disappointed that it was someone he worked with.

'I was having a drink at the Ermington Hotel when a workmate comes in drunk and starts calling me racial names,' remembers Olsen. 'I tried to leave but he blocked me and he made so much noise that I had to take him outside and try to talk to him away from everybody. He was out there with all his cheering mates and he swung first, but it was over quickly and his mates went quiet. I still feel bad about it. I hated fighting, but I knew what to do when I had no option.'

Leslie remembers a dark night of the soul: 'Olsen came home upset and crying. He was shocked that a person he knew could turn on him like that. He was less trusting and more wary after that.'

For a brief period, Olsen lived in fear of being sent back to New

Zealand and an even worse fate — getting caught breaking his promise to his mother: 'I decked the wrong guy. He was our union delegate and I thought he might go to the police and then my mum would find out.'

* * * * *

Despite the brawl and the racist abuse at Cumberland Oval, Olsen hit a purple patch of form playing alongside Percy Knight in the halves. Charles Christian, from *Rugby League Week*, reported that 'Olsen Filipaina has set an unofficial record' of four consecutive man-of-the-match awards.

'Dropped to reserve grade because of poor form,' wrote Christian, 'Filipaina has been an instant success since recalled to first grade as a five eighth. Filipaina has won club awards against Parramatta, Wests and Penrith and a Tooth Cup award against Easts in his only four games in Sydney as a pivot [five-eighth]. The awards have included a microwave oven, a three-in-one stereo and a video cassette recorder.'

The prizes were given to his adopted Dries family or sent to his family back home in New Zealand. Olsen remembers calling his mother to proudly announce: 'Hey, Mum — I won a Pākehā microwave!'

* * * * *

The relentless demands placed on Olsen by his father Aloese used to rile his 'Aussie mum' Margaret Dries: 'No one will say it, but Olsen was under big pressure from his father who was always calling the house to get him to send money home,' says Margaret. 'We froze his money for a while to make sure he got his act together to save for a house, but it was difficult. He would never think of himself and always did what his father said.'

'The boys loved their father and tried to block out the bad things,' explains Leslie. 'They always hoped he was going to improve, but Aloese would take advantage of their love and ask them for money. Olsen was the cash cow and he always sent money and went without himself — he wouldn't even buy new clothes. Aloese had a gambling addiction and Olsen was the enabler.'

Olsen was not alone in sending money to his parents, a common practice among Pacific athletes. When Tongan-Australian Israel Folau was playing with the Melbourne Storm he shocked rugby league fans when he shared his financial arrangements in a story in the *Sydney Morning Herald*.

Folau said that he gave his A$1 million annual salary directly to his parents who gave him an allowance of $150 a week. He even asked his father's permission to go to the movies.

* * * * *

Olsen's homesickness — which he had struggled with since his first day in Sydney — grew more acute and for emotional sustenance he relied heavily on talking to his family on the telephone, his umbilical cord back to New Zealand.

For every Pasifika, Māori or Aboriginal player that made it in Sydney, far more succumbed to homesickness and left, with some moving to other sports.

In 2004, Tana Umaga was selected as the All Blacks captain, the first of Samoan origin to achieve the honour. In 2005, he led the new haka named 'Kapa O Pango', a landmark moment in New Zealand rugby and society.

The 74-test legend may never have played for the All Blacks if the Newcastle Knights had known how to manage homesickness. In 1988, Umaga went to trial with the Newcastle Knights, having played league all his life and represented the Junior Kiwis.

Enveloped by homesickness, the teenaged Umaga returned to New Zealand on a plane after three weeks, opening up an opportunity for the All Blacks to leverage his talents and create history.

* * * * *

Homesick and floundering under Frank Stanton's system, Olsen's application to training, which was never a strong point, began to waver.

'Frank Stanton didn't like Olsen and gave him a hard time,' says Margaret Dries. 'Olsen would come home from training, wretched from the way he was treated. He would get on the phone to his mother and family for four or five hours and then get up and go to work. One time he put $800 for the phone bill in my husband Phil's bank account.'

Leslie says Olsen's feelings or problems were not a priority to Frank: 'If Olsen tried to explain his side of things he would be ridiculed. We always hoped Frank would come around because at times he could be a nice man and very charming.'

For Frank Stanton, a man steeped in the stiff-upper-lip, Anglo-Celtic world of Sydney rugby league, Olsen was a difficult player to reach.

'Olsen was a less than enthusiastic trainer, but he wasn't the only one,' recalls Stanton. 'The whole team had to live up to the training expectations I had, which were hard and difficult. Where I had come from, the harder you trained the better.'

* * * * *

The cultural differences did not just manifest themselves in application to training but also in playing style where there was a clash between the exuberant Polynesians and Aboriginals and the increasingly structured systems of Sydney clubs.

'For Polynesians and Aboriginals, it was twice as difficult to make the progression from being natural footballers to structural footballers,' explains Balmain Tigers halfback Percy Knight.

'For us Aboriginals it was easier to score a try from 70 metres out than battering them 20 metres out, when their defence was organised. Frank squandered my talent, Olsen's talent and Larry Corowa's talent — who some would say are three once in a lifetime talents. He homogenised us back to boring routine, robot players.'

Frank Stanton does not agree with Knight's view on his coaching: 'Percy had an opinion on a lot of things, but I didn't see it that way,' says Stanton. 'There were no racial implications at Balmain, no cultural clash and we all got along. My interest was to have a team regardless of who they were, fit and well and capable of playing the proper football I wanted them to play.'

Stanton feels that he represented the coaching norms of the time and was a man of his era: 'Regardless of who they were, and there were some internationals in that team, no one was treated any differently from each other. All were treated the same and the expectations were the same. I had coached Larry Corowa for the Kangaroos and encountered Indigenous players at Manly. It wasn't something that was new to me.'

Olsen's teammates had differing views on Frank. For players like Steve Roach, Ben Elias and Wayne Pearce, Frank would be a guiding light and pivotal in their success in becoming greats of the game.

For Wayne Wigham, Olsen's centre partner and friend, Frank Stanton's style was a cultural mismatch — a one-dimensional approach serving a mix of different thinkers and cultures. 'His transplanted Manly game plan didn't work and it's a great example of culture working in one place but not another,' says Wigham.

'We were multicultural and really working class with some free spirits and his Manly style was disciplined and regimented and dulled some of the guys who can win games. A lot of players lost their love for the game.'

For Wigham, the Stanton culture was not an environment that encouraged innovation and creativity: 'A lot of us were scared to try things because of what Frank would say. When you did something on the field that didn't work out, you knew you were getting an ear blast at halftime.'

* * * * *

Olsen was not enjoying his football, but he managed to hold on to his first-grade starting spot, oscillating between the centres and the five-eighth role for the second half of the 1981 season. In the final four games, as captain Percy Knight fell out with Stanton and was dropped to the bench, Olsen crossed over for a try in each outing.

After a 17–8 win over Western Suburbs in the second-to-last match of the season, Filipaina scored a 9/10 for his performance. The *Rugby*

League Week match report read:

'Filipaina was a match winner. Balmain were clearly the better side with Kiwi five eighth Olsen Filipaina turning in another outstanding game, capping a fine match by scoring a try.

'The pivot spot is undoubtedly Filipaina's role in the Balmain side and coach Frank Stanton must be wishing he'd discovered the fact much sooner, particularly when Filipaina went through the mid-season horrors and spent a stint in reserves. Filipaina was at his brilliant best using his brute strength to break up the defence before unloading superbly to supports.'

In the final match of the 1981 season, Balmain beat Penrith 25–6. 'I was playing lock forward and after a scrum I was moving across the field in cover defence,' says Royce Simmons, a Penrith and future Kangaroos legend then in his second year of first-grade football.

'Olsen got the ball and passed it to his winger and our winger wrapped him up. I thought we had done our job containing a line break when the winger popped the ball to Olsen who had wrapped around the winger. Not many guys wrapped around in those days and there I was facing Olsen, flat footed and him in full flight. He ran straight over the top of me, did a war dance on my chest and when I got up, he was putting the ball down between the sticks. I had never ever experienced anything like that power, and I had a bruised chest.'

It was all too late for Balmain, however, and under Stanton, the club finished bottom of the ladder with just 13 points. It was the Tigers' third wooden spoon in 73 seasons.

'1981 was a year to forget,' says Olsen, who despite it all, was awarded Balmain's Best and Fairest Player for the year. 'When you come last, the fans have every right to stick it to you. We had no confidence and were all a bit scared of Frank. Whatever we tried seemed to make it worse. Reaching the end of the season was like an escape to fresh air.'

* * * * *

The off-season held some different and new challenges for Olsen. Three days after the final game against Penrith he was corralled by his 'Aussie mum' Margaret Dries and they both drove to Royal North Shore hospital to witness Leslie give birth to their first child, Louise.

'Olsen was terrified of being a father, with the responsibility it entailed, but to his credit he was there for a tough caesarean birth,' Leslie recalls.

'His football wasn't going that well and he was unsure about a lot of things. It all changed when he held Louise in his arms and his eyes lit up. She gave him inspiration to deal with his situation at the Balmain Tigers.'

For Olsen, the arrival of Louise was a moment to savour: 'I remember holding her up and thinking — I'll go through anything for you.'

* * * * *

Sydney rugby league in the early 1980s was the domain of the white man. Aboriginal players, of which there were only a few, were viewed by some as stereotypically unreliable and 'flashy'.

The men on club committees were all Anglo-Celtic, as were all of the head coaches, and with the exception of Olsen and Aboriginal Percy Knight, so were all of the players in the key 'spine' playmaking positions — half, five-eighth, hooker and fullback.

This racial uniformity led to limited exposure for players, fans and administrators to the nuances of other cultures, creating a perfect environment for cultural miscommunication and negative stereotyping of outsiders.

Roy Masters was coaching Western Suburbs and remembers the colour line: 'It was a massive cultural leap for black players to finally break through in the decision-making positions and not just as a finisher or winger. When the five-eighths of Sydney lined up against Olsen, it was the first time any of them had faced a Polynesian playmaker. He was the one who broke through.

'I remember always having a special game plan for Olsen,' says Masters. 'He was a combustible player who could destroy opposition defences. You had to pick your players who could move up quickly to contain him.'

Masters, who would coach St George from 1982 to 1987 before establishing himself as a journalist, was 'fascinated' by Olsen: 'As a coach I would have loved to have got my hands on Olsen. He would have been better with me at Wests or St George. We had a culture that allowed people to be individuals. We played to people's strengths.'

* * * * *

In the end, the 1981 season belonged to the Parramatta Eels, led by one of rugby league's all-time great coaches, Jack Gibson. A mix of laconic genius, hard-man, philosopher, man manager and dry comedian, Gibson was a hero for Eels fans for delivering the club its first premiership.

Gibson was a man-management pioneer among Australian coaches. He had studied the best of American coaching techniques and come to the conclusion that personalised man management was the best way to blend teams of different individuals and to bring out the best in performance.

This meant learning about the player's life off the field in order to assist their development as people, not just as footballers.

Parramatta, NSW and Kangaroos legend Brett Kenny, who thrived under Gibson, remembers an honest, straightforward man with a wicked sense of humour: 'Jack would sit you down and he would tell you straight how he thought you were playing and you knew where you stood,' Kenny once explained in an interview in *Rugby League Week*. 'He could read players well. That's why players liked to play for him — he treated them with respect.'

During his career at Parramatta, Kenny would build an outstanding career, playing 265 first-grade games and scoring 110 tries. But in 1981 he was still a fresh-faced 20-year-old. Gibson had liked what he had seen in Olsen and looking to defend his premiership he made a decision to acquire some fresh blood to bolster his backline.

Olsen was off contract and Gibson sent his right-hand man, Ron Massey, to the Dries house in Ryde to secure Olsen's signature for the 1982 season.

'We didn't know how good Brett Kenny was going to be, and we thought Olsen could play,' Massey later told News Ltd journalist Paul Crawley. 'He was a bit of a lone wolf, Olsen, but a nice bloke to talk to. Anyway, I went to the place where he was living and we talked and he agreed to come to Parramatta. So I got in the car and drove back.'

Imagine Massey's shock, then, to hear that Olsen had decided to stay with Balmain. Massey was still travelling back to Parramatta along Victoria Road when he heard the news over the radio.

In hindsight, Olsen's decision now seems insane. Why, when he was clearly unhappy under Frank Stanton at cellar-dwellers Balmain, would Olsen back out on an agreement to join the premiers Parramatta?

Leslie believes Olsen's loyalty to his teammates was the decisive factor. 'I remember asking Olsen, "What do you want to do?" Olsen said he was getting on well with most of the Balmain first graders. It was always about the players with Olsen.'

'I was very close to joining Parramatta,' Olsen later explained. 'But Parramatta had just won the grand final and I didn't understand why they would want me with a winning team. We were all embarrassed to finish with the wooden spoon and it felt like I was jumping ship on my mates. We knew we were a better side than we showed that year.'

For Olsen, one of the biggest regrets in not signing with Parramatta was that he never got to play with Mick Cronin, his all-time favourite player. 'He was such an amazing player in attack and defence,' says Olsen.

Had their fates intertwined, Olsen may have been a key pillar in the Parramatta dynasty of the 1980s. Cronin recalls: 'It's a funny world. I remember Jack Gibson talking a lot about getting Olsen to Parramatta to play with me in the centres.'

Cronin feels that Gibson would have been a good mentor for Olsen: 'Jack would have been a different experience for Olsen compared to

Frank. I played under Frank on the 1978 tour of Great Britain and he was black and white. Jack would help people out and simplified the game for people. He would have made allowances for Olsen's unique body shape and as long as he put in on the field, Olsen would have thrived with us.'

Cronin remembers one plan to contain Olsen going astray: 'Before one match Ray Price announced to us in the change room that he had a theory to stop Olsen. Ray had a theory about everyone, and he kept saying, "You gotta go in low to stop Filipaina." First tackle of the game he tried to tackle Olsen low and got laid out flat. Brett Kenny and I burst out laughing and said to each other, "There's another theory down the drain."'

Little did Olsen know that Parramatta would become the club to beat in the 1980s, winning a historic and dynastic 'threepeat' by taking out the premiership in 1981, 1982 and 1983.

Who knows how Olsen's life and career might have changed had he joined the house that Jack built?

4
FREE-SPIRITED FOOTBALLER

'We've come too far to give up who we are.'

— Pharrell Williams, 'Get Lucky'

After Round 5 of the 1982 season of the freshly renamed 'Winfield Cup', *Rugby League Week* splashed with a story on Frank Stanton's new-look Balmain Tigers. 'Blond power!' read the headline. The article profiled Balmain's three new fair-haired signings: Garry Jack, a 20-year-old fullback recruited from Wests; Steve Martin, a 25-year-old half from Manly; and Gary Bridge, a rookie winger plucked from bush football.

When Olsen Filipaina joined the club in 1980, Balmain fielded the first 'First Nations' backline in the Sydney competition. Now, under the direction of Frank Stanton, his teams were increasingly Anglo-Celtic. Māori Lloyd Martin had moved to the Canberra Raiders, while Indigenous players Percy Knight and Larry Corowa would spend most of the season on the outer, playing generally in reserve grade.

With his new-look team in place, Stanton stepped up his commitment to conservative, mistake-free football and superior fitness. 'It's the teams that start training in November that are up there in September,' he told *Rugby League Week*. 'We'll be a much fitter side than last year and that will be a big factor.'

Led by trainer Les Hobbs and golden boy Wayne Pearce, the Tigers strived to be the fittest team in rugby league. Hobbs opened up his private gym for the players who wanted to do extra training. The media soon dubbed his house: 'the mecca for the motivated'.

'Olsen wasn't beating down the door to do extra training, but I had a special trick for him,' says Hobbs. 'I built a handball court in my gym and Olsen was so keen on ball sports that I could lure him in with the promise of a game. Funnily enough, in the entire time I had the handball court, Olsen was the only guy who could beat me.'

Olsen's aptitude at various sports astounded Hobbs. 'He was great at squash, basketball, tennis you name it. He would play tennis all day after finishing his garbage run. You couldn't keep him away from a racquet sport and he came alive when there was ball handling involved. Not so keen on training without a ball and I'll never forget the looks he used to give me when running was involved. He wanted to save himself for match day.'

Nothing could get Olsen motivated for long road runs, however. He was still rising every morning at 2 am to empty metal garbage bins, which took a heavy toll on his body, and at 100 kilograms, pounding the pavement had a terrible impact on his knees.

'With my garbage run and the training, I was turning up to matches footsore and my knees were hurting,' Olsen explains. 'One day, Kerry Hemsley and I didn't turn up for a road run. He gave a good excuse, but I'd had enough and just said, "They don't play rugby league on a road." After a $3000 fine it was the last road run I missed.'

* * * * *

One of Olsen's closest friends at the club was his partner in the centres, Wayne Wigham. During 1980 and 1981 they developed an almost telepathic relationship. Wayne watched Olsen closely, calculating how many seconds it would take him to get his hands free to deliver a pass.

'I studied Olsen's game and had worked out how I could work with him, get the most out of him. I would count to two as everyone was fighting to take him down,' says Wigham. 'I would take off at three, let him know I was there and receive a soft pass on the fly that put me in space and made me look good.'

Before long, Olsen was communicating with Wayne through darting eyes or a raised eyebrow. Off the field, however, Wigham noticed that his friend had become more introverted.

'In his first year at Balmain, Olsen was very social, coming back to the Leagues Club, playing tennis with the boys, and he was a bit of a celebrity at the Ranch pub in North Ryde, even though he wasn't much of a drinker,' says Wigham.

'Then under Frank, he just dropped out. He stopped coming to the pub and would race into the change rooms after training and matches and leave before some of us had even gotten back in there.'

By the 1982 season, Olsen had become a recluse. His triangular routine was work, football and then home to Leslie and his daughter Louise. Reporters, such as *Rugby League Week* editor Ian Heads, began to notice his absence.

'After the game Filipaina showed he has lost none of his dash in the dressing room,' observed Heads after a pre-season hit-out against Wests. 'He was dressed and gone before half his team was showered. Filipaina is no social butterfly. He plays his football professionally and well, but has no hankering for the social life afterwards. For him the words "training" and "playing" mean just that. As soon as both are finished he's off.'

Olsen remembers a dark time with minimal contact with the outside world: 'I became a homebody and as soon as I had done whatever had to be done I was gone a minute later.

'It became hard to deal with people and socialise and I kept it simple, in survival mode. I'd try to avoid getting my head blown off at training and meeting more people would bring more problems and I had enough piling on top of me already.'

What Heads and Wigham didn't realise at the time was that Olsen was struggling with depression. Later, after Wigham was diagnosed with melancholia, a form of depression and subsequently treated, he came out in the media in 1999, one of the first league players to admit suffering from mental health issues. But in the early 1980s, a man was supposed to 'suck it up', suffer in silence and get on with life.

'The hardest part about depression is that it takes away your energy,' says Wigham, who now works with the Black Dog Institute, a charity aimed at educating communities on identifying and managing depression. 'When I was younger I took energy for granted but without it, it's harder to function. So if you're really suffering before the game, you get out of the car, even walking round to the change rooms you'd feel like: "I've got no energy; how am I going to play today?" Then you'd feel bad — "What's wrong with me? I'm selfish, why am I feeling like this?" It's a disease.'

Reflecting on his time with Balmain, Wigham feels that Olsen showed every sign of depression. 'It would have been so easy to pick up now but back then no one was talking to us and there was all this pressure,' Wigham explains.

'We didn't know how to look after our minds and for years Olsen put on the face of bravery while he was struggling, which is exhausting. You're exhausted by pretending to your teammates and from putting on your mask. It was brave of Olsen and I'm in awe of him, dealing with the homesickness, the racism and the coach. If the coach doesn't love you and that's what you need, it's hard. It takes your energy and becomes hard to function. You just want to go home and hide, and Olsen did that — he stopped being social and became a loner. At the time I didn't know why but now I understand.'

Aboriginal Balmain teammate Percy Knight recalls Olsen going through a tough time in their three years playing together: 'Frank would publicly humiliate Olsen and he would just absorb it, and we wouldn't know what he was thinking. I remember him looking down at the ground with the shame of it all.'

When Knight was made captain of Balmain he remembers approaching Olsen about his welfare: "I could tell something was wrong with him and I remember asking him if he was OK and he said he was. We were taught not to show anxiety or emotion and he would suffer in silence.'

In Māori terms, Olsen's silent siege led to a state of 'mauri noho' or slumbering life force, which leads to withdrawal from participating in society. Education Aotearoa defines the outcomes of suffering the 'dormant spirit' of mauri noho as 'loss of hope, a clouded mind, a tortured body and relationships that are disempowering and humiliating'.

Olsen remembers the time with sadness: 'Some days I was bursting out of my skin, others I didn't want to come to the ground and I felt like shit. I remember talking to myself saying, "Get out of this mood. What are you doing?"'

His attitude on match day in Sydney was different to Auckland: 'Growing up, every day I was excited for match day and I couldn't wait all week. In Sydney it was different. Some days when I was thinking about off-field stuff, I couldn't find the spark. I was trying but nothing was happening.'

Looking back, Leslie agrees with Wigham's assessment and feels that Olsen went through a long and dispiriting phase: 'Olsen was depressed and it felt like he didn't like the game any more. I would try and find out what was wrong with him and he would say, "You don't understand the game." He would say he was tired and you have to remember, back then men showing emotions was taboo.'

* * * * *

After Olsen's solid finish to the 1981 season at five-eighth, Frank Stanton and club management expected big things from him in 1982. Secretary Keith Gittoes told reporters that he was to be the club's permanent goal-kicker. His efficient two-step toe-bash style had impressed the Tigers, prompting Gittoes to proclaim Olsen one of the best kickers in Sydney. 'There's no doubt he'll do the job for us,' said Gittoes.

The media termed Olsen a 'reluctant goal-kicker' and they were close to the mark. Olsen says: 'I only kicked in Māngere because nobody wanted to kick, and I was relieved when Wayne Miranda put his hand up for Balmain. If asked I'll do it, but it's stressful and you get abused by everyone so I would do it as fast as possible.'

Olsen's quick-fire two-step goal-kicking style would dismay his forwards, who were hoping for a break to regain their breath. 'I always kicked my goals quickly, but the big men would always beg me to take my time and give them a rest.'

* * * * *

Olsen's depression manifested itself though off-season over-eating and he did himself no favours with the extra kilos he was carrying to start the 1982 season. Ian Heads noted in *Rugby League Week*: 'Olsen Filipaina has not been the star pupil at Leichhardt this year. The Kiwi star came back from summer vacation many kilos overweight and is battling a weight problem.'

The season did not begin well for Balmain with three losses in a row. Balmain were ripe for a change and Stanton took action by dropping Olsen to reserve grade. He was the only back to be dropped, and he didn't take Stanton's decision well.

When the Tigers' reserve-grade coach, Laurie Freier, called a midweek team meeting, Olsen turned up late, preferring to play squash with a friend.

Olsen's attitude tormented Freier and he recalls an incident: 'I remember the squash court door flying open and Laurie came storming in furious that I was late for the team meeting. But I was in the middle of a tight squash game with my mate that I had promised him for weeks. I couldn't let him down.'

Luckily, he played well that weekend and was recalled to first grade for Balmain's Round 5 clash against South Sydney.

Starting on the bench, Stanton sent Olsen on after halftime with simple instructions: 'to blow up the bridge'. Trailing Souths by one point, Olsen was tasked with shutting down their main attacking threat, Queenslander Mitch Brennan.

FREE-SPIRITED FOOTBALLER

In the 65th minute, Brennan received the ball in a backline movement and Olsen lined him up. 'I was in the centres and Mick Pattison was five-eighth facing Olsen,' says Brennan. 'I agreed with Mick that he was to draw Olsen to him and I would take the hole outside him. Well, Mick sold me the best dump. Olsen was roaring in at an angle and Mick just passed the ball straight away. I was trapped between Olsen and my centre and he cleaned me up big time. He was a beautiful guy off the field, but he showed me no mercy that day.'

Olsen's thunderous tackle speared Brennan into the ground, dislodging the ball, which was swooped on by Olsen's teammate Wayne Wigham. On the next play the ball swung out to the Balmain backline for winger John Davidson to score the winning try, the Tigers triumphing 12–8.

'League matches can rarely be encapsulated in one instant,' reported the *Sun Herald* the next day. 'But that's the way it was yesterday with Filipaina's battering ram tackle jolting the ball loose from Brennan and leading directly to the try that won the match.'

Olsen's hit on Brennan reverberated around the competition. It was, for many observers, typical of Olsen — just one week after being dropped to reserve grade, he had come up with a game-changing tackle that would be spoken about for years to come.

Journalist Ian Heads' match report in *Rugby League Week* read: 'Olsen Filipaina's ferocious, game-breaking tackle on Souths' Mitch Brennan was an indication of the power of the enigmatic New Zealander.'

Although Olsen's intervention had delivered Frank Stanton a win, his coach was measured in his praise and after the match he called out Olsen's attitude to the waiting journalists: 'He did well and turned the game our way with a thunderous tackle. Where to fit him in will cause a lot of soul searching but I'd be happier if his attitude to training changed. He's not fair to himself, he turns up at training, but he won't push himself.'

Stanton noted his potential: 'Olsen has absolutely tremendous natural ability. But he's one of those blokes who is a gifted ball player, but he finds it hard to apply himself to do the hard work to back it all up.'

Olsen says it was all one-way communication: 'Culturally, I couldn't talk back or argue with Frank — I needed some body weight to throw around; it was my difference. I was match fit, but Frank wanted to make me marathon fit.'

* * * * *

Thirty-seven years after 'The Tackle', journalist and author Ian Heads is still in awe. 'That may well have been the most devastating tackle I ever saw. I saw some of the big hitters — Charlie Frith, Terry Randall, Bunny Reilly— but that one topped it. There was a gasp from the crowd and he almost snapped Brennan in half.'

It also changed the trajectory of Olsen's season. The following week, he laid on two tries for Wayne Wigham in a 12-point win over Wests. He celebrated in the dressing rooms after the match — a rarity noted by his fellow teammates and reporters alike. One Balmain official cheekily asked if someone had chained him to the leg of the change-room bench. 'Olsen,' observed one reporter, 'has been an inspiration.'

For the next 19 rounds, he didn't miss a single first-grade game. By mid-season, *Rugby League Week* polled 30 Winfield Cup players in two categories — who is the hardest player to tackle and who is the hardest defender.

In the first category Olsen was officially voted the 'hardest man to tackle' in Sydney, an overwhelming winner who was mentioned by a large majority of the players polled, who gushed over his attacking ability.

Manly's Max Krilich said Olsen was 'difficult to contain when firing'. Easts' Marty Gurr said that due to Olsen's low centre of gravity 'he can bump players off because very few can reach and grab his stocky legs'. St George's Graham Quinn shared his memory of being bumped off by Olsen, admiring 'the way he travels low to the ground and drops his shoulder into tackles'.

South's Tony Melrose noted being bumped off by Olsen's attacking technique and praised his well-balanced attacking skills. For Wests' Jim Leis, Olsen was a complex puzzle to work out due to the size of his chest and strong fend. Cronulla's Steve Rogers spoke of the difficulty of bringing Olsen down due to his overall strength.

Olsen earned the vote of Kiwis teammate Kurt Sorensen who said he was something special in attack, with the balance and power to bump off defenders with ease. One of the game's most famous defenders, Parramatta's Ron Hilditch, said he considered Olsen to be one of the hardest footballers around, acknowledging his 'tremendous all-round strength and his power when he uses his hip is quite incredible'.

Penrith's Lew Zivanovic voted for Olsen, saying he is a bulldozing type who doesn't know when to stop, while Canberra's John McLeod said: 'Olsen is a nugget with good balance and the way he pushes you off makes it look so simple.'

St George's Brian Johnston spoke of his personal experience, noting: 'Olsen can push people away with a virtual shrug of his shoulder — I know because he has done it to me on several occasions.'

In the second category: 'Who is the hardest tackler in the Winfield Cup?', established hitmen Terry Randall and Ron Hilditch were the top two selected, but Olsen came third in the voting.

Parramatta's Mick Cronin mentioned that 'Olsen Filipaina is quite strong and has got me down a few times'. Olsen's Balmain teammate Steve Martin also shared some of his experiences from playing for Manly against Olsen: 'A couple of tackles by Olsen Filipaina two years ago made me feel like I had been broken in two.'

* * * * *

Across 'the ditch' in New Zealand, rugby league was experiencing a boost thanks to a selection of Kiwi footballers plying their trade in Sydney. In 1982, in addition to Olsen at Balmain, front-rower Mark Broadhurst had signed for Manly Warringah and the Sorensen brothers Dane and Kurt continued their rise at Cronulla.

Fred Ah Kuoi was signed by the North Sydney Bears, joining Mark Graham, who had moved there the previous year from Brisbane. Graham played so well in his debut year in 1981 that he was featured in the NSWRL's 'Greatest Game of All' television promotion. The Kiwis had well and truly arrived.

'Never before have New Zealand Rugby League followers given so much attention to the code in Australia,' reported John Coffey in *Rugby League Week*.

'Interest in Australian rugby league has been boosted by delayed telecasts of highlights of the Tooth Cup competition. Many fans from other sports also take in the action over Sunday dinner. Bumper viewing audiences are assured whenever Cronulla, Manly, Norths and Balmain are involved because of the New Zealanders in their ranks. The Kiwi tour of Australia is being looked upon as a chance to improve rugby league's status in New Zealand and both tests will be televised live.'

For Mark Broadhurst, Manly Warringah's Christchurch import, the brotherhood of Kiwi pioneers helped him cope with Sydney life: 'The Kiwi players in Sydney always loved catching up because we were going through the same things,' Broadhurst explains. 'I didn't receive the racial slurs, but they would threaten me with "Kiwi this or that" or "We're going to run you out of the league".'

Sporting a boxer's bent nose, imposing size, a permanent scowl and a Viking demeanour, Broadhurst had arrived in Australia with the media labelling him 'The Rocky of New Zealand Rugby League'.

Like boxing movie hero Rocky Balboa, Broadhurst had worked in a freezing works and had earned the tough guy tag from a four-fight amateur boxing career in Christchurch. He also gained notoriety for punching Australian prop Craig Young to the ground in the 1980 test series. Broadhurst said of the incident: 'Young swung at me and made the mistake of missing, so I let him have it. He got what he deserved.'

When asked by *Rugby League Week* whether he expected any repercussions in Sydney, he replied: 'Hell no! If they want to carry it on, it is up to them. But I am hoping to go to Manly to play football. The first season will make or break me, but I think I can handle it alright.' Broadhurst was a marked man.

Whenever the Kiwis played each other in Sydney it was a match Broadhurst looked forward to: 'We would come together and share stories with a laugh — we enjoyed each other's company and I loved any time I spent with Olsen.'

The inability of Australian coaches to get the best out of Olsen irked Broadhurst: 'Olsen was one of the best I played with or against and they should have known in Sydney that if they let him play his natural game, he would cut the opposition to pieces. But it took Australian coaches a long time to wake up to that.'

Today Broadhurst still works in the same freezing works in Christchurch and reflects on his time in Sydney: 'I did what I needed to do in Sydney, but like Olsen I had a problem with the training. I was always worn out before I got onto the paddock.'

In Christchurch, Broadhurst played his best football when the training methods were varied and he loved the social aspect of the game, explaining the difference to Sydney: 'We would all go back to the home team's clubhouse in New Zealand, but that wasn't the case in Sydney. It was all about results and less about meaning — it was antisocial.'

Some of Broadhurst's teammates appreciated his efforts in Sydney. Manly's Paul Vautin wrote in his autobiography *Fatty*: 'You couldn't hurt him — and there was plenty who tried. No matter what sort of punishment he had to cop, he'd take it and keep coming back for more without complaining. He was as tough as any man I ever saw on the football field. For some reason [Manly coach] Ray Ritchie never really went for him and he spent a fair bit of time in second grade. I couldn't believe it. I thought he was a sensational player. He should have been a superstar at Manly.'

On his departure from Sydney in 1983 to play for Hull Kingston Rovers in England, Broadhurst told *Big League* magazine that although he had enjoyed his final year with the Illawarra Steelers, his two years at Manly were 'dehumanising — you are nothing more than a number there'.

When Broadhurst settled in to northern English life, he finally seemed happy. In an interview with the Yorkshire journalist George Dunkerley, he said: 'A thing I like here is the crowds. In Sydney it seemed that a lot of people went to the football mainly to bag the players. Here they appreciate a good break or a good piece of play and they don't get onto you about the odd little mistake. It makes it a very good atmosphere to play in.'

* * * * *

The 1982 Kiwis tour of Australia, which began in Brisbane with a trial match against Queensland in late June, ended up being powerfully illustrative of the insularity of the Sydney competition.

Mid-table Cronulla refused to release their Kiwis stars Kurt and Dane Sorensen to play in the test series. Cronulla Club Secretary Arthur Winn argued that the Sorensens' legal contract with New Zealand Rugby League had expired.

The press took a different view. *Rugby League Week* reporter Brad Boxall called Cronulla's decision a 'disgrace' and an 'outrage', while his editor, Ian Heads, worried about the future of international football.

'This year's tour by the Kiwis is heralded as the first real international contest in years,' wrote Heads. 'The appearance of the Sorensens in black and white would add real meat to the menu and thousands more to the gate. It could mean the rebirth of interest in international matches. Too often in recent years, a new Australian player's debut in his country's colours has met with as much interest as a repeat of *Gilligan's Island*.'

The Sorensens, who were in fine form for Cronulla, were keen to join the New Zealand Kiwis team. 'Public opinion is in our favour,' said Dane Sorensen to *Rugby League Week*. 'It's amazing how many people have come up to us and said they hoped we were able to play against the Aussies. I feel I have improved greatly since I joined Cronulla and I have to admit that the thought of playing tests again is appealing.'

* * * * *

'Has Frank created a Monster?' screamed the headline of a Peter Peters front-page story of *Rugby League Week*. The story read: 'A galloping garbo from Ryde — hounded into shape by the likely Australian coach — is sure to provide plenty of headaches for the Aussies in the coming test series against New Zealand. Manly's young centre Michael Blake got a taste of Olsen Filipaina's tremendous power when he was speared into the Brookvale Oval kikuyu like a human dart. Filipaina has ripped off almost two stone [12 kilos] since the start of the season under the personal supervision of Balmain coach Frank Stanton.'

Stanton, now in his alternate role of Kangaroos coach, said in the story: 'I'll worry about how to combat Olsen when the tests come around. Olsen is a dynamic player particularly with the ball in his hands. Once he gets momentum up, he is very fast for such a big man.'

* * * * *

The coach of the Kiwis 1982 touring team was Ces Mountford MBE, a 63-year-old former coal miner from the proud rugby league tradition of the West Coast of New Zealand's South Island. Known in his playing days as 'The Blackball Bullet', Mountford was a pioneer himself, moving to England and starring for Wigan as a five-eighth and going on to coach Warrington before being appointed Kiwis coach in 1979.

A believer in expansive rugby league, he shocked the Australians in a pre-test function by saying he was 'more interested in playing good attractive football than winning'.

Mountford was particularly unimpressed by the treatment of the Kiwis in Sydney. He also had five players — Clayton Friend, Gary Kemble, Gary Prohm, Gordon Smith and Kevin Tamati — returning from club football in England to join the Sydney contingent of Fred Ah Kuoi, Mark Graham, Mark Broadhurst and Olsen.

His key playmaker, five-eighth Fred Ah Kuoi, was not getting access to top-class football, miserably withering away in reserve grade for North Sydney. Meanwhile at the Tigers, Olsen had been shifted positions from five-eighth to the centres and even to the second row.

In frustration, Mountford requested an early release for Ah Kuoi from Norths to run him into some form in the Kiwis' lead-up games. 'If Norths do not want him,' he explained, 'why not let him play for us? Maybe he is out of form at present, so why not give the Kiwis the chance to play him back to form?' Norths refused Mountford's request.

In the warm-up match against Queensland in Brisbane, Mountford fielded an understrength line-up without his Sydney stars and the Kiwis suffered a heavy loss. When he met his professional players off the plane at Brisbane Airport a few days later to prepare for the test match, the Sorensen brothers were nowhere to be seen.

Cronulla had released Steve Rogers to play for Australia, but in an act of flagrant hypocrisy and defying media pressure, would not release Kurt and Dane Sorensen for the Kiwis. 'The men of Cronulla who made the decision should hang their head in shame,' wrote Ian Heads.

To make matters worse, Balmain recalled Olsen from the Kiwis camp to play in the Wednesday night KB Cup match, forcing him to fly back to Sydney and giving him only three days to recover for the upcoming test.

Balmain argued that the KB Cup match was too important for Olsen to miss, but their coach Frank Stanton — who was also the coach of Australia — was not ordered to return to Sydney. Instead, reserve-grade coach Laurie Freier guided Balmain to defeat and Stanton remained in Brisbane. One reporter called it 'a shameful act'.

Olsen's time in Sydney was split between two distinct realms — playing for New Zealand and playing for his club: 'It was like moving between different worlds, going from Balmain to the Kiwis,' Olsen says. 'At the Tigers it was every man for himself and the coach was negative and rude. Then in the Kiwi camp I had Ces Mountford, this tiny little coach that loved us and was always positive. We would burst onto the field to make him happy. It was always such a sad thing at the end of a Kiwis camp when Ces was in charge.'

The *Big League* test match programme team profiles paid begrudging respect to the motley group of travelling Kiwis. Olsen's player profile was laced with backhanded compliments: 'This blockbusting star sometimes has trouble with his weight and his approach to the game, but on his day is a match winner.'

* * * * *

Ces Mountford came agonisingly close, but there are no fairytales in New Zealand rugby league. For 77 minutes out of the 80-minute first test match, the Kiwis were in the lead and heading for a richly deserved upset. With three minutes to go, the Australians finally crossed their line to win 11–8.

The new Kiwis competitive era had been landmarked by surely one of the biggest hits in international rugby league history. Kevin Tamati led the Kiwis' haka and in the first few minutes was fuelled with fire, purpose and mission. The big moustachioed Māori prop hit debuting Kangaroo Rohan Hancock with a crushing legal tackle that knocked him cold, face down like a fallen statue. Hancock bravely rose and continued to play, but a new standard was set.

In his autobiography Paul Vautin describes the tackle: 'Tamati absolutely smashed him. I've never seen anyone hit that hard in my life and Hancock was lying there in Disneyland.'

Hancock today is a cattle buyer in the tiny Queensland town of Killarney and says, 'I have no memory of the hit and watched the video afterwards and I was shocked.'

He has one other enduring memory of the test: 'That test confirmed that Olsen Filipaina was the hardest man to tackle that I ever played. He would bump me off and I could never get my hands around his thighs.'

In the forwards, Mark Graham, Bruce Gall and Kevin and Howie Tamati tore into the Australians. In the centres, Olsen and his childhood teammate James Leuluai had a battle royale with Mick Cronin and Steve Rogers, holding the legendary duo scoreless.

The commentators noted Olsen's performance as 'a constant threat to the Australians' and at various times he manhandled Cronin, Rohan Hancock, Paul Vautin, Wally Lewis, Les Boyd and Greg Brentnall.

The match report noted Olsen's defensive performance and attitude: 'Australia faltered against the brick-wall defence of the Kiwis. New Zealand moved up, turning the match into a slogging encounter with centre Olsen Filipaina very prominent in defence.'

The Kiwis were heroic, leading for most of the match before Australia stole the match in the dying minutes. Ces Mountford was left to rue the one that got away, daring to tell reporters in the New Zealand dressing room: 'I thought we were the better team tonight. We have 13 broken hearts in here.' Mountford's team had offered the first serious challenge to Australia's supremacy in more than a decade.

The apparent change in Olsen was noted by some media who watched New Zealand's three-point loss to the Kangaroos.

'Filipaina,' wrote one bewildered journalist, 'produced more enthusiasm last night in 80 minutes of football than he ever has with Balmain.'

The next morning, Olsen farewelled his Kiwis teammates and flew from Brisbane back to Sydney. He collected Leslie from home and turned up at Redfern Oval to watch Balmain play South Sydney as a spectator.

The *Sydney Morning Herald* reported a difference of opinion on Olsen's availability: 'Balmain thought otherwise and after an interesting dressing room debate, Olsen went back to his car, got his gear and played.'

Battered and bruised from the test match the day before, he had not brought his playing gear. Twenty minutes before kick-off, however, he was told he was in the starting line-up. Shocked, he borrowed a pair of boots and gear and began to warm up.

'I had picked up some injuries in the test but could still walk and function,' Olsen says. 'He made me play and I hardly slept that night and was up manning the bins at 2.30 am. I was stiff like a mummy.'

Leslie was disgusted at Olsen's treatment. 'He got praised as a hero playing at the last minute, but I was there and I was so pissed off,' she remembers. 'It just wasn't right, and it wouldn't have happened to another player. He had also been celebrating the night before with his Kiwi mates and just turned up to support the Tigers. It really was exploitation of someone they knew wouldn't complain.'

Balmain were superb that day, winning 35–16. Despite his sore limbs, Olsen scored a vital try in the first half. The 'One Eyed Tiger' from the Ryde *Weekly Times* praised his contribution, noting 'his tree stump-like legs in top gear would be strong enough to generate nuclear power if harnessed to the national grid'.

It was Olsen's third game in five days, having played in the KB Cup match on the Wednesday, the test match on the Saturday and the Balmain game on the Sunday. 'Not bad for a bloke who has been taken to task at times for a lackadaisical approach to his club duties,' concluded the *Sydney Morning Herald*, acknowledging that Olsen was 'a true Tiger' who 'has been able to buy a house and set himself up comfortably in Sydney'.

With the help of Phil and Margaret Dries and the intervention of Sir Peter Leitch, Olsen's personal sponsor from Auckland, Olsen had stopped sending everything back to his father. He and Leslie were able to squirrel away enough money to buy a three-bedroom brick house in Lane Cove Road in North Ryde.

Leslie was excited about the milestone but says Olsen was most excited about the swimming pool. 'I was pregnant with my second child John and it was a good time to settle down. Olsen thought it was like being in a holiday resort and half the Māori community would splash around in the pool.'

Olsen has great memories of the house: 'It was more a place for my family to stay. I remember my blind Uncle Ray, who is buried next to my mum in Awarua, came to stay with us and would amaze us by somehow catching the bus to and from the city.'

He had bought a house and laid down roots in Sydney, but it was never home, Olsen remembers: 'Home was always New Zealand, that's where I was welcome.'

* * * * *

In mid-July, the second test between Australia and New Zealand was to be played in Sydney. Club officials, reported the Sydney press, were waiting for the Kiwis with chequebooks in hand.

For Olsen, who had continued his solid form for Balmain with another try against Wests, another controversy was waiting. Once again, it was not of his own making. 'I was trying to keep my head down, avoid distractions and hopefully the media would stop calling,' he remembers. 'I lived for these Kiwis team camps and I just wanted to enjoy it in peace — but something always popped up.'

In an arrogant move, Balmain attempted to force Olsen out of the Kiwis camp and back to club training with Balmain, enraging New Zealand's team management and causing a sensation in the press. 'Sabotage' read one headline. 'Kiwi Fury' read another.

'The Aussies were trapped in another world and in many ways they were a mystery to us,' says Sir Peter Leitch. 'We were still blown away by the cricket underarm incident the year before and now, typical Aussies, their clubs were not releasing our players, which obviously weakened our preparation. Kiwis just aren't a win at all costs sportspeople and events like these showed we were very different in the way we approached life.'

The chief of New Zealand Rugby League, Ron McGregor, tried unsuccessfully to broker a solution with Balmain secretary Keith Gittoes.

'Balmain has told us they want centre Olsen Filipaina to attend their training sessions this week, although he is in camp with the New Zealand team,' McGregor told *Rugby League Week*. 'We are demanding that Balmain release Filipaina from all club commitments this week.

Norths and Manly have not imposed any restrictions on their Kiwi players so why should Balmain be any different?

'The Balmain attitude is petty and one we can't comprehend. We have come here to win the test series and Filipaina is a vital part of our team. Balmain have an agreement with us that he will be available for test football and surely they know that we need him in camp this week.'

With relations at a flashpoint, the Australian Rugby League intervened and informed the NZRL that Olsen would not have to break Kiwis camp for his club training.

Instead, Olsen focused on the upcoming test match, where he was to line up against Mal Meninga — a 22-year-old Queensland prodigy and the first player of South Sea Islander (Melanesian) ancestry to play for Australia. 'The clash between the giant Meninga and the powerfully built Filipaina,' predicted Ian Heads, 'should rattle the SCG Stands.'

In the end, Meninga left the field early with an elbow injury and the Australians won convincingly, scoring four unanswered tries. In the aftermath, Kiwis hard-man Kevin Tamati blasted the Kangaroos as 'overpaid impostors'.

He also aired his disgust at the racist elements in the crowd. 'They were personal loud-mouth insults of the worst kind,' Tamati told *Rugby League Week*. 'There were racist overtones and I was angered and disappointed by that sort of attitude. Some people seem to have paid their money just to go along and shout abuse at us. I have doubts I would be welcome back again.'

* * * * *

'The crowd racism in Sydney and Brisbane for those tests was terrible, like a competition to see who could say the worst thing,' Kiwis five-eighth Fred Ah Kuoi later explained. 'After a while you don't hear it, but I distinctly remember Olsen copping it. My father said to me, "Son, you represent Samoans everywhere." I carried that with me onto the field and was able to take anything anyone threw at me. My parents left the life they were familiar with and sacrificed for me. That gave me armour against any names.

'It was different for Olsen, because nothing in New Zealand had prepared him for hurtful language and racism,' says the street-smart Ah Kuoi who is today a church pastor. 'It was a shock to him. I had a sharp mouth and if they called me black or Chinese, I would tell them how proud I was that they knew my name. Then they realised it wasn't working and would move on.'

For Ah Kuoi, what was more crippling was that he never got to show his wares in Sydney: 'I never got an opportunity to show what I could do. The best coaches don't change players — they are the brave ones who trust the player's instincts and not just stick to the plan.'

Ah Kuoi found Sydney coaches' endless rules stifling: 'I was told there was a strict rule not to chip kick in your own half. I mean what is that? Everyone played scared, flair was a bad thing and it led to not taking clear opportunities. It goes against everything I believe in — sometimes you have to run to where nobody's at.'

Whenever Norths played Balmain and Ah Kuoi got together socially with Olsen they would share bewilderment: 'It was always — what's wrong with them? Why can't you check us out so you know what you've got? You've paid for us, why don't you use us? Why are you wasting your money?'

Reflecting on his time in Australia, the cultural incompetence of the coaches was a standout memory for Ah Kuoi: 'Olsen wasn't a great trainer but there are examples through history of coaches making allowances for talented players,' Ah Kuoi says. 'But they were one size fits all and flogged a thoroughbred to prove a point. Then he would play like a champion under Ces or Lowey and they would scratch their heads. There was no mystery to us — just mismanagement.'

According to Ah Kuoi, Frank Stanton had a simple job — bring out the best in Olsen: 'Why would you level him back to the pack? A coach today would be sacked quickly if they don't personally man-manage expensive talent under the salary cap. To get the best out of our PI players, coaches have to work holistically with a player and their family who keep it tight and accountable.'

Ah Kuoi was proud to be the first Samoan captain of the Kiwis in 1979 but says the principles of Fa'a Samoa did not help him on his Sydney journey: 'I was born in Samoa and Olsen had a Samoan dad so respect for elders is locked in, it's not an option and it's our core humility,' explains Ah Kuoi. 'It was to our detriment in Sydney because we couldn't question coaches or answer back which was perceived as weak. We were easy to drop and more expendable.'

Within 18 months, Ah Kuoi would leave North Sydney to play for Hull in England. The Hull FC website records him as a fan favourite who played 126 matches and was 'an outstanding player whose organisational skills and explosive ability was the key to unlock many defences'.

'It was a shame Olsen never got to play with an English club,' Ah Kuoi says. 'Because although Sydney was closer to home, the English people were much closer to Kiwis in temperament, manners and culture.'

* * * * *

The 1982 New Zealand tour of Australia marked the end of the road for Ces Mountford, whose contract was not renewed by the NZRL. If it wasn't for the constant battles against the myopic but powerful Australian clubs, who tried to disrupt New Zealand with dodgy off-field antics, perhaps he might have presided over a famous upset victory.

Those upsets were still to come, however, and the players themselves recognised Mountford's contribution to their growth as a competitive football team. 'We had taken a big step forward and a lot of us were still amateur,' said Kiwis captain Graeme West years later. 'Ces Mountford had taken us to a level where we could compete. He brought in systems and a defined style of play. We were getting closer and closer to the Aussies.'

Despite the close scoreline in the first test, the Kiwis had lost 14 tests in a row against the Kangaroos since 1971. A whole generation of Kiwis players had come and gone without ever defeating Australia and a new approach was required.

* * * * *

Upon his return to Balmain, Olsen was again saddled with the goal-kicking duties — a role that club secretary Keith Gittoes had flagged for him earlier in the year. It was an extra responsibility that he did not want.

'It was fine in New Zealand,' Olsen recalls, 'but in Australia it means you cop extra abuse from fans and you would disappoint your teammates if you missed. When you are lining up the kick is when you got the most abuse so I got it over with quickly. Two steps and gone. You didn't get any extra pay for doing it and people were angry if you missed. Who needed it?'

In the final five matches for Balmain in the 1982 season, Olsen played four games at centre and one at five-eighth and played very strongly. He kicked 18 goals, including six from six in the final outing of the season against Illawarra.

Olsen's sparkling form was captured in a piece by journalist Tony Adams who wrote of Olsen's final game of the season in the *Daily Mirror*: 'Can you play less than half a game and still be man of the match? Normally you wouldn't think so. But the 3874 hardy souls who were at Leichhardt Oval know better. They saw Olsen Filipaina do his own impression of a runaway steamroller for an amazing 34-minute burst. In his short stay on the field Filipaina set up two tries and scored one himself in a bruising run in which he swatted off three defenders. Filipaina tore a hamstring and stunned the crowd by calmly leaving the field even before being congratulated by his teammates. After Filipaina's exit the game deteriorated noticeably, the match was like a Fred Astaire movie without Fred Astaire — very dull. Astonishingly after looking champions for the 34 minutes the big Kiwi was on the field, Balmain didn't score a point in the 46 he wasn't.'

Balmain coach Frank Stanton said the loss of Filipaina had an obvious effect on the team.

The *Canberra Times* match report described Olsen as 'a one-man Panzer division' and Dick Tucker wrote in his match report: 'the burly New Zealander waged a virtual single-handed battle against the hapless Steelers'.

* * * * *

In 1982, Olsen played 23 first-grade matches and scored 63 points — second only behind Wayne Miranda in total points for the season for Balmain.

It was Olsen's best-ever season. Not only had he been voted by his peers as the hardest hitter in the competition, he had also scored tries, kicked important conversions, and dazzled crowds with his unique combination of beauty and brutality. There were few more complete footballers than Olsen in 1982.

'Olsen Filipaina was in full cry for us that year,' wrote Wayne Pearce in his autobiography, *Local Hero*.

'Olsen was something different, one of the most enigmatic players of my experience. At his top he was devastating: I can still picture the avalanche tackle he hit Mitch Brennan with at Leichhardt. But Olsen was a player of moods. One day he'd be switched on and the next . . . well, he'd be in a different world. He worked on garbage trucks from four in the morning to 8 am, even on match days. He was a quiet polite guy, an individual playing a team game. When he played it well, he was dynamite.'

Olsen loved playing alongside Pearce, who Leslie says was a loyal gentleman and always encouraged Olsen. Olsen recalls the weight of on-field expectations from his captain: 'I remember Wayne Pearce in many games coming up to me and saying: "You can do this, it's up to you to win the game."'

It was a confusing time for Olsen with mixed messages between the two key Balmain decision makers: 'I've got the coach off field saying

I'm shit and then Pearcey saying that I'm the match winner and it's down to me. Sometimes it happened when I was straight out of reserve grade and I would think — hey I'm not the only man in the team, what about the others? Share the pressure around.'

Pearce says he enjoyed playing with Olsen: 'He was one of those guys who could turn a game on his own.'

* * * * *

It was a good year for the Balmain backline and Olsen was overjoyed that his best mate, Wayne Wigham, ended the season as the club's top try-scorer. Yet Wigham remembers he and Olsen remained unhappy playing under Frank Stanton: 'The coaches didn't understand that there were different motivators for different cultures and personality types and that some people went better with a kick up the arse and others with a pat on the back.'

For Wigham, the worst part was Olsen being humiliated in front of the team about his injured knee: 'They treated him differently, like an outsider, and we couldn't get why they treated him that way.

'We could see at training he wasn't on 100 per cent legs — his was a collision game and he was hobbly and you can't fake it week after week. Even now at player reunions they bring up Olsen's knee and why they didn't believe him and take him to a specialist. But they milked it as far as they could and said in front of all of us that they didn't believe him. It ended up being a simple cartilage problem, easily fixed.

'They had no sports medicine knowledge; they were primitive,' Wigham concludes, and feels like players were treated like 'beasts of burden', not as assets: 'Olsen was right all along. Now we know that bigger men don't do road runs. Pretty much all my mates are getting knee replacements because of road running. There are other ways to build stamina and they got it wrong. They flogged us mercilessly and we are all paying the price now.'

For Wigham, Balmain's treatment of Olsen's injuries was a symptom of a larger problem of cultural misunderstanding: 'In hindsight, I now understand how ignorant we were about Olsen and never thought how tough it might have been for him moving to a new country away from family and friends and having to deal with injuries. Frank Stanton never sat down with him and said, "What's in your head? What makes you enjoy the game?" One size fits all never works with different men who have different motivators.'

* * * * *

During the season, Balmain Tigers trainer Les Hobbs's role extended to being Frank Stanton's second set of eyes on game day. His role was simple — to help with feedback sessions during the week.

'Olsen stood out in 1982,' says Hobbs. 'He was ahead of his time with his skills. It was a real shame that he was perhaps the ultimate example of the free-spirited footballer who played for fun and Frank was the ultimate example of a disciplinarian and structured coach.'

For Hobbs, Olsen and Frank were a cross-cultural mismatch: 'Frank got frustrated with Olsen because he knew his ability, he knew what he had and he tried to bring it out in him. He was a disciplinarian coach — that's all he knew. Olsen knew what he could do but couldn't convey to Frank on how to access it. It was frustrating for everyone involved because when Olsen was on, we were a powerful force.'

Hobbs recalls one clash where Olsen came off second best: 'Frank was trying to change the attitude at Balmain and bring in a uniform for the players to wear — a polo, trousers and dress shoes. Olsen had been on the garbage truck that morning and arrived in a black singlet and a pair of shorts. Frank said, "Where's your gear?" When Olsen told him he didn't have his uniform, Frank didn't let him play the next week.'

The media portrayal of Olsen was off the mark according to Hobbs and part of a herd mentality: 'It was absolutely unfair the way they treated Olsen. He had way more good games for Balmain than bad ones, but they were all over his weight and consistency.'

The constant media reference to Olsen's weight was at odds with Hobbs's experience: 'Olsen didn't ever have a gut when I was there, he just had a big strong Polynesian arse and thighs and the media had never seen that before. He wasn't a great trainer, but he always gave the best on the field.'

Perhaps the saddest memory for Hobbs is the racism he witnessed and its impact on Olsen: 'He came up against some guys with much lesser ability who had to rely on words to put him off. You could hear them clearly on the sideline. He wouldn't say anything back, but at times it made him play worse and lose interest and other times he played better and his intensity lifted. Frank and I could tell when they had said something to upset him. He would smash people in tackles and sometimes we used to joke that we should pay the opposition to upset him.'

* * * * *

The early 1980s were a time of cultural upheaval in Sydney. Inter-generationally isolated from non-Europeans through the White Australia immigration policy, a culturally homogeneous Anglo-Celtic community had developed over 75 years.

In 1982, Australia was only seven years clear of the official end of the White Australia policy and was undergoing a slow learning process to unglue the belief that Asian and Pacific migrants were not a fleeting phenomenon but were Australians as well.

Anglo-Celtic Australians had been hardwired by their experience and the new migrant communities were seen as a threat to a way of life, which at times manifested itself in racism and other forms of discrimination imposed on 'outsiders'.

'I couldn't believe how many rednecks were calling out racial abuse — things were said at games that would never be said in New Zealand,' remembers Sir Peter Leitch. 'People try to play it down and say it wasn't that bad, but it was. It was disgusting and cowardly and when I saw it happen to Olsen it was devastating.'

* * * * *

International football was a lifeline for Olsen during a season in which he had been dropped to reserve grade by Stanton, used and abused by his club, and played in three different positions. It was a pattern that would continue during the next five years of his career — misunderstood in Australia, loved and respected in New Zealand.

In 1982, Balmain had finished the season in 11th place in what was yet another disappointing campaign. The Tigers faithful, who had waited five long years for the team to make finals football, were growing increasingly impatient.

Frank's melancholic summary of Olsen's season was simple and direct in a *Rugby League Week* interview: 'I don't think anyone has really been able to get the best out of Olsen.'

5

'I DON'T LIKE LIVING HERE. I TOLERATE IT.'

'Show me a reserve grader and I'll show you a bloke who doesn't like the first-grade coach.'
— Canterbury Bankstown Coach Warren Ryan, 1984

In the heart of pre-season training in February 1983, Ian Heads, the editor of *Rugby League Week*, ventured to Leichhardt Oval to interview Olsen Filipaina. Like most reporters in Sydney, Olsen's three seasons at the Tigers had left him intrigued and wanting to know more.

'He was quiet and amiable and not the easiest of interviews but a real enjoyment considering my respect for him as a player with power and great ability . . . a bloke with a real difference,' says Heads. 'It took me a long time to organise the interview and Wayne Pearce had to work hard to get him to do it. He didn't want to do any interviews or have anything to do with the media.'

Heads knew that Frank Stanton had big plans for Olsen. The Balmain first-grade squad for 1983 had an average age of just 22 — the youngest in the Winfield Cup — and Stanton now saw 25-year-old Olsen as a senior figure.

Olsen had trained hard over the off-season and landed at the Tigers 'in great shape' according to *Daily Mirror* journalist Jon Harker. Coach

144

'I DON'T LIKE LIVING HERE. I TOLERATE IT.'

Frank Stanton agreed with the assessment, telling media: 'Olsen looks better at this stage of the season than he has in three years. We'll be looking to him for a big season and the way he has come up is very encouraging.'

There were good reasons for Stanton to expect more from Olsen. He was coming off a stellar club and representative season in 1982 and had been joined at Balmain by forward Bruce Gall, a tough Taranaki fencing contractor and hunter who had been one of Olsen's Kiwis teammates in the 1982 test series against Australia.

Stanton had also shown faith in Olsen's ability by giving him the goal-kicking duties. 'He's a sheer natural,' enthused Stanton, adding that Olsen was 'one of the best goal-kickers I've ever seen'.

Away from football too, Olsen appeared more settled than ever. He had moved into a new home with his again-pregnant partner Leslie and his baby daughter Louise.

Yet in his interview with Heads, Olsen was typically unforthcoming with his responses. Heads noted that he was 'the strong, silent type' — 'something of a mystery man' whose answers 'were limited to the bare bones'.

Voicing his dislike of life in Sydney, Olsen told Heads: 'I don't like living here. I tolerate it. I certainly won't be living here when my football career finishes.'

He also shared his thoughts on training under Frank Stanton: 'I don't enjoy it; I'd rather just go out there and play.'

Olsen had, however, trained strongly in the off-season and was looking forward to the new season like never before, telling Heads: 'I'm looking forward to this year. We've got a lot of young blokes and great team spirit. It's because of that I have trained harder than ever before.'

After patiently waiting for the interview, at the completion Heads was sold: 'Filipaina looks fit, really fit for this time of year although his opponents will be disappointed to know that the tree-trunk legs have not diminished in size. Filipaina at his top is simply a devastating player.'

How to solve a mystery like Olsen Filipaina?

For Frank Stanton, everything came down to training. 'If Olsen had trained harder, he would have been sensational, but he came from an amateur system where he trained as hard as he felt he had to train,' Stanton explains.

'I'm sure to this day that if he had trained harder, he would have been a hell of a lot more successful.'

For Stanton, a major blockage for Olsen's development was his tough, menial second job as a garbage collector: 'Olsen's work ethic was very high and the type of job he had sapped a lot of his energy,' Stanton remembers. 'That had a lot to do with the attitude he had when he came to training because training was hard.'

* * * * *

The 1983 Winfield Cup season began at the tail end of one of Sydney's hottest summers on record. In Round 2, temperatures reached 38 degrees at Penrith Park. Across town, in Cronulla, Sharks prop Gavin Miller was photographed lying dazed and distressed from heat exhaustion on the dressing-room floor.

And at North Sydney, Mark Graham, the big Kiwi enforcer, went 'troppo' after being concussed. His mind altered by heat and a heavy collision, Graham had to be physically restrained as he began furiously attacking the walls with his fists.

Olsen, who was due to line up in the centres against Wests at Lidcombe Oval, did not want to play in such oppressive conditions that he described later as 'just madness and not worth risking someone's life for'.

He sent Leslie as an emissary to ask Stanton's permission to be excused from the match. The answer, says Leslie, 'was unprintable. Olsen played.'

Thankfully, Olsen was at the peak of his powers: fit and healthy after an off-season of careful eating and regular games of squash and tennis. It was the first time he had committed to a solo fitness programme, which impressed trainer Les Hobbs no end.

In a comprehensive 28-point victory against Wests, Olsen overcame the heat and was one of the standout performers for the Tigers, potting eight of nine attempts at goal.

'He's got to be the hardest player to tackle in the game,' said Wests coach, Len Stacker, after fulltime. 'I don't know if there's a stronger player going around and he's got that ability to offload in tackles.'

By Round 5, Balmain were undefeated at the top of the Winfield Cup competition ladder. According to Ray Chesterton, from the *Daily Telegraph*, 'the club's success has much to do with Filipaina's lift in form'. Olsen had contributed 40 of the Tigers' 130 points and was a crowd favourite at Leichhardt Oval.

In the Ryde *Weekly Times*, 'One Eyed Tiger' adopted Olsen's old Kiwi nickname of 'Bumper' for his high-contact running style. 'Anyone who saw the big centre in action against Cronulla on Saturday would vouch for its aptness,' he wrote after Balmain's Round 3 victory.

'Bumper, a garbage collector by profession, literally cleaned up Cronulla half Robert Lane with two ferocious tackles. On both occasions he tossed the little man aside as if he were a bin lid — such is his amazing strength. In attack there was no respite. Time and time again, Olsen bumped off would be tacklers who must have felt they were having a go at the dodgems in Luna Park.'

It seemed, to the Leichhardt faithful, that Olsen could do it all. 'He is also our goal-kicker,' continued 'One Eyed Tiger', 'and I doubt whether any side has ever had a man more reluctant to handle the job. Reluctance or not Olsen looks like taking the kicks for the rest of the year.'

An optimistic halo surrounded Olsen's early 1983 form.

Ray Chesterton wrote a story in the *Daily Telegraph* titled 'The Quiet Kiwi finds form' which was an ode to Olsen's form and fitness:

'If words were dollar bills, Olsen Filipaina wouldn't have much to show for his footballing efforts this year. Filipaina, Balmain's block-busting centre, is not one for wasting time with words when deeds on the football field speak much more eloquently. Usually at this stage of the season, Filipaina's efforts are more of a whisper as he runs his nugget frame into condition. This year Filipaina has raised the volume of his performances to a shout. In four matches Balmain is unbeaten and the club's success has much to do with Filipaina's lift in form.'

Chesterton also noticed a personality change in Olsen: 'Filipaina, a man seemingly dedicated in the past to keeping out of the mainstream of rugby league socialising is also coming out of his shell more this season. A non-drinker, he was famous for quickly disappearing after matches or training in the past, offering the reasonable excuse that he had to be up early each morning for work. This year Filipaina is less of a recluse.'

'I'd say he is playing better than he ever has for us,' added Balmain legend Keith Barnes.

* * * * *

Despite his burst of form, Olsen was feeling restless and he told Dorothy Goodwin of the *Sun Herald* of his plans to play in England after his contract expiry and that he had received offers from English clubs.

His reasons for wanting to migrate were laid bare: 'I have been in Australia three years and have had the one steady job, but I've never felt entirely settled. I've never felt at home.'

Goodwin asked Olsen about his improved fitness and whether it was due to long-distance running. Filipaina was aghast at the idea: 'I do enough of that at work behind the garbage truck. I start at 3.20 am and I'm on the job for four hours. But I like the job because it gives me the rest of the day to play tennis or squash.'

Olsen also revealed the unconventional secret of his fitness and flexibility — jazz ballet classes.

Keith Gittoes added: 'We've never seen Olsen in this mood before. He's quiet and relaxed and he's a loveable character. And what a ball handler — he's got glue on his fingers.'

* * * * *

'I DON'T LIKE LIVING HERE. I TOLERATE IT.'

Heading into the fifth game of the season against the Canterbury Bankstown Bulldogs, the Tigers were flying high, on top of the ladder and threatening a big year for their fans.

Yet just as the supporters were beginning to believe, Balmain narrowly lost against Canterbury, spiralling them into a four-match losing slump.

On the match day of the Easter weekend Round 9 match against St George, as pressure began to mount on coach Frank Stanton, Olsen rushed late into the Kogarah Oval dressing rooms, dressed in his garbo outfit — a blue singlet, shorts and thongs.

Olsen was replaced in the second half, the Tigers were thumped by 33 points, and Olsen was subsequently sacked from first grade. Roy Masters, the coach of St George, was clearly bemused by Olsen's antics. 'His dress and his playing performance resulted in his being dropped to second grade,' wrote Masters in his weekly column in the *Sydney Morning Herald*. 'His poor form could be partly put down to his working on a garbage truck the night before the game.'

Gary Lester's story in *The Sun* was headlined 'Dropped for Wearing Thongs' and he wrote: 'Balmain's Kiwi test centre Olsen Filipaina has been sacked from first grade for wearing thongs and a T-shirt to Monday's match against St George.'

For the media, it was yet another chapter in the unfolding story of 'Olsen the Enigma'. Here was the last of the amateurs, trapped in the headlights of the new professional world.

'Stanton was as miserable as any coach,' reported Alan Clarkson of the *Sydney Morning Herald*. 'I thought his blood pressure would go through the roof when he found out that Filipaina had worked overnight and morning on a garbage truck and then come directly to the match. When he learned about the night owl activities of his burly centre, his reaction was unprintable.'

It was a classic confrontation between the establishment and the free spirit. Knowing that he was up against a strong team, Stanton had wanted everything to be done with discipline and purpose and his key playmaker turned up in thongs. His casual nature in this case made Olsen his own worst enemy.

Olsen says, 'I had my gear in the truck but didn't have time to change. All the fans were cheering me as I ran. Just so many rules and fines and all I wanted to do was play footy.'

Thirty-six years later Frank Stanton can still remember the incident: 'That's proof of the attitude Olsen had towards his work. He never missed a day's work for the local council and football seemed a secondary thing to him.

'The effect on the team was more alarming, because everyone else had done the right thing, prepared properly, turned up on time; it wasn't fair on them,' explains Stanton. 'I couldn't ignore it nor could the committee who fined him. Balmain was a proud club with standards and that wasn't acceptable. I didn't do the fining.'

Olsen was hauled before the committee to explain himself. 'It's really simple,' Olsen recalls telling Keith Gittoes. 'It was public holiday rates and they gave me a long shift. Triple time!'

In the end, though, the fine handed to him by Balmain exceeded the extra money he had made from hauling the bins. Worse still, he spent the next four weeks training and playing in reserve grade alongside his Kiwis teammate, farmer Bruce Gall — who was also trapped in the reserves. The pair were miserable and their homesickness grew stronger.

Gall enjoyed getting to know Olsen but was dismayed at the way Frank Stanton treated him: 'Olsen was a real decent bloke, a hard worker who got a raw deal and they treated him badly — the way Frank spoke to him was terrible,' says Gall.

'I remember they used to dress him up in a wetsuit and run him around in the heat, trying to get his body like a European's by wrapping him up like a sausage. It was ridiculous. But despite it all, Olsen's record and play were stellar and many times I saw Leichhardt Oval go quiet when he ironed someone out.'

For Gall, it was his coach Frank Stanton's treatment of outsiders that was the most disappointing element of his two years with the

Tigers: 'Frank had a definite prejudice against outsiders and unless you were from Sydney, Frank didn't want to know you,' Gall explains.

'Look at how he treated Wally Lewis who was so obviously the best player in State of Origin, but Frank replaced him in the Kangaroos with Sydney player Brett Kenny. Frank's man management was terrible and he ruined me from day one.'

Olsen confirms that he had to talk Gall out of physically confronting Stanton one night after he was humiliated in a coaching session: 'I had to spend a long time talking him down. He was absolutely ready to go Frank.'

Leichhardt Oval, Gall recalls, 'was directly under the flight path and I always looked up at the planes and wished I was on one of them'.

After the 1984 season Gall fled Sydney rugby league to find happiness in a captain-coach role for tiny Lake Cargelligo in the Central West of New South Wales.

'Going out there restored my faith in Australians,' says Gall. 'They were larrikins but not vindictive.'

* * * * *

For both Gall and Olsen, the light at the end of the 1983 tunnel was the upcoming test series against Australia in June. The first match was scheduled for Carlaw Park, meaning a return to family, teammates and their adoring fans.

Olsen, who finally returned to first grade in Round 14, could not wait to pull on the black and white of New Zealand. His knee was shot — in part due to years of punishing road runs — but he was confident that he could manage the injury. 'I'll have an operation at the end of the season,' he told the *Daily Telegraph* before Balmain's Round 15 clash against Souths.

After counting down the weeks, Olsen prepared for his final Balmain game before the first test match in Auckland. Olsen lined up in the centres in first grade against Souths, now free of the dreaded goal-kicking duties.

After just 10 minutes Olsen ran the ball up and while standing up in a tackle, heard a snap in his ankle. He remembers his captain Wayne Pearce telling him, 'Don't worry about it; it's nothing.'

Olsen played on but realised it was something serious: 'Nah, something is wrong,' Olsen remembers thinking, 'I can't run, I can't move so I was helped off. I'd never heard of a busted fibula before.'

Leslie groaned from the sideline when Olsen was leaving the field: 'I saw him wince when they were carrying him off and it was so bad he couldn't drive me home. I was pregnant with my second child John and two days later Olsen had to somehow drive me to the hospital.'

The injury put him out for the rest of the year, sidelining him for the two-test series against Australia and Balmain's first finals appearance since 1977. 'I'll never forget the sound and instantly knowing I was out of that test series,' says Olsen. 'I was devastated. I lived and breathed to play for the Kiwis and to get injured in the final match before the first test was the worst.'

A photo of a sorry Olsen being helped from the field was published in the following edition of *Rugby League Week*.

'Olsen Filipaina hasn't had many bigger disappointments in his career than the one captured in *Rugby League Week*'s photo,' wrote Ian Heads. 'Olsen is a true-blue Kiwi. He doesn't like Sydney much and I suspect there's nothing more he cherishes in sporting life than putting on his Kiwi jumper. Now a broken ankle has ended all that.'

* * * * *

Two days after Olsen's ankle snapped, Queensland outclassed New South Wales in Game 1 of the State of Origin series. It was the Maroons' fifth victory in six Origin games, representing a historic turning point in Australian rugby league.

From 1908 to 1979, New South Wales had absolutely dominated Queensland in the annual interstate series, confirming its position as the home of the game in Australia. State of Origin, which began in 1980 and allowed Queensland to recall and select its Sydney-based players, spelt a dramatic end to that era of dominance.

At the centre of the Queensland renaissance was a young Brisbane five-eighth by the name of Wally Lewis who in 1981 had been made captain of Queensland at the absurdly young age of 21.

In many ways, Wally was to Queensland as Olsen was to New Zealand — a mercurial player who frustrated and confounded the Sydney establishment. Both were 'wunderkinds' who relied on natural instinct rather than training, and who would be remembered as pathfinders for their people — Queenslanders and Kiwis.

Like Olsen, Wally was a talented rugby union player who faced discrimination for his love of rugby league. After Lewis returned from the unbeaten 1977–78 Australian Schoolboys rugby union tour of Great Britain, he was told by the Queensland Rugby Union that if he continued to play both league and union he would no longer be selected in Queensland representative union teams. Bristling at the ultimatum, Lewis decided his future lay with rugby league.

Lewis also had problems with Frank Stanton. He was clearly the best player in the 1982 State of Origin series, yet was controversially dropped from the Kangaroos starting team by coach Frank Stanton for the following 1982 tour of Great Britain. Stanton cited Wally's attitude to training and fitness as the reason behind his demotion.

'I don't want to be disrespectful to Frank, but he was trying to fix something that wasn't broken, with both Wally and Olsen,' says Sir Graham Lowe. 'I don't think the game's seen a better player than Wally and Olsen is one of the only players to get the better of Wally.'

Lowe is adamant that Wally and Olsen were similar types of players: 'Both were very coachable and no challenge was too great to burden them with,' says Lowe.

'They could both totally change the game if they put their mind to it, defence, running, setting play up. A good five minutes from both of them could totally alter a game and there are not too many that can do that at all levels. Players like that don't need to be humiliated on their weight nor should playmakers be treated exactly the same as others.

You need them the most. The worst thing you can do with true talent is over-coach and over-train them, and the Aussie coaches were guilty of that.

'I don't want to get caught up in old people's talk, but perhaps the best players were the Olsens and Wallys who were crossing over from the amateurs to professionals and played with a mix of intuition and structure,' says Lowe.

* * * * *

Lowe was well placed to comment on the parallels between Wally and Olsen. After a successful start to his coaching career in Auckland, where he won back-to-back premierships with Ōtāhuhu Leopards in 1977 and 1978, Lowe had moved to Queensland to coach Brisbane Norths in 1979. At just 33, he was the first Kiwi coach to 'cross the ditch'.

In the tough Brisbane Rugby League competition, Lowe witnessed Wally's brilliance first hand while coaching against Fortitude Valley. 'Wally back then did not have the pressure that came later in his career where he had to show courage to cope with it. Back then he had freedom of expression and it was amazing, what he could do as a loose forward. It was like he was bringing his backyard footy onto the big stage.'

Wally Lewis agrees on some playing style similarities between him and Olsen: 'We both had free will and I've always had a belief and I'm sure Olsen's the same, that if you stick to the one plan, it's going to be easy and comfortable to plan a defensive line against you,' explains Lewis.

'When you have that free spirit, it's impossible to plan to stop you because if you yourself don't know what's going to happen, the defence is always in two minds.'

Lewis also sees a similarity with Olsen in fitness and training. 'I was the first to put up my hand and say I wasn't the fittest player, but come at me if I let you down on the field,' says Lewis.

'Olsen and I both got insults from media about our fitness, but Olsen could run all day and make life a misery for defenders.'

Another shared experience for Wally and Olsen was receiving a tough time under coach Frank Stanton, a fitness fanatic who made no allowances for 'special players'. Lewis was a State of Origin-winning captain in 1982 when Frank Stanton dropped him from the Kangaroos.

To rub salt into the wound, Frank did the deed on Wally's home soil in the Kangaroos training camp in Brisbane, sending Australia's best player to turn out for the second-string 'Emus'.

'Frank just had this belief that it was his way or the highway and if you didn't do exactly what he asked, you were dropped,' remembers Lewis. 'I had some drama with Frank and it's no surprise Olsen found his approach discouraging as well.'

Lewis played under Graham Lowe for Queensland in the 1991 State of Origin and experienced the contrast in coaching styles. 'I'm prepared to let Frank be rewarded for his record. I won't go much further than that,' says Lewis.

But according to Lewis, Graham Lowe was in a class of his own: 'Lowey was the next level — he was extraordinary at being able to get the best out of each and every player,' he says.

'He did it in different ways, used different formulas and different game plans. One thing that he had that few coaches were able to match was that he had genuine feeling. He had the honesty in his address to the players, he felt the mood of the game as much as each and every player on the football field and he was prepared to put just as much into that match as any player. It was real integrity.'

* * * * *

There was method in Graham Lowe's man-management coaching revolution and he had a proven model. Brisbane Norths, the club which Lowe was tasked with turning around, had finished last in 1978 and 26 first-grade players had walked out of the club — some after learning that an unknown New Zealander would be taking charge in 1979.

As a 'blow-in outsider', Lowe had no playing pedigree to lean on and had no allies in Brisbane. He had been handed a poisoned chalice, coined by the press as a 'riches to rags' mission with all the ingredients of failure. Yet the Ōtāhuhu automotive mechanic who left school at 16, presided over a stunning two-year turnaround, which saw Norths finish fifth in 1979 and win the premiership in 1980. It was one of the most unlikely stories in Australian rugby league history.

What's more, Lowe managed to get the best out of players like 'Smokin' Joe Kilroy, a sometimes-wayward Aboriginal winger, and big Stan Napa, a Cook Islands Māori and classic confidence player who had followed Lowe from Auckland to Brisbane.

The importance of managing genius was paramount for Lowe, who feels gifted players require gentle handling. Lowe wasn't alone in the sporting world as a personalised man manager and he is a big admirer of Manchester United's Alex Ferguson who applied similar methods in managing his troubled genius players like Eric Cantona, Wayne Rooney and Roy Keane.

In his book *Leading*, Ferguson reveals his strategy for managing his genius players: 'When you are dealing with individuals with unusual talent, it makes sense to treat them differently. Creative players can see things that others cannot and you have to set each individual up for success.'

The taming and harnessing of Manchester United French legend Eric Cantona's football genius is one of Ferguson's great managerial triumphs, but it did not come at the expense of the team, with Ferguson noting: 'Eric was a sensitive person who was easily bothered by all sorts of things and I did things for Eric Cantona that I did not do for others. I don't think it was resented because the players understood the exceptional talents had qualities they did not possess.'

Resentment among teammates at a talent getting special treatment was manageable according to Ferguson, who wrote: 'You might think that teammates would resent another player who was treated differently. That would probably be true if he was an everyday character. But once in a while, someone appeared who required something special. Eric Cantona fits into that category. I would make a point of talking to him every day.'

Ferguson, like Lowe, would embed himself in his players' lives:

'I couldn't count the number of times where I helped players with personal matters and I'm proud of the fact they trusted me and they knew that discussion would stay private. In these situations I acted as a priest, father or lawyer — whatever it took to make the problem go away.'

Deep personal understanding of his players was a crucial key to his success: 'Unless you understand people it's very hard to motivate them. Unless you know their background situation and have an understanding of someone's personality, it is impossible to get the best out of them.'

* * * * *

In the emotionally constipated world of Australian rugby league, Lowe's secret ingredient was love. For players like Brisbane Norths prop forward Campbell 'Zulu' Dews and future Kangaroos halfback Mark Murray, Lowe's approach was a revelation.

For Murray, Lowe's ability to successfully talk about love to Queensland rugby league players was unique: 'If you went to 9000 other coaches, no one would come up with that whereas Graham honestly believes it and he's not frightened to let his emotions go and talk about it.'

'I gave those boys a lot of love,' Lowe says. 'They started to love themselves and then they loved each other. Love wasn't a term bandied around by the rugby league community in Australia, and talking about loving yourselves and each other were alien concepts. Taking off the emotional masks and talking to each other worked. Deep down people want the connection: to feel wanted, feel part of something . . . a quest, a journey. Why not express it?'

For Lowe it was all about empathy: 'I was able to empathise with the players and understand them. Empathy as a concept wasn't a thing at that time. But that's what I did. Once I had empathy with a player, I then knew what made them tick. I would visit them at their home, their places of work, meet their families, get into their world. All of a sudden they will run through walls for you.'

An additional element that Lowe instinctively understood was the underlying honesty and street smarts of working-class rugby league players: 'Footballers are different and special. You can't lie to them or cheat them because they will sniff you out,' Lowe says. 'If you talk about simple concepts — truth, honesty and love and sometimes hate — I could always get them in a receptive mood and if they are listening then you can do great things.'

Later in his career, in 1991 and 1992, Lowe would become the first foreigner to coach Queensland in State of Origin and he was given the highest honour available to an outsider — anointed an 'honorary Queenslander'.

Former Queensland Rugby League Chairman Dick 'Tossa' Turner is clear on Lowe's legacy: 'We were concerned that we no longer had anybody who could motivate and coach the side to the level to beat NSW. It was a revolutionary step and what Graham did was extraordinary. We owe him way more than he owes us. The man is deeply admired and loved in this state and we will be indebted to him forever.'

Wally Lewis was one of his staunchest advocates. Recalling Lowe's earlier Brisbane triumph at Norths in 1980, Lewis told author Joe Gorman: 'No one thought they'd even make the Grand Final. It just showed how much emotion was tied to his pre-match presentations. I remember Mark Murray saying to me once, "When you're away from the footy you have so much respect for him. We'll talk to him all night long — he's one of the boys." He had a very clever rugby league mind.'

After witnessing Lowe's turnaround effort with Brisbane Norths, and having ended Ces Mountford's stint coaching the Kiwis, the New Zealand Rugby League made Lowe the new Kiwis coach in 1983. At 35 years old, he was 28 years younger than Mountford and represented a fresh start.

He was the right man at the right time. Freshly anointed, he burdened himself with glorious purpose, while remaining unburdened by the emotional baggage of the Kiwis' stultifying losing streak.

Lowe's first job, he knew, was ridding the players of their inferiority complex, a crucial enabler in ending a gruesome procession of losses against Australia dating back to 1971.

'We had low self-esteem and worshipped Australia,' he later explained. 'We used to go to training in Australian club jerseys — the Aussies were our heroes. The blind reverence had to be removed from our culture. I'd only ever been in winning cultures and it was really apparent to me that, in many ways, we were in awe of the Australians and I wanted that out of them.'

To make matters worse for Lowe, for the 1983 two-test series against Australia, he was missing Kevin Tamati, his highly skilled and ferocious Māori prop, and the injured Olsen, whom Lowe had admired since his rookie years in Auckland's Fox Memorial Cup. 'Olsen had a major role in our game plan and I was shattered not to have him in my first outing as New Zealand coach,' says Lowe.

With Olsen injured and watching from home on his television, New Zealand lost the first test 16–4 at Carlaw Park. On a positive note, the Kiwis performed commendably and scored their first try against Australia since 1978.

After the match, the Sydney-based Kiwis players returned to their clubs. Lowe kept up the momentum, hitting the phones and calling them every other day, reaffirming that they could match it with the Aussies in the second test.

To change up his team's mental preparation, he introduced a new theme — 'tears of joy' — in which he encouraged his players to cry only when they won. To reinforce the message, Lowe showed the Kiwis squad videos of members of the New Zealand men's rowing team crying after they won gold in the 1978 Munich Olympics.

Lowe reminded the players that they were playing to honour the sacrifices their families had made. Before the kick-off in the second test, he prevented them from leaving the Lang Park dressing room until the referees were bashing the door down.

And perhaps most importantly, he listened to his players. When Howie Tamati requested that the haka be performed after the game and only if the Kiwis won, Lowe acquiesced.

With protocols sorted, Lowe went to work on the Kiwis' emotional side. His personalisation and empathy skills were applied to the Kiwis team and are glimpsed in Richard Becht's biography of Lowe.

Lowe tapped into his players' deepest emotions in his final dressing-room speech before the match: 'I began reminding the players of what their families had done for them, the sacrifices they had made. I talked to the Sorensen brothers that all their father Peter wanted was to be proud of his boys knowing they'd given 100 per cent. Said to Nicky Wright that all his father Jack would want was to be able to go to work and say, "That was my son".'

The players responded magnificently, drawing a line in the sand for New Zealand rugby league. The upset 19–12 victory over the Kangaroos in Brisbane broke a 12-year drought and immediately re-energised the international game. Suddenly, the Australians had a challenger for the throne.

'I was at home laid up with my babies and a busted ankle,' says Olsen. 'But I was leaping up and down with excitement. We had finally beaten them and as a player and a fan I was rapt. The pain in my ankle went away for a night. It was the best medicine ever.'

The Kiwis had beaten Australia with an emphasis on style over structure; love over macho aggression. Later, in his autobiography, winger Dean Bell expressed his early reservations over Lowe's 'tears of joy' strategy.

'At the time I was thinking "Oh come on, Lowie. This is a tough rugby league player here. What are you talking about?"' wrote Bell. 'Little did I know that after that test I would be absolutely bawling my eyes out.'

The post-match haka was led by Howie Tamati and performed with a feverish emotion. Graham Lowe told journalist Peter Peters at *Rugby League Week* that he had learned a valuable lesson.

'I didn't realise how ignorant I was of my country's customs until

The Filipaina family in front of the family car in Māngere East. Olsen is fourth from left.

The New Zealand Secondary Schools team at the Rothmans national tournament held at Greymouth in 1972. Olsen is 15 years old and captain of the team, located fifth from left in the bottom row.

Olsen, far right, part of four Māngere East Hawks Centurions in 1979 commemorating 100 games played for the club. The other players in the photo are C. Hyndman, O. Gallagher and T. Robinson.

Olsen in full flight for Balmain Tigers against Souths at Redfern Oval in his second game for the club on 6 April 1980.

Left: With future coach and Eastern Suburbs, Parramatta, Queensland and Kangaroos star Arthur Beetson in front of his Ryde house on Olsen's early-morning garbage run on 31 January 1980.

Below: Olsen and partner Leslie, freshly returned from the hospital with newborn baby Louise in 1981.

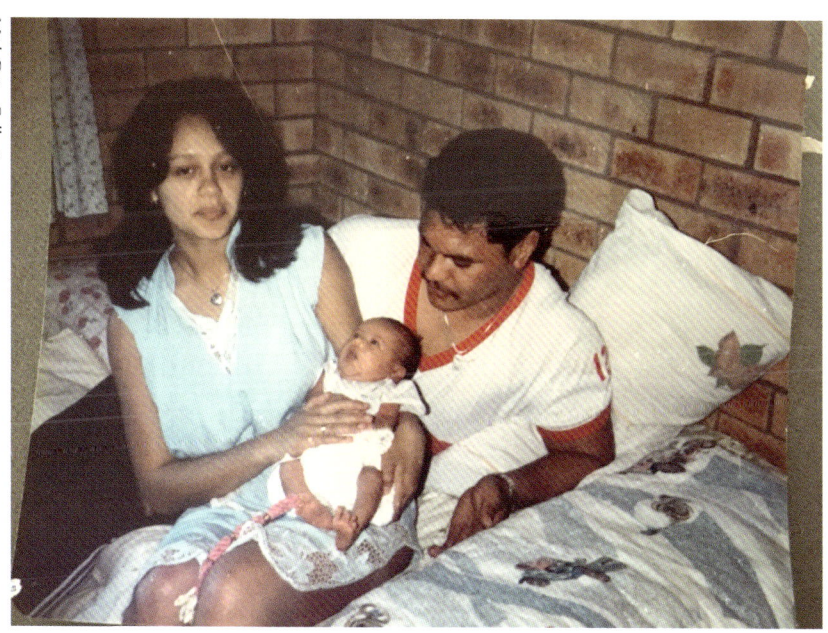

Taking the ball forward for the Balmain Tigers in 1982. 'Olsen was in full cry for us that year,' said captain Wayne Pearce.

Olsen charges at Cronulla-Sutherland Sharks captain Steve Rogers in Round 1 at Endeavour Field on 28 February 1982.

All smiles after a big hit on Western Suburbs' Tom Arber at Leichhardt Oval on 4 April 1982.

Above: For Olsen it was always a thrill when he played against his Kiwis teammates, especially the North Sydney Bears when their team included Mark Graham (centre) and Fred Ah Kuoi (left). The happy trio were captured together in the change rooms after their match at North Sydney Oval on 10 April 1982.

Left: Olsen proudly displaying his Polynesian culture by wearing a puka shell necklace for his 1982 Scanlens 'footy card'.

Playing traditional drums and sporting a 'Mr. T' mohawk hairstyle at the start of the 1984 season. Olsen shared a fear of flying with Mr. T, his favourite character from the American TV series *The A-Team*.

A devastated Olsen on the couch nursing a broken ankle, with daughter Louise. The injury happened against South Sydney in Round 14 in 1983 and cost him his spot in the Kiwis team to take on the Kangaroos a week later.

Olsen looks ready for action in the 1984 season, pictured in front of his pool at his home in Ryde in Sydney.

Swatting off a Great Britain defender in the 1984 test series in New Zealand. His friend and halves partner Clayton Friend is providing support.

The 1985 Kiwis team that changed New Zealand rugby league forever. Olsen is seated in the front row, third from right.

An imperious Olsen Filipaina evades the tackles of Kangaroos Mal Meninga and former Balmain Tigers teammate Garry Jack in the second test at Carlaw Park on 30 June 1985. Olsen went on to win his third consecutive international man of the match in the Kiwis' unlucky 10–6 loss.

Olsen makes a line break in his first match for the North Sydney Bears in Round 1 on 9 March 1986, helping them to a 16–12 victory against the Illawarra Steelers at the Wollongong Showground.

Happy times for the Kiwi connection in the Belmore Oval change rooms after the North Sydney Bears defeated the defending premiers Canterbury Bankstown Bulldogs 19–4. Olsen is seated on the right alongside teammates Clayton Friend (centre) and captain Mark Graham (left).

NRL Imagery

Olsen kicks a successful conversion with his famous two-step 'toe poke' style in the first test against Australia at a waterlogged Carlaw Park in Auckland on 6 July 1986.

Bursting through the tackles of Kangaroos Wayne Pearce and Royce Simmons in the second test, in front of 34,000 fans at the Sydney Cricket Ground on 19 July 1986.

On the charge in the second test against the Kangaroos, at the Sydney Cricket Ground on 19 July 1986.

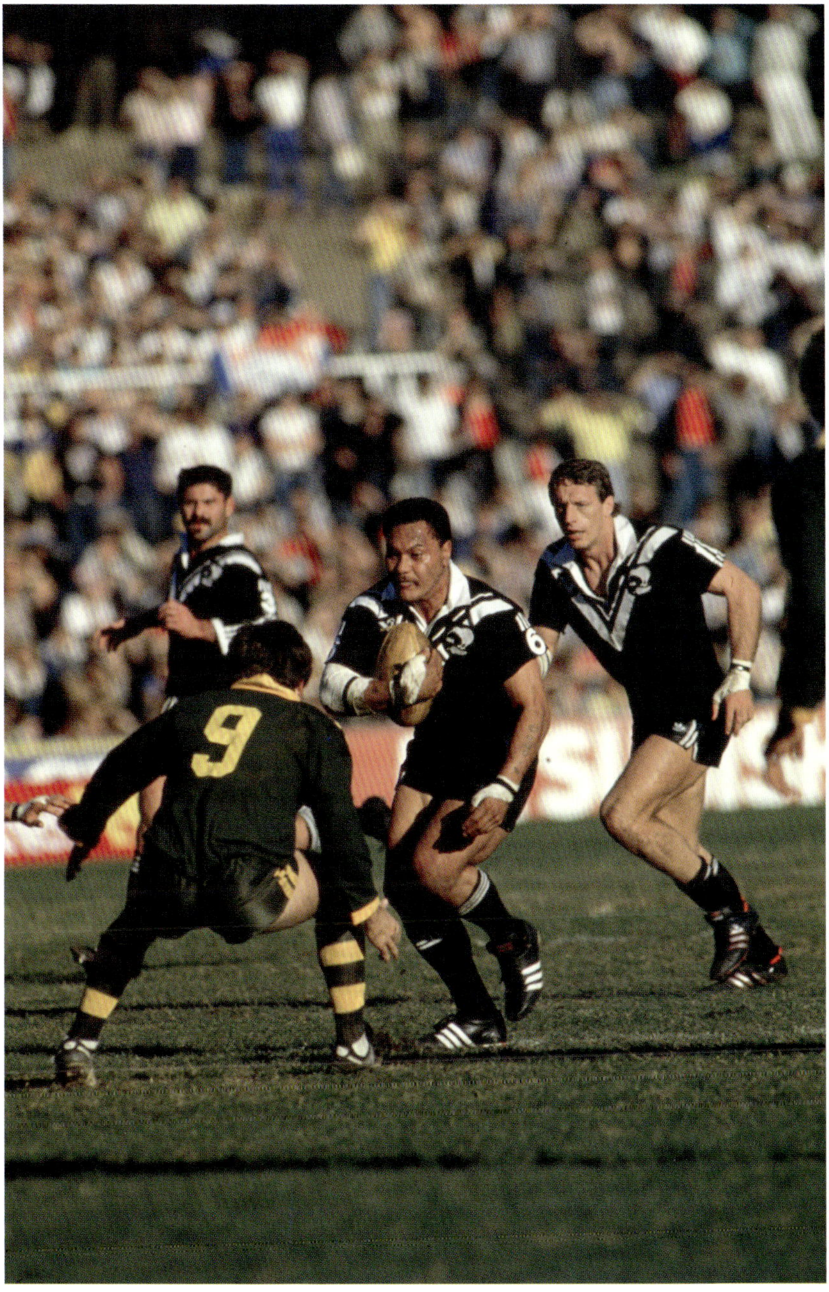

NRL Imagery

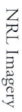

Olsen about to steamroll Kangaroos hooker Royce Simmons on 19 July 1986 with captain Mark Graham in support.

The 1985 Kiwis touring side of Great Britain in training. Olsen was the tour vice-captain and is in the centre wearing an AUTEX T-shirt.

The victorious Kiwis' post-match haka after their thrilling 24–22 first-test victory against Great Britain on 19 October 1985. The haka is led by Kevin Tamati and Olsen is second from the left.

Olsen playing his beloved tennis as part of his intense training regimen in the 1988 off-season before trialling for the Balmain Tigers. When Olsen arrived at Leichhardt Oval for the first training session, his old teammates were shocked at his weight loss. 'I had to look twice to make sure it was Olsen,' said teammate Wayne Pearce.

Olsen in Brisbane with his son Quin and All Blacks Jonah Lomu and Eroni Clarke in 1996.

Olsen with All Blacks legend Sir Bryan Williams in 2017 at Western Springs Stadium, the home ground of Ponsonby Rugby Club in Auckland. Williams was one of Olsen's heroes and is considered to be the first Polynesian sporting pioneer of the modern era.

Olsen and partner Leslie Anne Taylor in front of Te Huruhi Marae in Awarua, 23 kilometres from Kaikohe in Northland. Olsen's mother is buried in the cemetery here and he was born 500 metres away on the Filipaina family farm.

Mick Dries Collection

Olsen the proud father with family members Quin (left), John (centre), partner Leslie and Louise (right).

I returned home this year after four years in Australia,' he explained. When Tamati approached him about changing the haka to after the game, continued Lowe, 'I knew it had great meaning to him and the rest of the side. They are proud people and it shows when they play football.

'I'm a little ashamed for being ignorant of the customs. Tamati told me the haka would have more significance after the game and he was right. . . . To do it before the match wouldn't have had the same effect and it may not have received the respect it deserved.'

* * * * *

Back in New Zealand, the conservative European outpost was experiencing a historic period of social, cultural and political upheaval. In early 1984, 'Poi E', a song by the band Pātea Māori Club that featured traditional Māori language and dancing, spent four weeks at No. 1 and 22 weeks in the charts.

'It was an exciting time to be a Māori,' says Leslie. 'We had our own pop song in our language, but it also had breakdancing and other modern bits. It was who we are, an ancient people adapting to a modern era. And didn't we dance to "Poi E"!'

Nineteen eighty-four was a big year in New Zealand on all levels. The conservative government of Robert Muldoon was becoming deeply unpopular and the Labour opposition, under the leadership of David Lange, was gearing up for a July election, cooking up a plan to defeat Muldoon and end his nine brutal years in power.

And the Kiwis rugby league team, after its historic victory over Australia the previous year in 1983, was enjoying serious momentum. Television ratings were up and the team, headed by Graham Lowe, was more popular than ever.

Yet despite this momentum, the Sydney establishment which ruled Australian Rugby League seemed totally oblivious to its responsibilities in spreading the gospel of 'the greatest game of all'.

In an act of pure treachery and self-interest, the ARL reneged on its promise to hold a test series in 1984, robbing the in-form Kiwis of the opportunity to challenge its great rivals.

'Internationals between countries have always been the highlight of any rugby league season but it seems like Australia, unlike ourselves, give their club competition greater priority,' said Ron McGregor, the president of NZRL.

The drums of war were beating and Graham Lowe was furious at the snub and loss of momentum. In international rugby league, Australia and England had shared the number 1 and 2 rankings since the early 1900s and the Kiwis were primed for disruption. Lowe challenged the Aussies in *Rugby League Week*: 'We'll play Australia midweek or even at midnight if they'll turn up for the game.'

Instead, the Kiwis were to play a three-test home series against a touring Great Britain side. Olsen, after missing the 1983 tests, was looking forward to going home. 'It's hard to describe how much it lifted my spirits being with the Kiwi team and how much I wanted to play for them,' he later explained.

* * * * *

Under the Stanton Tigers regime for the new 1984 season, Olsen was still not getting any enjoyment out of playing at Leichhardt Oval. At the beginning of the season he had his hair cut in the mohawk style of Mr. T, the famous African American star of *The A-Team* TV series, making him appear even more outlandish.

He copped some flak for it from the short-back-and-sides world of Sydney rugby league, but to Olsen 'it was the best haircut I ever had'.

'Leslie called me an idiot and my daughter Louise cried when she saw me, but Mr. T was my hero for a different reason,' he says. 'Anyone that watched *The A-Team* knew that Mr. T was the toughest guy but he was totally scared of flying like me. That's why I liked him.'

Tigers coach Frank Stanton spoke to the media publicly of the pressure building on Olsen: 'He's only 26, so there are a few more years of football ahead of him. This is his last year on contract and he knows he has to produce. He is as fit and keen as I've ever seen him and others who have known him longer than me say the same thing.'

By Round 3 against Manly, Olsen was match fit and back in the starting line-up at five-eighth. The match preview in *Rugby League Week* celebrated his return: 'Olsen Filipaina makes a welcome return to first grade after a frustrating run of luck through injury. Filipaina hasn't played a full game in first grade since he injured his ankle in the seventh round last season. Up until his injury, Olsen was in the best club form of his career. He's raring to go now and is keen to make the most of his chance back in first grade.'

The Tigers beat Penrith 16–8 in Round 5 and Olsen was in imperious form. His opposite Brad Izzard struggled to contain Olsen, telling Charles Christian from *Rugby League Week* that Filipaina was 'impossible to stop'.

Izzard was bumped off three times by Filipaina in the match and said: 'Olsen is the player I least like facing. I haven't got any set plans on how to stop him. He just prepares himself so well. If I go low, I can't hug his legs because he crouches lower to bump me off. If I go higher, I get tossed.'

After two consecutive wins, the Balmain Tigers were on top of the Winfield Cup ladder and ready to take on heavyweights Canterbury Bankstown at home in Round 6. Canterbury took the threat of Olsen very seriously and moved Steve Folkes, their super-fit tackling maestro, from the forwards to five-eighth to counter his attack.

Canterbury coach Warren Ryan said to media before the match, 'Olsen was an influence in how we selected our halves. He can cause all sorts of strife but Folkes' defence should be able to handle things.'

Although he was fresh out of reserve grade, Filipaina was still Canterbury five-eighth Terry Lamb's danger man. Lamb told the *Daily Mirror* in the lead-up: 'I don't think he's played much first grade this year, but we have great respect for his ability. Out of all the players in Sydney football, he's got to be the most difficult to tackle. He's sort of built low to the ground and he's really powerful once he gets moving. I've seen him carve up plenty of teams before.'

Lamb would later rate Olsen very highly in his list of five-eighths he played against: 'Olsen would be in my top four. You'd have Wally Lewis, Brett Kenny, Olsen and Cliffy Lyons. I've got to throw Olsen in there for sure. If he turned up ready to play football you had to be on your game and a lot of the times Balmain won, he would get man of the match.'

Despite the plaudits, Olsen was dropped by Frank Stanton after Round 7 and would not be picked again in first grade until Round 19. In the opening 19 rounds of the 1984 Balmain Tigers season Olsen had played just eight games — two of which he started from the bench.

At the beginning of the season he had used an ancient Māori treatment in an effort to overcome his ongoing knee injury. His mother, Sissie, had flown in with the healing substance and a week later Olsen was back on the pitch.

But Balmain and particularly Frank Stanton remained culturally incompetent, unable to find a way to motivate Olsen. Stanton's decision to drop Olsen to reserve grade mystified opposition players.

'It was an absolute relief to us when Olsen wasn't picked. We were confused but grateful to Frank Stanton for that,' recalls Brad Izzard who dominated in Penrith's Round 18 win over the Olsen-less Tigers.

Izzard played many times against Olsen and will never forget the impact he had on opposing players:

'All the players would read the *Big League* magazine for the team line-ups and who they were playing opposite,' says Izzard.

'Whenever we came up against the Tigers I dreaded playing Olsen. We all did. You faced up without fear and did your job, but he was just so hard to handle.'

For Izzard one match stands out: 'I was coming back from injury in reserve grade and for whatever reason Olsen had also been playing reserves. When the *Big League* magazine came out that day, I remember rubbing my hands together when his name wasn't in there. I would have a good day in the office and get back to match fitness.'

When Izzard ran out onto the field his mood changed: 'There he was, standing opposite me. The big man with the big grin and those massive thighs that were guaranteed trouble. We had our normal tussle, but thankfully they took me off at halftime to rest. Then we had an injury in first grade after 20 minutes and I went on the field and lo and behold who was standing opposite waiting for me — Olsen again with a big grin. My Olsen-free day had turned into a double dose.'

Izzard tried to take Olsen on and paid the price: 'I thought I can't escape him so I'm gonna get him. I went low on him and his hip caught my head and I was knocked cold. I was trying to line him up, but he lined me up big time. In those days we just got up and I wobbled around the park until they took me off. I have no memory of the rest of the day until I woke up around 11 pm with a headache.'

Olsen had different weapons at his disposal according to Izzard: 'You never knew when he was going to bulldoze forward or be the playmaker. If you rushed up he had quick footwork; if you hung back he would get momentum with that stocky frame and it needed two or three guys to bring him down and we all found it so hard to stop him. He would make breaks out of nothing, and his defence was brutal. There was real sting in his tackles. They would shake your bones. Olsen was always in our thoughts in attack and defence.'

Izzard had a similar chunky frame to Olsen and copped the same treatment from the media: 'I feel for Olsen on that one. I had my weight criticised all the time even when I was fit and playing my best football. It was the trend to always pick on something and weight was a real thing for the media. He got extra because he was an outsider.'

Where Olsen sits in the ranking of five-eighths is simple for Izzard: 'Olsen, Cliff Lyons, Brett Kenny and Terry Lamb are all 9s in their own different ways. Wally was just above them, but Olsen was up there. I enjoyed playing against him; he made me a better player and best of all we always shook hands afterwards, had a laugh and all the on-field stuff was forgotten.'

* * * * *

Canterbury's Terry Lamb, who went on to win the 1984 Rothmans Medal for the best player in the Winfield Cup, was always relieved when Stanton buried Olsen in reserve grade. 'Ask the players about Olsen, don't ask the media who loved piling in on individual players,' says Lamb. 'They didn't have to tackle Olsen or be tackled by him.'

Olsen's Kiwis teammate Mark Graham had his own view of the situation from across the harbour at North Sydney Bears: 'I didn't know Frank very well but I knew for certain that Olsen wasn't very happy. Olsen was the last guy you would punish if you wanted the best out of him, but the Aussie coaches had no idea.'

* * * * *

In the final year of his contract with Balmain, Olsen was feeling the pressure. By the time he flew into Auckland for the three-test series against Great Britain, there were just six rounds left in the season and his future at the club was increasingly uncertain.

'When I got off the plane in Auckland everything was so familiar, people were so polite,' he recalls. 'I had always taken Auckland for granted but now it seemed like a kind of heaven. The moment I got to sit down in the living room and answer a million questions from Mum and my brothers, I knew I could finally relax. I hated being always on guard.'

Transitioning from Stanton's strict and cold regime to Graham Lowe's love-in was equally liberating. He lined up at five-eighth in the first test and helped New Zealand to a 12–0 victory over Great Britain at Carlaw Park in Auckland. The match itself was a low-scoring, old-school dogfight, and Olsen's four points went a long way to securing the win.

Although Olsen limped off late in the game with an ankle injury, he received a standing ovation from the Carlaw Park faithful and praise from the English newspaper *The Guardian*, which noted that Olsen's 'heavy build and direct style was ideal for the grim conditions'.

The significance of the result was perhaps overshadowed by the

'I DON'T LIKE LIVING HERE. I TOLERATE IT.'

outcome of the election that day. While Olsen was swatting away defenders from Great Britain, another empire was crumbling in Wellington, the political capital of New Zealand.

The New Zealand Labour Party crushed the National Party in the 1984 election, abruptly terminating the nine-year reign of Robert Muldoon. The new Prime Minister David Lange, a South Auckland old boy from Māngere and Ōtāhuhu College, promised to chart a new path for New Zealand.

'Although Lange was white — a Pākehā and Palagi — for us he was the first Pacific prime minister,' says Olsen's brother Alf. 'He was one of us. To the other guy, Muldoon, we were invisible, and our communities can never forget the fear of the Dawn Raids — he made us feel like outsiders. Lange was funny and charming and understood us.'

Lange had a vision of a more coherent, hybrid New Zealand identity that embraced both its history and geography. At the youthful political age of 41, Lange saw his election win as an opportunity to resolve the nation's identity crisis and break down and rebuild its character.

'It was a chance to make a different kind of country in New Zealand,' Lange wrote in his autobiography. 'We had to start getting a bit of joy back into the place. I wanted New Zealand to be a voice for good in the world.'

In the years preceding the election, the two rugby codes had mirrored the social and political differences between National and Labour. Muldoon was a rugby union fan and had no time for the multicultural, working-class communities that played rugby league.

On Muldoon's watch, the All Blacks rugby union side had defied the international community and inflamed his Polynesian and Māori constituents by touring apartheid South Africa in 1976 and hosting the Springboks' inbound tour in 1981.

The 1981 tour confirmed New Zealand's status as an international pariah following on from the Montreal Olympic Games in 1976, where 25 African nations had boycotted the Games in protest at New Zealand's sporting links with South Africa.

Both the All Blacks tour of South Africa in 1976 and the Springboks tour of New Zealand in 1981 were in defiance of the global 'Gleneagles Agreement' in which South Africa was to be isolated from all international sporting events.

The Springboks would only return to international sport when South Africa dismantled its apartheid regime that trapped the majority black population in segregation as second-class citizens.

* * * * *

The All Blacks of the late 1970s and early 1980s looked very different ethnically to the All Blacks of today. They were mostly white, acting as cultural ambassadors for Muldoon's version of New Zealand: an industrious, conservative and mainly rural people.

The captain of the All Blacks, Graham Mourie, fitted this image perfectly. He was a Pākehā from a farm in Taranaki. Yet before the 1981 Springboks tour of New Zealand he examined his conscience and decided to remove himself from All Blacks selection in protest at their support for South Africa's apartheid regime.

Rugby union, concluded Mourie in his autobiography, 'seems to breed isolationists wherever it is played, particularly those who aspire to be administrators. Nothing else matters.'

Despite angry objections, the 1981 South African Springboks tour of New Zealand went ahead, and the people that Muldoon had spent years scapegoating — unionists, academics, Māori, Pacific Islanders and journalists — rose up to create his worst nightmare.

'The Tour' sparked something akin to a civil war with flashpoints at barbed-wire-ringed stadiums and furious debates that tore families, friends, couples, churches and workplaces apart. The 56-day tour featured the worst intercommunal violence since the waterside workers' strike of 1951 and was effectively a proxy battle for the cultural soul of New Zealand.

In the blue corner was the National Party with its dour, monocultural Scots/English identity. In the red corner was the Labour Party with

'I DON'T LIKE LIVING HERE. I TOLERATE IT.'

its vision of a new outward-looking multicultural nation of which its citizens could be globally proud.

When the 'Barbed-wire Boks' finally left New Zealand, what remained was a country ripped in two pieces, both sides bleeding and bruised, with rugby union as the culprit. A 100-year toxic epoch, driven by the insecurity and arrogance of rugby union's powerbrokers, had finally reached a tipping point and triggered consequences that cast long shadows.

All Black Murray Mexted said in a later documentary on the tour: 'We had a country torn apart.'

New Zealand historian Gordon McLauchlan, who in 1976 wrote the best-selling book *The Passionless People*, provided a historical background to the attitude that underpinned the 1981 Springboks tour — the inability of New Zealand rugby fans to see outside their cultural bubble.

'The common British background, the long isolation and the narrow streams of immigration, the rigorous discrimination against difference, dissent and non-conformity,' wrote McLauchlan, 'has led the New Zealand population to be the most culturally inbred of any developed country in the world.'

In this context, rugby league offered a progressive alternative. In the Kiwis' starting 13 that defeated Great Britain in 1984, for example, three Pākehā players — fullback Gary Kemble, winger Dane O'Hara and halfback Shane Varley — lined up alongside 10 New Zealanders of Māori, Tongan, Samoan and mixed heritage.

The Māori and Polynesians were a crucial part of the Kiwis' success, not bit players. In the Kiwis' 12-nil victory over Great Britain in the first test, Olsen, the Samoan-Māori, and Tongan Kurt Sorensen laid on tries for Samoans James Leuluai and Fred Ah Kuoi.

And they were led by Graham Lowe, a culturally competent Pākehā coach who, like new Prime Minister David Lange, had been raised on rugby league at the Ōtāhuhu Leopards.

Lowe was ready for his finest hour, and he truly was rugby league coaching's rags to riches story. He had an unremarkable start in life, leaving Ōtāhuhu College at 16 to start an apprenticeship as an auto electrician.

Lowe found school uninteresting and it did not suit him. What it did teach him was a key principle for his later success. Lowe says: 'I wasn't treated as an individual at school and it showed me how important it was to treat people as individuals and not be one size fits all.'

Anyone who witnessed Graham Lowe's underwhelming playing career could not have predicted his success as a coach. He was certainly not to the manor born. He came through the 'tradesman's entrance', starting his coaching in eighth-grade local football with the Ōtāhuhu Leopards and setting a path to becoming the best coach in the world. The journey took him from his launch pad of hardscrabble Murphy Park in Ōtāhuhu to packed stadiums around the world.

In a documentary on Auckland rugby league, Kiwis test player Owen Wright remembers Lowe being 'all business' from the outset in 1973: 'The first time I ran into Graham at Ōtāhuhu we were doing our pre-training stretches on the back of an Austin A40, having some cigarettes and telling jokes to each other and this bloke walks up along the park and he's got this clipboard and whistle and a hat and a brand-new tracksuit and everything.

'We look at him and we're thinking who the hell is this bloke? The next minute he comes up and says, "I'm looking for Ōtāhuhu eighth-grade. Can you tell us where they are?" And we said, "We're it." He looked at the car and us and said, "You'd better go and get 13 more blokes for Thursday night." Wright asked Lowe why and he replied, 'Cause you blokes aren't playing.'

Lowe's meteoric rise led him to a first-grade coach appointment in 1977 at the improbably young age of 31. Lowe was an oddity in New Zealand, a young pup in the elite coaching ranks, normally the domain of gruff and grey-haired ex-players.

Lowe was the first coach in Auckland to move towards a professional style with his Ōtāhuhu Leopards. They were the first club to move from two to three training nights a week and his team lapped it up. Lowe says: 'It was a big commitment, but we trained three days when everyone else trained twice and that's why we won everything.'

It was in the 1950s and 1960s that Lowe absorbed the unique Auckland rugby league playing style that he would later use to ambush the Kangaroos: 'It was fast with uncompromising defence and great attacking play. It was filled with great characters, great footballers who were not necessarily the fittest but were football fit. Kiwi football was based on instinct, it promoted the instinctive players. I absorbed that entertaining style and would never let it go regardless of where I coached.'

From the outset, Graham Lowe showed his ability to get the best out of 'unfashionable' players who had confidence issues, a troubled past or came from broken homes. He also aimed to make them better men through empathy — by entering his players' mindsets to see their hopes and dreams he could bridge any social divide. He would visit them at places they felt comfortable and, most importantly, he would listen to them.

* * * * *

In many respects, Graham Lowe was to rugby league what David Lange was to politics. 'My mum loved Lowie and she loved Lange,' says Olsen. 'They were a new breed of Pākehā and were both men of the people. They listened to us and had faith in us. For the first time it felt good to be a Pacific person in Auckland.'

Lange had deep roots in Māngere East and he had extraordinary personal experience with Māori. A lawyer, he had started his first legal aid practice in Kaikohe — Olsen's mother Sissie's Ngāpuhi hometown in Northland. He had taken on almost exclusively Māori casework including a large amount of pro bono clients from remote Māori communities.

Later, after his switch to politics as the local member for Māngere Bridge, many of his constituents were from the Pacific communities and he had helped provide legal advice to them during Muldoon's Dawn Raids. Sissie Filipaina would regularly attend his office for a chat and Lange was a regular at Fox Memorial Cup games as a fan of his beloved Ōtāhuhu Leopards.

In his autobiography, Lange proclaimed his love of rugby league and dissatisfaction with rugby union. Lange was once jeered by the crowd and punched by a wild spectator at an All Blacks test match against France in Christchurch. 'It certainly marked the end of my efforts to reach some sort of understanding with the rugby union public and I have not seen a rugby union game since,' Lange wrote of the incident.

Perhaps buoyed by the fall of the Muldoon Government, the Kiwis won the next two test matches against Great Britain, completing New Zealand's first-ever three-nil series win over the British.

Olsen started every match at five-eighth and contributed 24 points with the boot. Goal-kicking, which he hated doing in Sydney, suddenly didn't seem so daunting in front of supportive New Zealand crowds.

In the third test at Carlaw Park, won by the Kiwis 32–16, he was named man of the match for his brute strength in bursting the English defence and in acknowledgement of his softer skills including delivering a beautiful pass for James Leuluai's crucial try. 'That's why Olsen Filipaina is in the side,' gushed commentator Colin O'Neil.

'In difficult conditions he handled the heavy leather ball easily, and always gave you beautiful soft passes, not tricky spirals,' recalls Howie Tamati, who played all three tests as hooker. 'They couldn't put him down and he fed us into gaps. That year he really infected us with his attitude and the joy of playing footy. I was honoured to be Olly's roommate. He's a very tidy man for a garbo!'

In the third-test victory over Great Britain at Carlaw Park, Olsen's performance left an indelible imprint on English rugby league historian Tony Collins: 'I was watching the third test with my dad and we were completely blown away by Olsen's power — he had the size of a prop

'I DON'T LIKE LIVING HERE. I TOLERATE IT.'

but was so skilful and he tore our players apart. He just took over the middle of the park, which is the most contested space. Even then, I had a feeling that something had changed in rugby league.'

* * * * *

With a great test series under his belt, Olsen returned to Australia with mixed emotions for the final stretch of Balmain's 1984 Winfield Cup season. He was happy to reunite with his young family but reluctant to leave New Zealand. On his return to Sydney he was confined to bed for a week, struck down with the flu and so had time to reflect on his future. He was coming to the end of his second Balmain contract and a decision was required.

Was this the end of his journey with Balmain? Should he try his luck at another Sydney club, or follow his Kiwis teammates to England?

At the urging of his teammates, he hauled himself out of his sickbed to line up against Wests in Round 23. It was an important game for Balmain, who were hovering just outside the top five. In the No. 6 jumper, Olsen had a game to remember, guiding the Tigers to an eight-point victory.

'Olsen was the difference today,' admitted Stanton. 'He kicked the goals that we needed and played strongly.'

Out in his adopted hometown of Ryde, the 'One Eyed Tiger' was jubilant in his column in *The Weekly Times*: 'Fans — I've always maintained that Olsen Filipaina is the best thing to come out of New Zealand since Phar Lap,' he wrote.

'Filipaina got out of his sick bed, despite being as crook as a week-old railway pie and kicked the necessary goals and played his usual strong all-round game. Although choked up with the flu, Filipaina lived up to the adage that when the goin' gets tough, the tough get goin'. He advised coach Frank Stanton that he wanted to play for the club, as he knew it was a desperate game, and although short of breath, performed with greater shine than Mr Sheen.'

In his *Rugby League Week* match report headlined 'Olsen Bumps and Grinds', David Middleton wrote of his performance in the Wests match: 'A welcome return to form by Kiwi international five-eighth Olsen Filipaina rekindled the Tigers' semi-final hopes. Filipaina had spent much of the season in reserve grade before being called upon by New Zealand. The Tigers would have been hard-pressed to record a win had it not been for the bullocking runs of Filipaina. On numerous occasions he bumped and burst his way through the Western Suburbs' defence in his characteristic style.'

The following Sunday, Olsen scored a try and kicked seven goals in Balmain's 27-point victory over Canberra. His form was good, but his mind was elsewhere. In an interview with Peter Peters, published in the *Sun Herald*, he spoke of his dislike of goal-kicking, admitting that he refused to practise the set shots at training.

Olsen's fear of flying made a move to England seem unlikely, yet he had not been offered a contract with Balmain and his five-year association with the club appeared to be coming to an end. For the moment, at least, Olsen had no answers to questions about his future.

And so Peters, like many reporters in Sydney, fell back on a familiar trope. 'The 94-kilogram Kiwi,' he concluded, 'is a football enigma.'

On the positive side, Peters was impressed with Olsen's performance against Canberra and wrote: 'Olsen scattered them like ninepins.' Alan Clarkson from the *Sydney Morning Herald* was equally enthused: 'When Filipaina has a good game, the whole Balmain team fires and this happened on Saturday.'

Neil Cadigan wrote in *Rugby League Week* about Olsen's importance to the Tigers: 'Most talk was about the dynamic return of Olsen Filipaina. The times when Balmain have looked a threat in the past three seasons have been when Filipaina has been "in the mood". He has struggled in reserves all season while the Tigers top side has lacked spark. But after some sensational performances for New Zealand and with contract renewal time coming up, big Olsen has brought out his best.'

Ray Chesterton wrote in the *Daily Telegraph* that although his on-field form was good, Olsen's mysterious off-field behaviour continued:

'Balmain's match-winning five-eighth Olsen Filipaina was at his enigmatic best against Canberra. After playing a commanding role, Filipaina was among the first off the field, quickly into the showers and off home while many of his teammates were still slumped in the dressing room. No time for an interview with Olsen. He's a doer, not a talker and yesterday he was doing Balmain proud. He put on a burst of such power and strength that only those contemplating suicide would have contemplated intercepting him.

'Balmain coach "Cranky" Frank Stanton, not a man given to smiling without justification, couldn't repress a grin yet said begrudgingly to reporters: "Olsen's a great player when he's in the mood."'

* * * * *

Despite his excellent end-of-season form, the bells were soon to toll for Olsen. He heard whispers that Balmain were not going to retain him, and his suspicions were confirmed by Peter Frilingos of the *Daily Telegraph* who wrote a story titled 'Tigers' Hero Unwanted'.

'Olsen Filipaina fears his chequered career with Balmain may be over even after producing his best form of the season,' wrote Frilingos: 'On his day there are few more damaging runners than Filipaina. His contract will finish on grand final day, bringing to an end his five-year association with Balmain.'

The Tigers staggered to the final round needing a win and other teams to lose to make the semi-finals. Their opponent was third-placed St George who had enjoyed a strong and consistent year.

Sydney Sun journalist John Brady was on the Olsen bandwagon. His match preview was titled 'New-look Filipaina Tigers' trump' and he wrote: 'Rampaging Balmain five-eighth Olsen Filipaina is the key to Sunday's grudge match against St George at Leichhardt.'

In a pre-match interview, Frank Stanton shared with Brady his thoughts on Olsen's form: 'There aren't many players in the world who can stop Filipaina when he's in the frame of mind he's in now.'

St George coach Roy Masters announced his game plan in advance. He was to move his best defender Graeme O'Grady from the forwards to five-eighth to counter the 'Filipaina threat'. Olsen the danger man, being assigned the opposition's best tackler — a familiar scenario facing Olsen throughout his career.

The Tigers lost a close game to St George 26–18 and the Tigers' season was over.

In the end, Balmain finished eighth in the Winfield Cup in 1984 and missed out on finals football. Parramatta, meanwhile, were denied their fourth consecutive premiership by a stodgy, defensive Canterbury side coached by Warren Ryan.

In the grand final, Canterbury's gang-tacklers subsumed Parramatta's individual brilliance with a watertight defensive phalanx. The Bulldogs' negative brand of 'Wozzaball' eventually outmuscled, outswarmed and sludged Parramatta's entertainers to grind out a win four points to two — one of the lowest-scoring finals in history. 'I remember thinking, who wants to watch this stuff?' says Olsen. 'It was not good for the fans.'

What next for the 'Enigma'?

* * * * *

Olsen was not the only player labelled an 'enigma' in rugby league. From his northern stronghold in Brisbane, Queensland five-eighth Wally Lewis was completing one of the greatest individual seasons in the history of the game.

He was the captain of his club, Wynnum Manly, which won the Brisbane competition and the captain of the Combined Brisbane representative side that won the midweek National Panasonic Cup. He led Queensland to yet another State of Origin series victory over New South Wales and skippered the Australian Kangaroos to a three-nil series whitewash of Great Britain.

'Revered in Brisbane, confronted with fear and loathing in Sydney, Lewis this year has emerged as the game's true "superstar",' concluded

Ian Heads of *Rugby League Week*. 'He's rugby league's Carl Lewis, Edwin Moses, Dean Lukin and Viv Richards wrapped into one.'

Like Olsen, Wally played football for enjoyment, not punishment. Unlike Olsen, however, Wally was shielded from the conservative, soul-sucking Sydney competition and weekly negativity of the media.

Ignoring the streams of 'sports science' emanating from Sydney's Winfield Cup, Lewis boasted of his relaxed eating style. 'I eat what I like, when I like,' he told reporter Tony Durkin. 'All the food that's supposedly wrong for us — hot chips, cold chips, soft drink etc. doesn't seem to affect me.'

Like Wally, Olsen also seemed to cause issues for Sydney's golden boy five-eighth, Parramatta's Brett Kenny. In his *Rugby League Week* player profile, Kenny had named Olsen as the hardest player to tackle in the Winfield Cup.

* * * * *

At the end of the 1984 season and after five years' service, the Balmain Tigers chose not to renew Olsen's contract. Despite being in the best form of his Winfield Cup career, the Balmain Tigers retention committee decided that he was surplus to their requirements.

Frank Stanton does not recall any specific conversations regarding Olsen moving on. 'Recruitment and retention wasn't part of my job, it was done by a committee,' Stanton explains. 'Teams were selected by selectors; my job was to mould the team and get them to contend for the semi-finals.'

Stanton is surprised to hear of Olsen's unhappiness and depression during his time at the Tigers. 'That's disappointing Olsen feels that way and I wouldn't like to think that Olsen blames me for his career,' says Stanton.

'My only regret is that I would have liked to have had a better outcome. I'm sorry he feels that way and there was certainly no intention to be harder on him than anybody else.

'I don't look upon my coaching period during those years

specifically around handling Olsen,' Stanton explains. 'There's 16 or 17 other players in the club that needed to be attended to, needed to be coached, dealt with and listened to. It wasn't always about Olsen. Some people responded but obviously Olsen's level of response wasn't always as we wanted.'

Wayne Wigham, Olsen's first and closest friend at Balmain, always maintained that the Tigers had wasted Olsen's talent and the Sydney press had never properly understood him.

'Although the media had a lot of fun calling Olsen the enigma, it was bullshit,' says Wigham. 'He had a lot of great games for Balmain, won a lot of man of the matches and he was a sensation. You ask the players he played against — none of them call him lazy or an enigma. When he was on fire and injury free, he dominated most centres and five-eighths in Sydney. It's a bit of a good story, but it's not the truth and it gives me the shits.'

For Olsen, the feeling of sadness at leaving his teammates was tempered by relief. He was uneasy to leave the first club in his career, a club he wanted to stay loyal to, like his Māngere East Hawks in Auckland. But he was finally free of the tyranny of Stanton, and he had an opportunity to pursue his career at a new club.

Looking back, the ultimate insult, for Olsen, was when he says Stanton sent him to a psychiatrist instead of a physiotherapist. He told reporters in 1987 that he felt it was 'a slur against my half Samoan and half Māori background. It wouldn't have happened to a white player.'

'Frank sent me to what I thought was a knee specialist in North Sydney,' explained Olsen. 'I front up there and the guy starts asking me all these questions about my life and my family's mental health history. When I asked him about my knee he told me he was a psychiatrist. I went back to Leichhardt to do the time trials and just jogged around the field in protest. Balmain branded me a loony and I didn't like it. Now it's okay, but back then it was a source of shame.'

Frank Stanton has no recollection of the incident, reiterating that player welfare was not his responsibility but the club's staff.

* * * * *

Despite his treatment, Olsen would always love and appreciate the Tigers for giving him an opportunity. Leslie was less forgiving.

'I'll never forget it,' she once said, '. . . we were standing outside some changing rooms and we heard someone yell out: "Who does this black cunt think he is taking one of our spots?" Just imagine hearing that.'

Leslie's worst moment of Olsen's time at the Tigers came in 1984 when Graham Lowe was in Sydney to meet Olsen and check his form out for an upcoming test. According to Leslie, Frank — in front of Olsen — told Graham that he shouldn't pick Olsen for the Kiwis.

Leslie says: 'If Frank only knew the impact that had on Olsen. His coaches had all been father figures and Frank tried to sabotage his Kiwi chances. I remember the look of betrayal on Olsen's face. I'll never forget it.'

'I remember the incident and it wasn't pleasant,' says Sir Graham Lowe: 'I stuck up for Olsen and gave Frank a burst in reply, telling him he didn't know how to coach him.'

Olsen felt abandoned when Frank would talk about him negatively in the press. When once asked about Olsen, Frank replied to the awaiting media: 'If you don't have anything nice to say, say nothing at all.'

Leslie had grown tired of the cat-and-mouse game between Olsen and Frank and the impact it had on her partner: 'In my opinion, Frank didn't know how to handle the Pacific Islands boys and whether he realised it or not, he tried to break Olsen. Olsen would sometimes say, "Why bother?" but then he would tell me, "I've got a thing with the coach but can't let my teammates down." And on it went. I was relieved when it was over.'

Sir Peter Leitch remembers watching from Auckland in horror as the Olsen and Frank saga unfolded: 'I knew that Olsen might struggle with the wrong coach. Frank wasn't a bad guy, but he was very hard on Olsen and to get the best out of him, he should have done it in a different way. Really, none of the Aussies could handle Polynesians and the difference in culture. They tried to sanitise and sterilise them rather than set them loose. Frank tried to turn Olsen from a skilful and unpredictable playmaker into a battering ram. Every team needs an Olsen, not clones of each other.'

Rugby League Week editor Ian Heads was close with Frank Stanton and saw the cultural mismatch first hand, explaining:

'I don't think any of us understood Olsen, including Frank. Frank didn't really understand what he had in Olsen who was devastating at his best. He had a sense of mystery from the fans to the media to the coaches. It was a clash of cultures between those two at Balmain. One was the taskmaster and the other was the free spirit and they bumped up against each other. They were men of different cultures and different eras that stood for different things and neither backed down. And don't forget that despite what some of the media said, Olsen played a lot of unbelievable match-winning games for Frank.'

The Frank and Olsen story is best viewed as a story of two cultures crashing into each other like tectonic plates. Frank had the power as coach and was a man of his times, the product of a 70-year-old 'one size fits all' system based on Australian egalitarian principles.

The real villain is ignorance and the lack of intercultural understanding, and that gap has now been closed by succeeding generations of coaches. The old ways did not suit the new ways and the miscommunication was inevitable as very few understood the Polynesian and Māori cultures.

Olsen bore the brunt of a system that is now much more culturally attuned. Some pioneers have to sacrifice, to build the learnings for those that follow.

* * * * *

'I DON'T LIKE LIVING HERE. I TOLERATE IT.'

Olsen's record at Balmain Tigers — 77 first-grade games for 19 tries — meant that he could never quite shake the 'enigma' tag. In five seasons he had dazzled supporters and entertained journalists but had never played finals football or truly established himself in one position. And yet 'the reluctant goal-kicker', as he was often labelled, still left Balmain as the highest-ever points-scorer at Leichhardt Oval.

That record would not be broken for another 27 years. Perhaps fittingly, the man who would eventually overtake Olsen's tally was another Māori five-eighth who was adored by the Leichhardt crowd: Benjamin Quentin 'Benji' Marshall.

6
THE FILIPAINA AFFAIR

'The split is likely to remain permanent.'
— Arthur Beetson, 1984

After leaving Balmain, Olsen was faced with the brave new world of playing for a new club for the upcoming 1985 season.

Already on the table were offers in pounds sterling from three English clubs, each of which were reportedly happy to meet Olsen's financial demands of a A$50,000 a year contract plus car, accommodation and a job.

The English offers sparked considerable debate with his family and partner, but Olsen declined the offers due to his panic that the 24-hour flight to London would prove too much for his nerves.

Even the comparatively short three-hour flights between Auckland and Sydney required extensive cajoling from friends, teammates and family before he would reluctantly and fearfully step on a plane.

Graham Lowe had enrolled Olsen in special classes to help him overcome his 'aviophobia', but it had not been enough. In September 1984, Olsen announced publicly that he would not consider moving to an English club to join his merry band of Kiwis mates carving out fame for themselves in the northern hemisphere.

One headline in *Big League* magazine read 'Flying Fear Costs Olsen a Packet'.

His decision meant that playing in Australia was his only real option. Two clubs, led by two of rugby league's most respected figures, emerged as frontrunners: Cronulla, coached by supercoach Jack Gibson, and Eastern Suburbs, coached by Aboriginal legend Arthur Beetson.

Both sensed that Olsen had more to give in the right environment. After all, here was a man who could seemingly do it all when in the mood: he could operate in the centres, in the halves, in the forward-line and he could kick for goal.

Gibson, who had tried to recruit Olsen to Parramatta in 1981, was becoming the elder statesman of the game in Australia. He had been coaching for nearly two decades and Cronulla was his sixth club in Sydney. After delivering Parramatta its first premiership in 1981 — and then backing it up with two more in 1982 and 1983 — he had taken a year off coaching in 1984.

He had forged a reputation as rugby league's innovator-in-chief. He was the first to use video and computer analysis. The first to cross train and share knowledge with rival codes. The first to use Nautilus machines and the first to bring in the dreaded skin-fold test. He brought in 'the bomb' — an attacking high kick designed to put the opposition fullback under pressure in his own in-goal area.

And perhaps his greatest legacy — he was a pioneer in man management, believing that football could build better men and thus a better society.

'He was the first coach of my experience who was concerned as much about his players' progress and development off the field as he was with their performances on it,' Arthur Beetson said of Gibson in his autobiography. 'Almost single-handedly he dragged the game into the age of professionalism.'

Eastern Suburbs' coach Beetson, who was 15 years Gibson's junior, was a pioneer of a different kind. He was the first Indigenous captain of the Kangaroos, the first Indigenous captain to win a NSWRL premiership, and now at Eastern Suburbs, the first Indigenous head coach of a club in Sydney. Although he had retired as a player in 1981,

Beetson had already coached club sides in Sydney and Brisbane and taken the reins of Queensland and Australia.

Beetson was one of Gibson's many disciples. In 1974 and 1975, when Gibson coached Easts to consecutive premierships, Beetson had been his captain. To Artie, Jack was a friend and a father figure. They were weekly golfing buddies. It was Gibson who delivered the famous line: 'Arthur's idea of a balanced meal is a pie in each hand.'

Now, with the 1985 season looming, Gibson was back from his sabbatical and Beetson was returning to coach club football after three years coaching representative sides.

For both men, 1985 represented a significant challenge. Easts had not played finals football in two seasons and had not won a premiership since 1975. Cronulla, meanwhile, had never won a premiership since joining the NSWRL in 1963.

Gibson and Beetson were both keen to build squads of their own design. Both set their sights on Olsen Filipaina — perhaps the hottest free agent in Sydney. What followed in the next three weeks would live on in rugby league folklore — a saga known as 'The Filipaina Affair'.

Gibson had the inside running and they agreed terms to play for Cronulla by a handshake in early November. Olsen was open to joining a Cronulla side that included his Kiwis teammates Kurt and Dane Sorensen and he was keen to be coached by Gibson.

'It has always been my ambition to be coached by Jack,' Olsen told the *Daily Telegraph*.

Despite the handshake, Cronulla delayed getting Olsen a contract, which made him nervous. Feeling unmoored and uncertain, Olsen received a call from Ron Jones, the secretary of Eastern Suburbs, and agreed to meet him at the Eastern Suburbs Leagues Club in Bondi Junction.

Jones was ready with an aggressive offer — double the money on offer from Cronulla. It was more money than Olsen had ever been offered from an Australian club — $35,000 for a season, but the deal was conditional on him signing immediately.

Although located only 10 kilometres away, the plush Eastern Suburbs Leagues Club was a world apart from the working man's Balmain Leagues Club. At Easts Leagues Club, a strict dress code was in place including no hair over the collar. A gentleman's club with leather couches hosted serious business gatherings.

Olsen remembers a surreal scene in Ron Jones' office: 'A huge wad of cash appeared in a brown paper bag, just like in the movies. And then they ran it through a money-counting machine.'

'It was more cash than we'd ever seen,' says Leslie: 'We were astounded and it was then we realised they were a money club; whatever they said they could make happen.'

To heighten the drama, Jones offered Olsen and his cash an escort to his car, which he politely declined.

Looking back Olsen applauds Jones' strategy: 'No Polynesian sending money home to take care of their family could ever say no to that sort of cash, double the amount of any other offer. It was like being hypnotised, seeing it in that bag. The possibilities were endless.

'I had agreed terms for two years with Cronulla, quite soon after Balmain cut me but they hadn't produced a contract,' Olsen recalls. 'And then Easts offered me the same money as Cronulla but for a one-year contract not two. Double the money! Two years of pay for one year of work . . . it was hard for me and Leslie to say no.'

In late November, it was announced across Australian and New Zealand media that Easts had won the race for Olsen's signature, inflaming Cronulla.

'We are flabbergasted. The deal was done and Filipaina and Beetson knew it!' raged Cronulla secretary Peter Riley, who added: 'We had arranged for him to live in a unit in Cronulla and I was in the process of getting him a job.'

Confident that Olsen would honour their deal, Riley said Cronulla had stopped looking at other centres and focused on recruiting players in other key positions. 'Now we have missed the boat,' said Riley, 'and we are desperate for a centre.'

Easts secretary Ron Jones was having none of it. Olsen was a logical recruit for a club that had already signed Kiwi internationals Hugh McGahan and Dean Bell. 'When I knew Balmain had released him,' explains Jones, 'I asked Beetson what he thought of Filipaina and he said he liked him.'

The relationship between Cronulla and Easts oscillated from frosty to outright war. One journalist compared the drama the incident generated to the American soap opera *Days of Our Lives*. The *Daily Mirror* claimed it had 'stunned the rugby league world'.

Rugby League Week editor Ian Heads remembers the drama of the 'Filipaina Affair': 'Both coaches felt so strongly about him that they were prepared to end their friendship, which was one of the deepest in rugby league. Coaches that felt they'd get more out of him wanted to get their hands on him. It was the biggest story of the pre-season by far.'

Once again Olsen was the subject of intrigue and controversy. At the time, Heads wrote that the issue 'was simmering like a restive volcano'. Cronulla felt that Olsen's gentleman's agreement should stand and the friendship between Jack and Arthur went 'straight out of the window', according to Gibson.

'Let's get it straight,' Beetson told journalist Ron Casey in reply. 'There's no one outside my family who means more to me than Jack Gibson. Jack is from the old school and I reckon he expected me to automatically drop off Olsen Filipaina because we've been like brothers for the past 10 years. Jack should understand Filipaina was keen to sign with Easts because 15 minutes after the meeting he signed on the dotted line.'

Asked about the future of his relationship with Gibson, Beetson continued: 'I still think Jack is a good bloke and I hope our friendship survives this storm. But by the words Jack used, the split is likely to remain permanent.'

For a second time in three years, Jack Gibson had missed out on signing Olsen. The first time it had been due to Olsen's sense of loyalty to his Balmain teammates. Now, it seemed to be down to money.

'I felt terrible about letting Jack down,' says Olsen. 'It's hard to explain now, but it wasn't about how I was feeling, about which coach I should play for. I made the decision for my family. They didn't know about Cronulla versus Easts, or Arthur versus Jack. Easts were paying double what Cronulla was paying so it was Easts. I was so embarrassed when I called Jack and told him I was going for the cash.'

For Olsen, at almost 28 years of age, the decision was a no-brainer: 'It was potentially my last big contract to make for my family and my mother in particular,' Olsen says. 'My knee was troubling me, my elbow was in bad shape. In Sydney my game was a big collision game — I was always met by the best tacklers and lots of them. The collisions take a toll over time.'

According to Leslie, 'it was the brown paper bag that made the difference'. The image of Olsen returning from a cash-counting machine with $15,000 in hand, 'was like being in a movie'.

'Olsen could never tell his family how he was feeling,' Leslie later explained. 'He had to put on a front for them. Olsen would have loved to play under Jack, but he couldn't put his personal preferences ahead of the amazing money that he would be able to send back to his family.

'Easts offered a car and some other incentives that were above the contract amount. We both felt terrible about it at the time, but it was never about what Olsen wanted to do. Olsen did what was best for his family, in true Polynesian style.'

* * * * *

With rumours swirling about his integrity, Olsen played on. He began training with Easts immediately, settling into a new routine. He felt 'a bit strange' driving from Ryde across the Sydney CBD for training and into a different world.

In the first trial match of the pre-season, he performed well in an eight-point win over his old club, Balmain.

'I suppose he was a bit like me in the old days — play some and rest some — but what I've seen so far, Filipaina will be with us for 80 minutes every week,' declared Beetson in *Rugby League Week*.

In many ways, as an Aboriginal legend of the game, Arthur Beetson seemed to be the perfect coach to bring out Olsen's delicate genius. Like Olsen, he had started his career at Balmain. They were both big men that loved to eat and had unique ability to scatter defences, using their dexterity and strength to clear their arms and offload to eager support runners.

Beetson was equally adept on the court at tennis, racquetball and squash. And they both had their moments with Frank Stanton with Beetson once labelling Stanton 'a company man'.

Where they differed, though, was in their response to racism. 'Even five years in to playing in Sydney, virtually every game a player would call me racist names, and I would never respond,' says Olsen.

'It was shocking, and it just didn't stop,' says Kiwis coach Graham Lowe. 'When I visited Olsen at Easts in 1985, the language from players and fans to him and Hugh McGahan was foul, racist and very hurtful. Australia was ahead of us in rugby league professionalism, but we were well ahead of them in social behaviour. It was like they were living in frontier times.'

Beetson, who had grown up in Roma in country Queensland, learned to deal with racism from an early age including his local racially segregated 'picture theatre'. He developed a thick skin and used his fists or his charm to confront his assailants.

When he moved to Sydney he faced open racism from opponents, teammates and sometimes coaches. In Ian Heads' autobiography *Big Artie*, Beetson recounts being abused by captain-coach and Immortal Graeme Langlands on the 1973 Kangaroos tour of Great Britain.

Beetson said: 'Some of the terms he used to my face and in front of the team at training sessions were as derogatory and racist as they come.'

According to Wilfred Williams, an Aboriginal second-rower who also joined Easts in 1985, Beetson was relatively privileged due to his status in the game, and he operated mostly in a white world.

'Although Arthur was a blackfella, he was very much a part of the system,' says Williams, who grew up in Wiradjuri country in Cowra in south-western New South Wales. 'He had a lot of cultural pressures — Aboriginal activists hustling him on one hand; on the other the white rugby league community loving him as the first Aboriginal captain of the Kangaroos.

'Don't get me wrong,' says Williams. 'Arthur took me in to his house when I came here and changed my mindset and believed in me. I'd have been an alcoholic or dead if not for him. But he didn't get Olsen.'

Before the first 15-kilometre road run of the pre-season, Wilfred Williams sidled up to Olsen and asked if he could stick with him.

Williams says: 'I introduced myself to Olly who was the only other dark fella there that day. I asked him, "Do you mind if I run with you?" He laughed and said: "Don't go running with me, you might get a reputation".'

It was the beginning of a beautiful friendship. On one occasion, when Olsen saw Wilfred shivering on the sideline, he took off his jacket and draped it over his shoulders.

'It was this big, puffy beautiful Adidas thing and he just handed it over,' says Williams. 'He didn't know me from a bar of soap and I was a little lost Koori and here was this guy, taking me in.'

For Olsen the Māori-Samoan collective style of living was all he knew: 'It was just a jacket and poor Wilfred was cold. Nothing is mine, everything is ours, everything is shared. My Australian friends still can't understand it but it's our way.'

Later, when Wilfred and Olsen moved on from Easts to other clubs, Olsen told him he wouldn't hurt him in tackles. 'It's not talked about much, but the blackfellas used to look after each other,' says Williams. 'Not miss tackles, but tackle a little bit softer, not try to injure them, just put them on the ground clean with no whacking. Imagine what it was like hearing that from Olsen — he was one of us. He didn't play the game to bash people.'

Yet during their time together at Easts, Wilfred could see that Olsen was being mismanaged by the coaching staff. The road runs, for instance, did more harm than good. 'It was ridiculous. Anyone could see Olsen was a big musclebound man and would be better on a rowing machine. He would never be an 800-metre specialist.'

* * * * *

In the opening game of the season against South Sydney, Olsen started at five-eighth and Wilfred Williams was selected on the bench. Souths' aggressive forwards tore into the Easts players with special attention paid to their new Kiwi imports Hugh McGahan and Dean Bell, both of whom were making their Sydney debuts. The hits were as big as the language was feral. McGahan, a proud Māori, was called names 'that can't be repeated,' said Easts Secretary Ron Jones after the game.

'Souths were just lunatics that day,' remembers Bell, a Māori who played on the wing. 'At one stage, I picked up the ball from dummy half and passed it and about a second later, whack! [Michael] Pobjie, one of their centres, came around from marker and whacked me across the jaw, then stood over me yelling: "Come on, get up you Kiwi so-and-so." All these obscenities. I saw the fire in their eyes.'

South Sydney won 34–16 and Beetson rang in the changes. In training Olsen remained at five-eighth, but by the weekend he was dropped to reserve grade. Ironically, the Round 2 clash was away against Jack Gibson's Cronulla.

To Beetson's great delight, Easts won the game convincingly. Yet after the fear and loathing of the 'Filipaina Affair' that had raged only months earlier, it felt like somewhat of an anticlimax without the presence of Olsen.

For the next four months, Olsen would languish in reserve grade as Beetson tried to settle on a halves pairing. Laurie Spina, a talented Italian Australian cane-farmer from North Queensland, held down the halfback spot while Todd Riley, Mark Horton and Gary Wurth were all enlisted as stop-gap five-eighths.

'When Arthur told me that I would be staying in reserve grade it was a strange one,' Olsen says. 'He told me that there were other people in the decision and he felt like he was overruled. I told him I was fine with it, and that it was a relief for us to talk about it. When I told him that I was happy with whatever decision they made he looked relieved, like a weight was off his shoulders.'

In the grandstand Leslie felt isolated for the first time in her Australian experience: 'At games I was sitting with the WAGS [wives and girlfriends] and it was always cliquey so I stuck with the Kiwi girls. We never felt part of the club and the undertone was if you're dark, you're still not quite accepted. Some condescending and ignorant comments would ruin your mood and you couldn't enjoy watching the game.'

Trapped in the reserves, Olsen faced familiar problems with injury and was shifted between the backs and the forward-line. 'I tried everything I could to get the best out of him,' says Easts' reserve-grade coach Paul Cross. 'I didn't think he was a reserve grader and I knew how good he was. We all did. He didn't shirk training, but I just couldn't get him going, couldn't get him involved in attack.'

* * * * *

Meanwhile, in New Zealand, Kiwis coach Graham Lowe was methodically preparing for three test matches against the Kangaroos. Like his predecessor, Ces Mountford, Lowe was not happy with the way his players were being treated in Sydney.

For Lowe, the open and crowd-pleasing style played in New Zealand could be their advantage and according to *Rugby League Week*, told his training squad: '1985 will be the year of creative rugby league. Anyone who saw our clean sweep over Great Britain was watching creative football at its best, as good a brand of quality rugby league and entertainment that you would find anywhere in the world. We have the defensive pattern to back such positive play and will certainly not be changing our formula when we meet the Australians.'

At Manly Warringah, new recruit and Kiwis superstar James 'The Finisher' Leuluai had been greeted with guffaws by his teammates and kept in reserve grade. Admitting that none of the Manly players had ever played alongside a Polynesian, Paul Vautin wrote in his autobiography about meeting Leuluai for the first time at training:

'I just burst out laughing. He was a nice bloke, but he had the funniest head I've ever seen. I was pissing myself and the blokes behind me had got a good look at him and they were laughing too. Good fella, but rough melon.'

Years later, Leuluai spoke of his season of discomfort in Sydney. 'People are going to say whatever they want, but at the end of the day I know who I am,' he explained. 'We Samoan people respect everyone, especially our elders, and I'm not going to change that. I was only there for three months. Poor Olsen had been there six years.'

* * * * *

On Sunday, 26 May 1985 Lowe turned up early for the Round 12 match between Easts and Norths at the Sydney Sports Ground. He wanted to check on the welfare of his Kiwis captain, Norths lock Mark Graham, who had been mysteriously stripped of the Norths captaincy, and Easts' Kiwi contingent Dean Bell, Hugh McGahan and Olsen Filipaina.

The match programme informed him that Olsen would be starting on the bench — not for first grade, but for the reserves. 'I could not believe my eyes,' remembers Lowe. 'I thought to myself, what have they done to him?'

Olsen proceeded to destroy Norths in the reserves, while in first grade Mark Graham was the inspiration for Norths' four-point victory over Easts. Lowe had seen enough. Their performances convinced him that Olsen was still his best man at five-eighth, and that Graham was still his captain.

No matter what Sydney threw at them, Lowe knew his players would perform in the black and white of New Zealand. 'We will have a powerful side and this series is going to be a lot closer than a lot of people think,' he predicted to reporters.

7
KINGSLAYER

'Regard your soldiers as your children and they will follow you into the deepest valleys; look on them as your own beloved sons, and they will stand by you even unto death.'

— Sun Tzu, *Art of War*

For five years, Australian rugby league supporters had been enthralled and enraged by State of Origin. The series followed on from the old interstate matches between New South Wales and Queensland, but the major difference was that it allowed players to represent their state of birth, rather than their state of residence.

As many as seven Sydney-based Queenslanders would pull on a Maroons jersey, reunite with their Brisbane-based teammates, and beat the Blues with an extraordinary team spirit, bound together by the maroon jersey.

State of Origin totally re-energised interstate football, which had previously been dominated by New South Wales, and inflamed the rivalry between the two states. In five years, Queensland had won eight games to New South Wales' three, forcing the Sydney rugby league public to recognise their mortality for the first time.

Sydney's response typified the city's spoilt, born-to-rule attitude. In particular, they singled out Queensland captain Wally Lewis for abuse. Even as Lewis was commanding the Maroons to successive victories in State of Origin, players and reporters openly questioned whether he was good enough to make it in Sydney club football. And in 1984, when Lewis captained the Kangaroos in Sydney against Great Britain, he was loudly jeered by the crowd.

Wally had triggered the notorious Australian 'tall poppy syndrome'. He had grown too tall for Sydney-siders, who took it upon themselves to cut him down to size. 'Leading Australia onto the SCG for the first time was one of the proudest moments of my life that turned into the most disappointing of my career,' Lewis explained in 1985 of the scarring experience of his own Kangaroos supporters booing him.

* * * * *

When Olsen received a call from Graham Lowe to confirm his selection for the 1985 series against Australia, he remembers a wave of excitement: 'Lowey phoned me to say he was backing me at five-eighth, and soon after my phone started going crazy with friends and reporters. I had to take it off the hook!'

For Olsen, now preparing to line up directly against Wally Lewis during the three-game test series, the hatred towards Lewis by Sydney fans left him confused. On his garbage run, people would pat him on the back and implore him to 'give Wally the Wanker one for me'. Never before had Olsen been more popular in Sydney.

'I never made so many friends in my life,' he once recalled. 'How much do they hate this guy because he's a Queenslander? They hated him even though he played for Australia. I thought it was the strangest thing, how much people had tried to fire me up to play well against him.'

Graham Lowe, meanwhile, could sense that the intensity of the interstate rivalry was a potentially fatal weakness in the Kangaroos camp. During his time in Brisbane he became well-versed in Queensland's notorious chip-on-the-shoulder attitude towards New South Welshmen. And he could see that the Sydney establishment that ruled the ARL was more concerned with their own prestige than the national interest.

'I knew about the north–south divide in Aussie rugby league even before I even started coaching in Australia. I just needed a good team to expose the faultline,' says Lowe. 'I was always respectful to the media so when the time came I was able to use them to my advantage to play "divide and conquer".'

In the build-up to the 1985 test series, Lowe inflamed the Queensland camp by cheekily selecting his predicted Australian side for a media story and his selections were dominated by New South Welshmen. The powerful Sydney press, he knew, played a significant role in the psychological wellbeing of players and coaches in its orbit. There were several newspapers in stiff competition for readers and reporters in Sydney were relentless in their pursuit of a story.

As the Kiwis players arrived in camp in Brisbane, Eastern Suburbs and Cronulla met at the Sydney Sports Ground, bringing together coaches Arthur Beetson and Jack Gibson.

With Olsen now floundering in reserve grade, the Filipaina Affair was effectively over. After Easts beat Cronulla, *Rugby League Week* columnist 'Sherlock' published a story that mocked Olsen's fall from grace:

'Keen Arthur Beetson and Jack Gibson watchers rushed me with the following news this week. Jack and Artie are pals again having been seen playing golf together. You'll remember the big fall out at the start of the year over a player named Olsen Filipaina (remember him?)'

Lowe, meanwhile, was asked by Australian reporters how he expected an 'overweight, reserve-grade garbo' could possibly compete against Wally Lewis — the best five-eighth in the world. Surely it was a suicide mission for Olsen?

Lowe tried to educate them on the finer points of the unique Polynesian body shape, which has a lower centre of gravity and therefore can carry more weight, but felt his responses weren't getting through.

Tony Kemp was the next big-bodied Polynesian playmaker to make it in the Winfield Cup for the Newcastle Knights and echoes Lowe's sentiments. 'Aussie commentators and media had no idea how to categorise the heavier Polynesian build,' says Kemp.

'Olsen and I were both referred to as rotund and fat and they were not used to our shape. I showed up in Newcastle and they joked that I was the little fat kid. I was 20 kilograms heavier than the others, but it was always a joy to see the look of confusion on my teammates' faces when I won sprints.'

* * * * *

Out on the media circuit, Graham Lowe recalls one reporter labelling Olsen a 'journeyman'.

'One of New Zealand's best players of a generation . . . a journeyman?' he says. 'I stored that one away to motivate Olsen. We laughed about it — for us it was no mission impossible. They thought it would be an easy night's work for Wally, but we knew different.'

Lowe protected and supported his star playmaker. When asked how Olsen would contain Wally, he responded: 'I wonder whether Wally can contain Olsen.'

But behind the scenes Lowe wasn't so cocky. He knew Wally was a tremendous player. And Lowe's cultural competence was so attuned that he unleashed his secret weapon. He phoned Olsen's mother Sissie at her home in Auckland to explain the challenges facing her boy.

'No coach will ever have as much power as a mother and she is the best judge of what he is capable of,' Lowe later explained. 'Sissie was a unique woman with a strong influence over Olsen and if she had even the slightest doubt of him being able to handle Wally, I would've switched him to the centres. The right words from her would be ten times more effective than anything I could say.'

After a one-hour discussion, Sissie told Lowe that her son could handle whatever Wally threw at him. Then, according to Lowe, she announced that she would clip Olsen's ear if he didn't get on top of Wally. Lowe relayed the news to Olsen. 'Your mother said you're up to it,' he said. He also told Olsen that he was to be New Zealand's goal-kicker.

For a player like Olsen, regimentation and conformity made him feel inauthentic. He wanted to be creative, solve the problem of breaking defences and entertain. He needed the right environment to thrive.

'Lowey was different; he did the little things that made you comfortable, unlike the Australian coaches who were in your face and shouting a million words at you,' says Olsen. 'Graham Lowe never asked me to change my game — he knew I had played like this all my life. Within the game plan he would give me freedom.'

Olsen's trust of Lowe meant taking on the unsavoury responsibility and distraction of goal-kicking: 'I trusted him and would do anything for him. When he pulled me aside and asked me to kick, I said: "I'll tell you this, Lowey. If I kick — it goes over, it goes over. I'm not going to practise and start having to think about it".'

That was good enough for Lowe. With his playmaker sorted, he turned his attention to the rest of the team — a ragtag mix of players pulled from three different national rugby league competitions, some not yet professional.

From New Zealand amateur competitions came Taranaki hooker Howie Tamati and Auckland's Clayton Friend (halfback), Owen Wright and Riki Cowan (forwards). The Sydney contingent included captain Mark Graham from Norths, Kurt Sorensen from Cronulla, James Leuluai from Hull via Manly and the Easts trio of winger Dean Bell, lock Hugh McGahan and Olsen.

From England came forward enforcer Kevin Tamati, who had left Widnes to join Warrington, reserve back Mark Elia from St Helens, winger Dane O'Hara and fullback Gary Kemble who were club-mates of Leuluai at Hull FC, and centre Gary Prohm from Hull Kingston Rovers.

'You counted the days until the tour,' Kemble says. 'It had been slowly building since 1977. We were all mates and if you joined the group you were instantly mates. It was all about love, respect and shared experience and there wasn't a hint of ego or selfishness from any player. Lowey encouraged us to talk to each other about our fears and dreams, which bound us closer. The vulnerability bonded us quickly.

It seemed impossible to imagine a team more committed to each other or to their coach.'

For Kiwis players like Kemble, Olsen's temperament was a crucial part of their team chemistry: 'Regardless of what was happening in Sydney, Olsen was a key part of our leadership group. He balanced out some of the more intense guys as his mantra was enjoyment first. He always made the new blokes welcome and kept it light. And for us, Olsen and Mark Graham had such enormous mana for sticking it out in Sydney.'

The Kangaroos squad, meanwhile, comprised an even split of Queensland and New South Wales players, skippered by Wally Lewis and coached by New South Wales boss Terry Fearnley. Nine of the starting team played for clubs in Sydney, while the other four plied their trade in Brisbane.

Undeterred, Lowe predicted his lads were 'even money' for the series while the former coach of Australia, Frank Stanton, predicted the Kangaroos 'would win and win easily'. The chairman of the ARL, Ken Arthurson, was a little more diplomatic, announcing that the three-match series was 'legitimately the Championship of the World'.

Lowe went to work on building his team's confidence and stuck with his 'tears of joy' strategy from 1983, replaying the videos of New Zealand rowers crying after winning an Olympic gold medal.

Not all those in attendance bought into Lowe's strategy: 'One of our players said mockingly, "Oooh, he's got a tear in his eye,"' recalls Howie Tamati. 'Lowe stopped the videotape and pulled the player up, saying: "That's a tear of joy. They don't come easy. They are earned and only come after effort, striving, commitment. Let's be so happy we cry." We really took that on board and talked about it a lot.'

* * * * *

Once the psychological building blocks were in place for his team, Lowe switched to his planned on-field tactics, encouraging his players to execute an expansive game plan.

His English and New Zealand-based players were less fit than the

Australians, and he worried that the difference in conditioning might cost them in the second half. They would need to get into a leading position early and then defend at all costs.

'Because the Australian players are so regimented, we figured that if we could pass the ball around, not necessarily making yardage and maybe even losing some, they would have to tackle us,' wrote Mark Graham in his autobiography.

'We could then move their ruck from one side of the field to another and all their forwards would have to keep running across and back. Even if we were losing yards and then punting the ball downfield, they would have to run 40 or 50 yards and try and run the ball back. We planned to turn their strength into weakness. The idea was to work the ball from one side to the other with every Kiwi player involved in running it up, deliberately working their forwards first one way then another. If we could control the ball for 10–15 minutes they would be shot.'

Additionally, Lowe had studied the Sydney competition and realised that the Sydney players had been softened up by the NSWRL's three-year crackdown on violence and thuggery led by judiciary sheriff Jim Comans.

Supporting Lowe's theory was the selection of the referee for the series, a controversial Frenchman named Julien Rascagneres who was more accustomed and comfortable with the old-school, roughhouse and at times outright violent style of rugby league played in the south of France.

Lowe knew his Kiwis needed to create exploitable chaos and hit the Aussies with something they had not prepared for. He told his junkyard dog, prop Kevin Tamati, to start something to rile the Aussies. 'You're meant to be a tough bugger, and they say you can put up your hands,' Olsen remembers Lowe telling Tamati, arming him with a mandate of destruction. According to Olsen, Tamati turned to the rest of the team to issue them with a dire warning: 'If it starts and I don't see anyone hitting, I will hit you myself.'

Many of the players needed no motivation, according to Gary

Kemble. Kemble was one of four Pākehā players in the team, a minority in a Pasifika side of Māori, Samoans and Tongans. The Australians, on the other hand, did not select a single Indigenous player. The sole non-European in their side was Mal Meninga, of South Sea Islander heritage.

'We talked about racism in the team meetings and decided that we weren't going to back down this time,' says Kemble. 'Australia had gotten an advantage before with lots of racist, niggly chat and us not responding. This was the game we were going to take a stand.'

* * * * *

Lowe had a final secret weapon at his disposal — cultural competence. An understanding that his players, in particular his Pacific and Māori players, were wired differently than the Australians.

Lowe grew up with the Pacific community in Auckland and understood what made them tick: 'The secret was to take an interest in their personal lives. Know about their cultural upbringing, their church, their current living environment and get an understanding of their mindset,' says Lowe.

Lowe also learnt early in his coaching career that embarrassing and publicly reprimanding players did not bring out their best: 'Shouting and swearing and humiliating Pacific players in front of their peers like a military taskmaster just doesn't work,' Lowe says. 'It's best to deal with any issues in private — eyeball to eyeball. Bring in the support structure — their family or partner if you need to.'

Lowe loved having a diverse mix of players and he applied the same principles to the Kiwis that had delivered him championship success with Ōtāhuhu and Brisbane Norths.

For him it was simply executing his proven method to extract the best performance from his Pacific and Māori players: 'Always being respectful and honest and following through on your word builds the trust. And it is trust. With Polynesian boys or men, it doesn't matter, their parents are handing their beloved kid to you and as a coach you have an opportunity to give them the tools to be better men and citizens. When they see you working to improve them as human beings you get buy-in. And I always brought a sense of love to my players.'

Lowe feels the lack of cultural competence in Australia was not really the fault of the Aussie coaches: 'In fairness to Aussie coaches they hadn't dealt with Polynesian players before. They were just men of their times and didn't understand family orientation, shyness, not humiliating them individually, the seriousness of religion, the expectations of family members and the money-sharing situation.'

According to Lowe the Australian coaches ultimately did not have the tools to empathise and unlock the talent: 'There was no empathy at all and they didn't understand that the Polynesians are an exuberant, emotional, affectionate people who are also naturally shy with outsiders,' says Lowe: 'They saw it as weakness; I saw it as a strength and we were able to leverage it. The Aussies had no idea what they were about to face.'

* * * * *

For Olsen, the build-up to the first test was 'like a blur'. At Eastern Suburbs he had been operating in a depressive and crippling fog of uncertainty: 'I had doubts and I'll admit I was nervous. But when I tried on my new Kiwi jersey in the mirror, I felt instantly crisp.'

And he was about to face the best in the world: 'Watching Wally in State of Origin for six years, every year he would carve up NSW. I'd played against Wally before but never opposite him at five-eighth.'

Yet there comes a time in a footballer's career when to be great, retreat is not an option. Over the next three weeks, Olsen would take his stand. He would show that Wally — 'the King' — could indeed be toppled and ensure that his own name would live on in the memories of every Australian and New Zealand rugby league supporter that bore witness to his epic performances.

In those fateful days of 1985, Olsen would win over his doubters in the Sydney press, transforming their snide remarks of 'Remember him?' into the awestruck 'Where did he come from?'

* * * * *

The dressing room doors burst open at the first test in Brisbane, and the Kiwis players 'roared out of the players tunnel looking for blood,' says Olsen. 'The Lang Park crowd was deafening. Everything was set. Graham Lowe had drilled into me time and time again that if I could contain and rattle Wally, it would break their structure.'

For Olsen there were some early omens: 'After we ran on and were doing final warm-ups, I had my eye on Wally, and he didn't look at me. I knew it was my night.'

It was a night to remember for the Kiwis' Eastern Suburbs connection. The Australians scored early but in the 12th minute the Kiwis replied with their first try of the night featuring Hugh McGahan soaring through the air to catch and score off a perfect bomb by Olsen. The kick, McGahan later recalled, 'seemed to drift into the heavens'.

Six minutes later, winger Dean Bell broke the line showing an incredible turn of speed to stand up Australian winger John Ribot. Bell passed, the ball went loose and Olsen, socks down around his ankles, thighs pumping and with a big smile on his face, scooped up the ball to score and give New Zealand a 12–8 lead. The commentators were in shock with one bellowing: 'This score is unbelievable.'

Olsen targeted Wally, leaving the Australian five-eighth looking dazed and confused both in attack and defence.

For their previous meeting in a test series in 1982, Olsen had been a centre and Wally in the halves, meaning their contact had been limited. But there had been warning signs.

In the second test of 1982, they had ended up in a brief scuffle after Wally had illegally held Olsen's jumper and prevented him from scoring a try. They both fell to the ground and Wally came away second best after two quicksilver punches from an angry Olsen. In the final play of that test in 1982, Olsen had steamrolled Wally by running straight over the top of his would-be tackle.

Three years later, and a more seasoned Olsen was resuming hostilities, humbling Wally with brains as much as brawn.

'He would pick up the ball and charge straight ahead like a prop, get up, play the ball forward, chip the ball over the top, run through, pick it up and then weave his way all over the field,' wrote Mark Graham in his autobiography.

'He played like this for about five minutes — a virtuoso solo performance — and we were all standing around him on the blind, looking on with awe.'

In a blistering first half, Olsen had scored one try, created another, kicked three conversions and kept Wally quiet in front of his adoring Lang Park faithful. At one stage Wally stood staring at Olsen with his hands on his hips, unable to rationalise the ill Kiwi wind that had blown across Lang Park.

By halftime, the score was tied at 14-all courtesy of a long and brilliant kick for goal from Olsen right on the siren, which drew the scores level. The Kiwis came out breathing fire in the second half and went out to a 20–14 lead courtesy of a superb Dean Bell solo try.

The Kiwis fought on gamely but suffered a fateful blow when their skipper Mark Graham was disgracefully taken out of the game and heavily concussed in a late tackle.

Now rudderless without their captain and trying to hold on to their lead, the game Kiwis began to run out of condition in the middle of the second half.

The game turned Australia's way through a Steve Roach try to equal the scores at 20–20, but it was a dour struggle with Olsen continuing to restrict Wally from playing his normal dominant game.

With seven minutes remaining, Kiwi hearts were broken by a John Ribot try, which sealed a 26–20 victory for Australia.

But the main event had not yet begun.

* * * * *

Hard-man Kiwis prop Kevin Tamati, who in 1982 had publicly sledged the Australians as overpaid and overrated, had terrorised the Kangaroos all evening. With two minutes remaining, he had a fight with prop Greg Dowling and the referee sent them both off.

As they made their way towards the tunnel, the jostling and verbal exchanges continued. Push became shove, which became an elbow, which triggered an eruption of violence on the sideline.

Suddenly, the Lang Park crowd and viewers across Australia and New Zealand had ringside seats to a spectacularly violent brawl, which, according to Kangaroos forward Steve Roach, lit up the night sky 'like a barrage of fireworks'.

Roach was making his debut for the Kangaroos, and he had earlier been on the receiving end of Tamati's destructive brutality. Kevin Tamati, wrote Roach in his autobiography, 'gave me the worst hiding I'd ever taken on a football field. By the time Tamati finished with me I felt like one of those cartoon characters who take such a belting, the lumps all pop up on their heads and their hats sit on the top like a marble in a pumpkin.'

Now it was Dowling's turn as Tamati put an old-school bare-knuckle beatdown on him, peppering Dowling with savage uppercuts in front of both delighted and horrified fans.

The fight, which would be watched on YouTube for decades to come, became a defining image of the trans-Tasman rivalry. According to Tamati, who eventually broke his silence in 2008, it was caused by a racial slur.

'There was derogatory remarks about my colour, verbal abuse, racial abuse about who I was and my ancestry,' Tamati told New Zealand's TV3. 'As always, it's fucking nigger, you fucking black bastard. You're no fucking good for rugby. All you're fucking good for is fucking stoushing.'

Tamati's Pākehā teammate Dane O'Hara, corroborated his claim. 'I was right there on the wing where it all happened. It was loud and horribly racist. There is no dispute and Dowling would know that.'

The incident, and Tamati's response, had an immediate impact. 'We didn't hear too much racial stuff from the Aussies after that for the rest of the series,' says Olsen. 'Something changed.'

The Australians left the field with a narrow victory, although everyone could see that New Zealand had not only matched but for most of the match overwhelmed the surprised Australians.

Olsen was crowned the official man of the match and Kangaroos centre Mal Meninga acknowledged in his post-match interview that Olsen had 'a magical game'.

The man-of-the-match announcement did not go down well with rowdy Lang Park fans, with Olsen later telling media: 'I didn't get a good reception because of what I had done to their hero.'

Back home in Sydney, Olsen's partner Leslie watched the match unfold and was whooping for joy on the couch alongside Mark Graham's wife Carmen: 'My heart was jumping out of my chest for him to go from Roosters reserve grade to dominating Wally. I was originally just hoping he didn't get injured and it was surreal.'

Kangaroos prop Steve Roach summed up the mood in his autobiography: 'We trooped from the field knowing deep down that we had been lucky to win and that vast improvement was needed for the next two tests in New Zealand.'

Kangaroos winger John Ribot had delivered the killer blow but was in awe of the Kiwis' performance: 'They drew a mark in the sand and that was no normal game of rugby league,' he says. 'We got ambushed and had to pull out everything to win. We knew right then we were in for a hell of a series.

'Our forwards cancelled each other out so Olsen was able to isolate Wally and come to the fore. Olsen was a free spirit who stood up in the big plays.'

Kangaroos centre Chris Close was impressed with Olsen that night, who appeared like an animating force that verged on the supernatural: 'That night he was like a bolt of lightning out of the Kiwi sky that hit rugby league,' remembers Close: 'He was fast, strong and agile and I remember having conversations with Wally and us both marvelling and saying, "Where did he come from?"'

For King Wally Lewis it was a night to forget. He remembers having a torrid time handling Olsen: 'His performance on the night was a surprise. It was an extremely good performance and an eye opener not just for the Australian side but the bloke he was playing directly against. It was size and power and brute strength running directly at you.'

Lewis had been humbled on sacred ground but found a way to turn it into inspiration: 'I remember going home after training and watching the tape and using it as a way to inspire myself. Sometimes watching and facing up to your worst performances can turn you around for the next battle.'

* * * * *

Olsen had risen from reserve grade to humble Wally Lewis — a man known as 'the Emperor of Lang Park' — on his home turf. When Channel 9 named Wally as their own most valuable player, columnist Greg Hartley, of the *Sydney Morning Herald*, labelled the decision 'laughable'.

'Lewis wasn't among the top eight and had one of the worst games I have seen him play. Lewis himself said he was embarrassed. It's now painfully clear that the Channel 9 team can't see past Lewis, who is a great player but didn't play like one on Tuesday night. Players know themselves when they have played below their best and Lewis was the first to admit that he was below par. Certainly a good cross-section of the media thought that his opposite, Olsen Filipaina, had been far more impressive.'

Rugby league tradition dictated that opposition players share a drink after the game. Olsen was looking forward to sharing a beer with Wally — after all, he had admired him from afar for many years.

Most of the Kangaroos were sociable in the post-match function. Yet according to Olsen, when he approached Wally, the Queenslander 'left me hanging and brushed me'.

'You hear so much about the guy and watch him on TV, just to be able to talk to him would be a pleasure and something to tell my family about,' Olsen later told *Rugby League Week*.

'I thought test matches gave you the opportunity to talk to your opponents, but he pushed my hand away and gave me the cold shoulder. You have your good days and bad days, but I was taught that you should always be sociable after a match. I was devastated and felt put down.

'Who cares what happens on the field,' says Olsen. 'Unless someone has cheap-shotted you, we should always celebrate together afterwards. I always wanted to have a chat with Wally — the Origin legend. I tried to introduce myself, but he ignored me and made an enemy. I had beaten him on his own turf; all day I was in his face and he couldn't do anything. Now my goal was to mutilate him in front of a Kiwi crowd.'

Olsen's anger and embarrassment turned to steely resolve. He raised the black flag and promised himself that he would beat Wally once again, this time on his own sacred ground — Carlaw Park.

The early colonials in New Zealand found out the hard way that there was great risk in offending Māori. Captain Cook summarised both sides of their utu value system in his diary: 'Maori have a brave, open, noble and benevolent disposition, but they are a people that will never put up with an insult if they have an opportunity to resent it.'

* * * * *

'Wally has a lot of mana and was the most competitive person in the world,' explains Kiwis coach Graham Lowe, who loved coaching Wally as much as he did Olsen. 'An impertinent reserve grader had just knocked him off his perch. I don't agree with it, but I understand it. Wally was the great champion of our time and it was hard for him to digest.'

Lewis says he doesn't remember the incident: 'But I'll stick with Olsen's story and my apologies if I did that. I don't remember enjoying any game when I got outplayed and I probably had the shits big time.'

* * * * *

Rather than hit the nightclubs in Brisbane after the test match, the Kiwis huddled together in Mark Graham's room, concerned for the welfare of their fallen and concussed captain. According to Graham, it was illustrative of the family environment of the Kiwis camp.

Before the next test in Auckland, Mark Graham spoke to *Rugby League Week*: 'I'd like to play a big part to see New Zealand rated the world's best,' he said. 'That's what we're going home for. It hasn't been a good two years for me and I can't think of a better place to put it all right.'

Graham was also grateful for the licence to be creative and instinctive in the Graham Lowe environment: 'I love the freedom with the Kiwis that I don't have in Sydney and it's a lot of fun to run the ball and be creative. Graham Lowe is a great coach. I've never played under Jack Gibson, but I think Graham would be in a similar mould. He knows his football and he has this effect of uniting people.'

The Australian media, meanwhile, were trying to comprehend how a reserve grader had dismantled their king. Radio 2UE's Ray Hadley called Olsen 'Fine Cotton', in reference to Australia's biggest horseracing scandal. In that scandal, a horse by the name of Bold Personality had been painted white to look like a mediocre horse named Fine Cotton to get some good betting odds.

When Bold Personality won the race masquerading as Fine Cotton, people soon discovered the disguise. To Hadley, the Kiwis jumper was Olsen's white paint, transforming him into a much better player.

New South Wales legend Ray Price jumped on the comedy bandwagon, telling the press that Olsen should play for Western Suburbs Magpies, as 'he always does well in black and white'. The most common joke among media was that to boost his performance, Olsen should wear his Kiwis jersey underneath his Eastern Suburbs Roosters jersey.

Dean Bell felt the condescension for the first time. 'It was after that test that some of the Sydney scribes started ribbing me, like they had with Olsen Filipaina and Fred Ah Kuoi,' he recalls. 'They'd be writing: "Why can't he play that way for Easts? Why does he do it only when he pulls on the black jersey?" That sort of thing.'

The jibes only provided more ammunition for the Kiwis, who were determined to put on a show for their supporters at Carlaw Park. 'We just couldn't wait to get at them on Carlaw — in our house!' says Olsen.

* * * * *

The day after the first test, Wally Lewis was awarded the inaugural Adidas 'Golden Boot' award for the best rugby league player in the world in a major event at the Park Royal Hotel in Brisbane.

Wally was acclaimed as 'the High Priest of the Spectacular', and the front page of the newspapers displayed a picture of him kissing his 'Golden Boot' trophy.

Graham Lowe sat next to Australian coach Terry Fearnley at the black-tie function. Lowe remembers looking at Fearnley and thinking to himself with a smile: 'Your guy got the award this week and my guy Olsen is going to get you again next week on our turf.'

* * * * *

How Graham Lowe was able to unlock greatness from enigmatic, diverse, undervalued and troubled players like Olsen was a mystery to Australian fans, media and players.

Lowe says he always had a great laugh when an Aussie journalist called him a 'sorcerer' or a 'magician' or an 'alchemist that could turn any base metal into gold' or a 'wizard with mysterious levers'.

For Lowe there was no wizardry or special potions, but he has strong opinions on the Australian coaches of the time: 'Most Aussie coaches except maybe Jack Gibson and Roy Masters were not paying attention to what was happening in the world of coaching. They had no idea of the changes — that coaches were moving to a new model — getting close to their players, not distancing themselves and being aloof. Who wants to play for a coach who doesn't seem to care for you off the field?'

As for whether he had a magic potion the NSW media accused him of using to extract superhuman performances, Lowe responds with a smile: 'To look for the strengths in an individual not his weaknesses and try and build on those strengths. I don't think there's any magic about that.'

In Lowe's autobiography *Dreams Die Hard*, he wrote of the active role he took in his players' lives: 'Players aren't cattle; they're human beings. All human beings are affected in their professional lives by what goes on in their personal lives because it can have such a dramatic effect on on-field performance. No matter whether they were meat workers or judges.'

Lowe did things differently from the outset as he explained early in his coaching career to *Rugby League Week* in 1980: 'There's a lot more to a player than the bloke you see pulling up in the car park at training and pulling on his tracksuit.'

Lowe was different because he was open to harnessing the power of empathy.

In his book *Empathy*, author Roman Krznaric writes that the ability to empathise is one of the great hidden human talents: 'Entering people's mindsets and trying to see where they are coming from enables you to harness the power of empathy and bridge social divides.'

Krznaric maps out a clear path to success by engaging with empathy, writing: 'By stepping into the world of experience through immersion, exploration and co-operation we make quantum leaps in our understanding of other lives.

'Learning to empathise is like learning a language — hanging out with the natives is the only way. It's not about over sharing, but providing an emotional outlet rather than bottling up open lines of communication.'

Lowe says of his empathetic approach: 'I was always hungry to understand people. Lots of shared experiences meant ideas flowed and the connections became so strong that people were truthful with me. And then you could find out what was holding them back. I would write them letters that charted their progress and talked about love and friendship and the importance of the team as family.'

Krznaric noted another benefit of empathy — the boosting of creativity, a trait for which Lowe became famous in rugby league. Krznaric writes: 'Creative thinking is boosted with empathy — it enables seeing problems and perspectives normally hidden.'

Lowe agrees: 'There is also a link between happiness and creativity and that was one of my missions — creative rugby league. The happier the players, the more headspace they have to be creative.'

Lowe says his empathy-based, close-proximity approach with the players also delivered some dark moments: 'When you are trying to solve players' problems you get involved in some things that you would have nothing to do with if you kept your distance. Off-field dramas — family fights, affairs, pregnancies, drink driving, bailing guys out of jail. But it's all worth it when gratitude turns into loyalty and loyalty wins you premierships.'

For Lowe it was a deceptively simple process — knowing people. And once he knew them, he could tap into the power of treating his players with humanity. Through repeated exposure and care he could develop a portrait of the off-field player. Their inner world of dreams, fears, hopes, beliefs and ambitions, not only shared with him but with teammates. Once he had developed this crucial personal knowledge of his players, he could personalise their motivation so it was rich in meaning.

Olsen says: 'I used to dread calls from other coaches, but I used to look forward to Lowey's calls. He would know if I was homesick and I'm not much of a talker on the phone, but there I would be chatting away about life in Australia and my family and after a while I'd be laughing and feel so good.'

For Lowe it was a personal mission based on something he missed out on: 'I guess I could see myself in every one of those players. No one had ever taken the time to talk to me and find out what I had to contribute, so I made damn sure I did with those players.'

The revolution for Lowe came from getting the players to share their emotions and allow themselves to be vulnerable — to develop what is termed today as 'emotional intelligence'. His secret sauce was to open up his players, and many were initially reluctant to talk about their feelings or emotions. It wasn't the masculine way they had learnt from their fathers who saw exposing vulnerability as a weakness.

Lowe notes a special power in assembling men for story sessions: 'They would bond together in the feedback sessions and hear each other's stories.

'When players started to care for each other you could see it when they stood up in defence or in a great piece of teamwork. You could see they felt strongly for each other over time and then you have a platform to build on. It bound them like glue and made them happy so they can be creative and innovative and win games for you. It builds from the positivity.'

Graham Lowe's mentor, Jack Gibson, understood the power of positivity to make players happy and help players accept criticism. Gibson was famous for his positive first strategy in his man management: 'If you are going to say a bad thing to a player, say two good things first,' Gibson wrote in his autobiography.

Lowe also believed that a spoonful of sugar helped the medicine go down: 'When I had to deliver them a serve for playing badly or drop them to reserves I always started with a cuddle and said positive things before I flogged them with the barbed wire that I needed to do to get my message across. It always made the negative stuff much easier to take.'

In 2005 American psychologist Marcial Losada published the findings of a decade-long study on high- and low-performance teams in which he mathematically modelled 'The Losada Line' — the number 2.9013 being the ratio of positive to negative instructions to make players and a team successful. Those teams and individuals with lower ratios languished.

Gibson and Lowe were ahead of their time.

* * * * *

During the flight from Sydney to Auckland for the second test, Olsen clutched his lucky taonga, a Māori greenstone hei tiki that he had been given by a family friend, Neville Nepia, a descendant of legendary 1930s Kiwis and All Blacks code hopper George Nepia.

Olsen remembers the importance of his lucky charm, which he still carries to this day: 'If it's not in my bum-bag, I don't fly.'

The combination of his usual in-flight nerves, the feverish excitement to see his family in Auckland, and the sense of anticipation for the second test was almost overwhelming.

The Kiwis returned to a swarm of appreciative fans and reporters. Rugby league was the talk of the town. Graham Lowe was the conductor of the media orchestra, praising the Kiwi people's new passion for the game and telling *Rugby League Week*: 'People over here are so desperate to read about the game that they pay $10 a copy for *Rugby League Week* and rent Winfield Cup match videos.'

A documentary crew followed Lowe and his Kiwis team around Auckland, capturing their preparations, including training runs on Takapuna beach and card games in Mark Graham's room. Professionals from England and Australia mixed with local amateurs employed as meat workers, storemen and forklift drivers.

Captain Mark Graham was excited by the preparation: 'We definitely knew we could match them and were so dirty about losing in Brisbane,' explains Graham. 'The Kangaroos had lost their unbeatable aura and were there for the taking. What I liked was that Lowey organised everything — all our moves were on paper. We knew where to be on the field, where the kick would go, what attack moves we could use. And we always had a plan B for Olsen. If he saw an opportunity, to go for it.'

Free from the programmed structure of the Winfield Cup in Sydney, Olsen was playing pure football — for love not money. The remuneration was low, but the satisfaction was like nothing he had experienced before.

'Pulling on that black and white jersey was never a job and I would have happily done it for free,' explains Olsen. 'I would have even paid to play. It was so good for my spirit to represent my family and play with players I loved and respected. Plus there was a coach who knew about our lives and the people that mattered in our lives. My mum loved Graham Lowe and the respect he would give her. I would have taken a bullet for him for making my mum feel special.'

With the All Blacks rugby union side set to play the Wallabies on the Saturday and the Kiwis challenging the Kangaroos in rugby league on the Sunday, New Zealand sports fans were treated to a 'Battle of the Codes' weekend.

Graham Lowe cheekily told the media: 'And I am appreciative that the New Zealand rugby union have been kind enough to put on an All Blacks–Wallabies curtain-raiser on the Saturday before our second test.'

For the first time in 75 years, rugby league seemed to have the upper hand in public relations as the All Blacks played poorly and only just managed to beat the Wallabies 10–9 in an uninspiring match at Eden Park.

Many All Blacks fans had still not recovered or forgiven the NZRU for allowing the disastrous, violent and divisive 1981 Springbok tour of New Zealand.

'We had to upgrade our image in New Zealand with the public,' said All Blacks coach Brian Lochore to local media about life as an All Black after the tour. 'A lot of the public saw us as ogres and there was a stage when the All Blacks would not wear their gear downtown.'

On the Sunday morning of the second test match, Auckland crackled with rugby league fever. An estimated 21,000 people filed into a sold-out Carlaw Park — the most iconic and intimidating rugby league venue in New Zealand. It was the Kiwis' time to shine.

* * * * *

Prior to being converted to a rugby league ground, Carlaw Park had been a flourmill, a tannery and Auckland's first Chinese vegetable market garden. It was not a pretty piece of real estate. The drainage was poor, meaning the turf more often resembled a muddy rice paddy than an international venue, and the facilities were 'Z-grade', according to Graham Lowe.

Yet despite its flaws, Carlaw Park had been the proud home of rugby league in New Zealand since 1921. It was the site of Auckland's miracle 'Grand Slam' achievement in 1977, where the Olsen-inspired provincial side defeated Great Britain, Australia and France in succession. When Pacific boxers like Tongan Kitione Lave and Samoan Tuna Scanlan came out to fight, they sold out Carlaw Park.

Carlaw Park was the not-so-secret weapon of New Zealand rugby league, a binding agent that united the tribal communities of rugby league into one. Once the factory and wharf whistles blew to end their day's work, the working-class faithful counted the hours until Carlaw Park opened. Fans relished meeting each other and were so intimately close to the action that the players could hear their conversations.

Graham Lowe loved having a headquarters that opposing teams hated: 'Teams felt uncomfortable playing there. It was rough and ready, but it was ours. Owning it meant nobody from the outside could touch us.'

Historians John Coffey and Bernie Wood wrote of tough Carlaw Park matches that were often tagged on as the last stop at the end of long France and Great Britain tours of Australia: 'matches were played in the wet and cold of a mid-winter day or night. It was of no comfort to visiting professionals that those waiting to have a last crack at them were only playing for pride and possibly petrol money.'

Carlaw Park, more than any other place, developed a sense of social solidarity and belonging for working-class New Zealanders, bringing isolated communities together. Every week, they met at Carlaw. Families intermarried as future husbands and wives were introduced, kids formed lifelong friendships and babies screamed in their prams at the rain, the cold and the noise.

And as the displaced Polynesian communities blended together to form a new Pasifika identity, Carlaw Park was their social canvas and bricks-and-mortar HQ.

Most importantly, Carlaw Park gave working-class Kiwis a place to beat their chests and announce to the world that they too were worthy.

'Coming to Carlaw was always the highlight of the weekend,' says Olsen. 'I was never happier or more comfortable walking into this place. If you could get a win, the community was happy for the week after and talked about it and patted you on the back when they saw you. Even if you lost, they loved you as long as you tried your best.'

For Olsen it felt like home. He remembers his first time walking down Carlaw Park Lane: 'When I played my first match for Māngere East Seniors here and walked down the lane, it felt like I'd made it. We couldn't afford to come to Carlaw Park and if we could, we came in the workers entrance near the concrete stands where we sat with the labourers, garbos, meatworkers and concrete workers.'

Before he was a star for Māngere East, Olsen enjoyed roaming around the two grounds with the other children. Halftime was a particularly exciting time: 'I remember sprinting to get on the field. It seemed like halftime would go forever as you kicked, sidestepped and tackled your friends.'

Carlaw Park had its thorns, but Kiwis legendary five-eighth Tony Kemp would not have replaced it. For him entering the ground was like stepping through a magical door: 'The Aussies would whinge about the grandstands, the pitch, the drainage, the wind, the cold, the rain. But we loved it — it was a place that loved suffering and hard work. It was a temple that brought us all together — a uniquely New Zealand place. And since it's closed down, all our memories are now locked under tarseal and buildings.'

For Howie Tamati, there was always excitement arriving at the ground: 'I can never forget being on the bus coming to the ground for a test match and feeling goose bumps as the team was singing old Māori Battalion war songs. As human beings we have a need to connect and Carlaw Park was a place for all of us to put away our differences.'

The men that slugged it out every week in the mud of Carlaw Park would breed the next generation of New Zealand stars that would, in years to come, become the dominant group in the NRL.

For Troy Hardy, who runs the 'Carlaw Park Diehards' Facebook page, surrendering Carlaw Park to the property developers in 1995 was akin to 'an old beautiful church being burnt down'.

Hardy recalls a unique place that demanded unity: 'Carlaw brought six different tribal clubs together every Saturday and Sunday. One tribe, one love, all mixed together, all standing alongside each other.'

Olsen was the undisputed King of Carlaw Park according to Hardy: 'The reason Olsen has had longevity and they keep talking about him is that he was a man who could deliver pain in attack and defence with a big smile on his face. You can't fake how much he loved the game and loved to deliver for his people. And he was always smiling at Carlaw.'

* * * * *

Author Joseph Campbell once wrote: 'Your sacred space is where you can find yourself again and again.' For Olsen, Carlaw Park had echoes of the sacred and he fulfilled his mandate to thrill and be creative whenever he played there.

'The Carlaw crowd made me feel special and brought out the best in me, particularly the people in the concrete stands who were often poor migrants,' Olsen recalls.

'I loved entertaining them and giving them their money's worth. The fans were so close to the ground you could hear every word. When they walked out of the ground, I wanted them to feel good about themselves when they went back to their tough jobs.'

Legendary Kiwis halfback Gary Freeman was in awe of Olsen when he played at Carlaw Park: 'He was kind of the king. Every time he got the ball there was excitement, a special noise that the fans made that he was going to do something with the ball — give a pass, steamroll someone, chip over the top. In defence he was this little nugget brute who took great delight in big hits.'

For Māori Kiwis five-eighth Tony Kemp, a four-hour drive from Taranaki to Carlaw Park was nothing compared to the benefits he received: 'As a youngster I saw Olsen in the Kiwi change rooms at Carlaw Park and I'll never forget the feeling I had. It set my dreams in place that one day I would wear the black and white jersey.'

And when Kemp got to play there, it had even deeper significance: 'I loved playing at Carlaw; it was a place of mana. You left your heart there, you bled there. The crowd would come up behind the change sheds and talk to you at halftime and when the bus came in the fans would tap on the side — it was electric.'

* * * * *

Graham Lowe was thrilled to have his 'underperforming' Winfield Cup stars like Olsen and Kurt Sorensen embedded in his camp. He would have time to work on their confidence and unleash the talent he knew was inside: 'Any New Zealander with half a league brain knew these guys were not reserve-graders and somehow lost their talent at the customs line. I was in disbelief and it seemed to be a personality problem between the players and the clubs more than anything.'

Lowe later wrote in his column in the *New Zealand Herald* in 2015, 'In fact, they were top-line internationals who lacked the respect they deserved from their Australian coaches at the time.

'And because the likes of Filipaina and Sorensen did not fit the robotic mould that most coaches in Sydney encouraged at the time, their natural talent was rarely appreciated to the extent it should have been.'

Lowe felt having mavericks and entertainers was important to balance the mix with solid and reliable players: 'Both Kurt and Olsen had genius in the right environment, and it felt so good to prove people wrong about those two.

'With Olsen I would just keep telling him he was the best, which was the opposite to the Australian way where coaches would tear strips off players, tell them they were hopeless or scare them by telling them there was a hungry player in reserves after their spot. If you have a talented confidence player, why crush their confidence?'

For Lowe, the Kangaroos played with Winfield Cup-style structures, an orderly assembly line that focused on efficiency and reducing mistakes. He saw their strength as their weakness, and he had the perfect weapon to expose them.

For the second test, Kiwi spontaneity and creativity would trump structure: 'The Kangaroos' attacking instincts had been blunted by playing low-risk, low-percentage football in the Winfield Cup and they were stuck in a certain robotic way of doing things,' Lowe explains.

'They assumed we would play a rational, structured, percentages game and get crushed like usual and we would have been if we played them at their own game.'

* * * * *

The giant-killing strategy that Lowe was planning to execute dates back to Israelite biblical times. The venue changes — replace Carlaw Park with Israel's Valley of Elah and the Kangaroos with the Philistines — but the same fundamentals apply.

When underdog shepherd David conquered giant Philistine soldier Goliath, he negated the size differential by adjusting the terms of engagement until they were favourable to his own skill set. In his case, he chose to use a slingshot from a distance over a spear in close hand-to-hand combat.

The history and science of the underdog is documented in Malcolm Gladwell's book *David and Goliath: Underdogs, Misfits and the Art of Battling Giants*. Gladwell writes of the underdog scenario and the 'advantages of disadvantages': 'The act of facing overwhelming odds produces greatness and beauty. An important lesson in battling giants is that the powerful and strong are not always what they seem. They always have weaknesses. The same qualities that give them strength are often the sources of great weakness.'

Successful underdog strategies are the fruits of meticulous planning.

In 1954 at the Battle of Dien Bien Phu, Vietnamese Communist leader Ho Chi Minh led his forces to a shock victory against the French colonial army, defeating them after a four-month siege and shattering French confidence to the point they withdrew from their Asian colonies. It is not widely published that Ho Chi Minh spent two years preparing and planning for this single strategically important battle.

* * * * *

After his Kiwis' shock victory over the Kangaroos in 1983, Lowe had two years to prepare for the 1985 series against Australia. Lowe meticulously hatched plans to beat the Australians and he sought advice far and wide.

Lowe was obsessed with bringing the Kangaroos down and would watch videos in the dead of night, between 2 am and 4 am. He told *Rugby League Week*: 'I want to win that bad, I can smell it every day.'

Prior to the second test, Kiwis captain Mark Graham remembers Lowe was always looking to improve and he had ideas around the clock: 'He would call me at three in the morning with an idea on how to get through the Australian defence. And I would always take the call and listen to him because sure enough he was onto something. Then at test match time, his hotel room would become a war room.'

Lowe instinctively understood that rugby league in its essence is about territorial rights, with no more important space than the centre of the ground: 'In the first test we opened them up in their centre, their strongest area, and they had no Plan B. We went straight for their king with our king — King Olsen.'

Lowe also was a master of playing the underdog and ran a shrewd psychological game with the Aussies before test matches, aiming to never 'poke the bear'. Lowe says: 'Australians don't handle humiliation well so we never talked it up before a test. We were humble and never sledged and never provided them with motivation.'

Lowe was also able to exploit Australian hubris and says they had no inkling that there were other styles of rugby league that could challenge theirs. Lowe says: 'Even after we outplayed them in the first test, it was Australia's arrogance that was our greatest weapon. In their mind they think they invented everything in the game except the air that goes into the ball.

'But in many ways New Zealand has reminded them how to play football — whether they like hearing that or not, that's what happened. New Zealand's fingerprints are all over the current NRL playing style, and it all started with that 1985 team.'

* * * * *

On a crisp afternoon on Sunday, 30 June 1985, the Kiwis players erupted onto Carlaw Park for the second test greeted by a thunderous roar from a packed house.

As the players lined up for the ceremonies, awaiting them in the centre of the ground was New Zealand's highest-profile rugby league fan, Prime Minister David Lange. Lange had attended many rugby league games at Carlaw Park and was there to greet and inspire his beloved Kiwis. As captain, Mark Graham made the player introductions.

When he reached a beaming Olsen, Lange leaned forward to shake his hand. 'It's my old mate from Māngere,' Lange said with a big smile in front of the TV camera.

Lange and Olsen, both alumni of Ōtāhuhu College, had travelled wildly different journeys. Yet here they were, in the middle of a sold-out Carlaw Park, two pioneers of the new progressive New Zealand. Olsen grinned widely, enjoying the brief moment of familiarity and recognition, and then returned his focus to Wally Lewis.

His eyes were clear and steadfast, and he crackled with energy and restrained menace. Bouncing with anticipation, his superpowers were about to be activated in his black and white costume. Wally was now in *his* house.

From the moment Mark Graham returned Mal Meninga's kick-off with fire, until the 79th minute, the Kiwis physically matched and, after the first 20 minutes, dominated the Australians.

They manhandled the Kangaroos in the traditional 'softening up' period, and then moved the ball thrillingly from one side of the field to the other, to tire out the Kangaroos forwards.

After 20 minutes, the Kiwis broke the Kangaroos' line and James Leuluai finished off a brilliant 60-metre team try which prompted Australian commentator Darrell Eastlake to bellow: 'That's as good a try as you'll see in a test match.'

Just before the end of the first half, Olsen went into 'beast mode' and steamrolled Wally Lewis to make a 30-metre break. Five minutes before halftime Olsen made another line break which led to the first disallowed try in which Kevin Tamati gave a controversial final pass to Gary Prohm. Tamati says: 'No way that was forward; they got off the hook.'

Prior to halftime, Eastlake's match summary was gloomy for the Kangaroos: 'The Australians are certainly not playing like the champions they are. The Kiwis are swarming them.'

By halftime, New Zealand led Australia six points to four and jogged off Carlaw Park with purpose. Olsen says: 'When we got to the change rooms, you could feel we had them. We had taken their best early and were now on top of them.'

The trend continued in the second half, with the Kiwis' pressure continuing to force the Kangaroos into making mistakes. Commentator Ian Maurice was in a state of disbelief at the error rate, declaring: 'We haven't seen this from an Australian side.'

Five minutes into the second half, Olsen collected the ball from a scrum in the middle of the field and ran straight over Wally Lewis, making a 30-metre break only to be pulled down 10 metres short of the tryline.

A bemused Darrell Eastlake noted: 'New Zealand have made more clean breaks than Australia. They look very, very dangerous, when they run it, especially Filipaina with those big legs of his, he can make breaks so easily.'

Co-commentator Ian Maurice added: 'Olsen Filipaina has cut threads into the Australian defence. He's having a whale of a match.'

Midway through the second half the Kiwis swept forward, and in his own half, Olsen decided to chip the ball over the Australian defence. He regathered gracefully, brutally stomped over fullback Garry Jack, and passed to Dane O'Hara who put the ball over the tryline, only to be again disallowed by referee Rascagneres.

O'Hara says, 'Nothing surer than I scored that try. Watch the replays. I was clearly over the line and Mal then jolted the ball out. It was a disgraceful decision.'

Ignoring the traditional commentators' code of neutrality, Ian Maurice said of the reprieve: 'We were lucky then.'

* * * * *

With two minutes to go in the match, the camera panned to an anxious Graham Lowe who commentator Darrell Eastlake concluded 'is sensing victory'.

With just 90 seconds remaining, New Zealand was still leading by two points. Then, without warning, Wally Lewis clicked into gear and led a last-chance counter-attack. A brilliant long pass to Garry Jack ended with John Ribot scoring the last-minute match-winning try.

To any fair-minded rugby league fan, Garry Jack's final pass looked clearly forward, but referee Rascagneres waved it through. It was the second time in two games that Ribot had won a test match for Australia at the death.

For Ribot, the Kangaroos got out of jail. 'I remember being swarmed by relieved Australian players, we couldn't believe it,' Ribot recalls. 'The Kiwis have a good argument to feel they were the better side. We were down and out but a few things went our way and Wally sniffed out a half chance. I felt for the Kiwis, but character building is what our game is all about — it's the journey.'

Wally Lewis acknowledges the unfairness of the day. 'We got out of jail and Olsen and all of the Kiwis were robbed and deserved to feel insulted at losing that game. We got our arses kicked,' says Lewis.

* * * * *

Olsen had an imperious game, wreaking havoc on the Kangaroos with his big runs, elusive sidesteps, brutal broken-field running, silky passes, demonically possessed tackling, energetic diving on loose balls and wondrously dexterous chip kicks.

Olsen, wrote one reporter, 'churned the Australian defence into a lunar landscape'.

Wally, on the other hand, cut a forlorn figure.

Actor, comedian and author Oscar Kightley was 15 years old at the time and remembers watching with his extended family crammed into his living room. 'That day Olsen was a step above everyone else on the team, only because he was the man at five-eighth — the position that Australians should always dominate us in.

'King Wally was the dominant pinnacle. He looked like a freakin' woodwork teacher at secondary school, you know, but he was the man. But then Olsen was our man and Olsen schooled him and we just thought . . . my God.'

The Kangaroos' planning sessions under coach Terry Fearnley had covered the threat of Olsen but to no avail. Wally Lewis recalls the meetings: 'I remember every pre-match discussion we used to talk about Olsen — try to make a plan to nullify his strength and power. Those plans didn't work out that day.'

For Wally, Olsen's power game was a new experience: 'I remember Olsen was extremely powerful and strong and in that Kiwi jersey I was stunned that he was 10 feet tall and bulletproof. He was different to anything I had faced. In addition to his power he had every skill in the game and displayed it to the highest level.

'At one stage after he ran through me and I spotted him on the other side of the scrum calling for the ball and I didn't make much of a move to head to the other side. That was a compliment to Olsen. If you were marking him, you used to take a couple of deep breaths, because you knew he was going to be heading your way asap. He would seek you out.'

And, Lewis says, he wasn't alone in the Kangaroos: 'Ask any

Australian player if they enjoyed playing against him and it's a fairly simple answer.'

* * * * *

After the final siren, Wally Lewis slumped to his knees on the Carlaw Park turf in exhausted gratitude. Graham Lowe buried his head in his hands unable to process the nightmare that he had just witnessed. His plans had worked, they had outplayed the Australians, but they hadn't got the win. Carlaw Park was deathly silent. The old ground, remembers Dean Bell, 'had the air of a morgue'.

In the dressing room, Howie Tamati was physically sick and tears flowed freely among hard, working-class men. 'We were shattered,' says Mark Graham. 'We just sat in the dressing room, not saying anything . . . with tears running down our cheeks, all of us.'

Kiwis second-rower Hugh McGahan described the emotional scene in his autobiography: 'I was getting my wounds stitched up and started to cry and Gary Prohm who was next to me joined in.

'Lowey came in and he had his head down. It was as if someone had died. After about three minutes Lowe spoke and said next week we were going to train like never before and that champions don't quit. He then promised us that this time next week we would thrash Australia. That pulled the team up straight away.'

Olsen, who for the third Kiwis test in a row had received the man-of-the-match award, was numb. 'I was in a daze from losing and was lucky not to cry on camera. It was so sad, so unfair. We had them. I just wanted to get away from the media into the change rooms and home as fast as I could. Everything me and the team had worked for had come to nothing in 60 seconds. We were shattered and it was half an hour before we got changed and out of the rooms.'

In a television moment that enraptured two nations, Wally Lewis approached a teary Graham Lowe outside the change rooms and hugged him for a long time. Lewis explains: 'I went into the Kiwi dressing room and hugged Lowie after the game and he was bawling his eyes out. I felt uncomfortable winning that game, it didn't feel right.'

In a rare display of trans-Tasman respect, the chairman of the Australian Rugby League, Ken Arthurson, put an arm around his New Zealand counterpart Ron McGregor after the match. 'The better side lost,' admitted Arthurson to *Rugby League Week*. 'I would not have thrown myself off Auckland Bridge if New Zealand had won.'

* * * * *

The Australians knew they had been lucky. 'The Best Side Lost' read one headline. 'Justice was Not Done' read another. The *Sydney Sun* said the Kangaroos had been 'outrun and outgunned', while *Rugby League Week* declared: 'Wally Dethroned by "Enigma" Olsen'.

Later, in his autobiography, Kangaroos second-rower Paul Vautin described the sheer relief of winning that test. 'They were a good side, very tough, very mobile,' he wrote. 'The enigmatic Olsen Filipaina ran riot. The powerfully built five eighth saved the greatest performances for his country. Once he pulled on a black and white jumper, Filipaina was possibly the only player in the world to consistently bother Wally Lewis — and never more so than that day.'

Kangaroos winger and winning try-scorer John Ribot says the second test was even more intense than the first and Olsen was the difference: 'He dominated the game and you could see how comfortable and respected he was at Carlaw Park. He was just so hard to handle one on one.'

For Kangaroos centre Chris Close, Olsen's performance in the second test confirmed what he had learnt in the first test: 'Make no mistake, Olsen was the key to that game,' says Close.

'We got outplayed and we were in awe of Olsen just like his own teammates were. We were fans of the game and became instant Olsen fans and I remember talking to Wally and both saying we wanted to play against him and watch him. So competitive, such flair, so strong and such pace in his first strides with a real determination and identifiable pride.'

For New Zealand journalists like John Coffey, Olsen's dominance of Wally Lewis was not a surprise and justified the New Zealand media's mocking of Winfield Cup clubs' treatment of their Kiwi players.

Coffey wrote in the *New Zealand Rugby League Annual*: 'Filipaina far surpassed King Wally Lewis, illustrating how ludicrous is his rating as a reserve grader in Sydney. It is fair to say that no player has ever charged through Lewis' tackles as contemptuously as did Filipaina. He pushed him off at will.'

For neutral observers like legendary Great Britain halfback Alex Murphy it was the end of an era, bluntly stating to *Rugby League Week*: 'Lewis is gone and should have been the first player pulled from the field. Australia needed someone to lead and make a few breaks but Lewis did nothing; he wouldn't stand up to his opposite man.'

Some moments in sport go to a place that never fades and Graham Lowe says he'll never forget Olsen in that game. 'He reverted back to playing for Māngere East Hawks — he was home and comfortable. It looked like he had the ball on a string.'

The enduring memory for Graham Lowe, however, was what Olsen did off the field in the change room filled with broken men. 'The chieftain in Olsen came out,' he says. 'He sat with the young ones, told them stories, got them laughing and we started believing again. He's exactly the sort of man you need when the chips are down. A real asset in our darkest hour.'

8
DELIVERANCE

'Just remember, the Aussies had Wally and we had Olly.'
— Clayton Friend, 2017

When daylight broke on the Monday morning after the second test, Graham Lowe remembers waking up in the team hotel and immediately sensing his players were physically and emotionally spent, their confidence at breaking point. A protracted dissection of the game would only bring more pain and he had a week until the third test to transform the tragedy into a positive.

Lowe felt that something radical was required to shift his team's despondent psyche: 'I could see that the players felt a bit like me,' Lowe explains. 'I felt that I'd let the players down and they thought they'd let the country down. That they had missed an opportunity to put league on top of the mountain.'

The team was infected with a sense of gloom, according to Olsen: 'We just couldn't face the reality that we had missed our big chance to beat the Aussies at home and finally reward our fans. Every year they had walked away from Carlaw Park with losses all the way back to our last win when I was a 14-year-old boy in 1971.'

Second-rower Hugh McGahan told a documentary crew of his personal devastation: 'It was as if someone close to you had died. We'd lost something we thought we had and it slipped through our fingers.'

Lowe's challenge was clear: 'to somehow prove to the players that the people still loved them'.

An idea came to him that would become embedded in New Zealand sports mythology. Lowe called a few radio stations in preparation for his mission to rally as many people as possible to show their support for the Kiwis.

After a few lacklustre training sessions, on the Wednesday morning, he ordered his squad onto the team bus bound for Queen Street in the heart of Auckland's CBD. 'I know you're thinking everyone is pissed off with us,' he told the players. 'But I guarantee once we get to the top of Queen Street, you'll see that people still love you.'

Olsen remembers Lowe finishing his speech and no one on the bus moving. Lowe upped the ante, instructing his team menacingly: 'You're getting out of this bus even if I have to pull you out myself.'

The radio stations that Lowe had tipped off beforehand had done their job, and traffic had been brought to a halt as thousands of Kiwis fans clogged the streets to welcome the players. Construction workers slapped the players on the back. People were hanging out of windows to get a glimpse of the passing parade.

'The walk down Queen Street was a first for us and the support was unreal,' says Olsen. 'Everyone knew who we were, right in the city and not just South Auckland. There were builders on scaffolding yelling "Go Kiwis" and people running out of shops and offices. You could see the team change all of a sudden. We all thought, "What the hell is this going to do?" but Lowey kept saying "Don't worry" — and he was right.'

'By the time we got close to the Town Hall I knew that any team in the world would not stand a chance against us,' says Lowe. 'I just knew. The guys felt a million dollars.'

It was a life-changing experience for Olsen. 'I realised we hadn't let our country down. They were proud of us. It was like we were reborn and had a reason to live and it affected everyone. Nothing was going to stop us after that. I finally felt we were alongside the All Blacks in respect,' he says.

Kiwis hard-man Kurt Sorensen will never forget the moment: 'We got out and started walking slowly and it felt a bit strange,' Sorensen recalls. 'At the time I told Olsen that we might need helmets if they throw stuff at us, but it felt like the whole city had come out on the streets to see us. They shook our hands, slapped us on the backs, and cheered out to us from building sites. They went out of their way to see us in the heart of Auckland. It's hard to describe the feeling unless you were there.'

Lowe's masterstroke paid dividends and he knew that there is magic in hope and belief. The Kiwis' body language switched to positive and the talk turned to beating the Australians. Halfback Clayton Friend called it 'a positive vibe that just spread and built our strength'.

Lowe continued his team's reconstitution with some additional tactics. He upgraded the team to the best hotel on the North Shore. They had fun barefoot training sessions on Takapuna beach. Lowe remembers the key motivation behind his strategy: 'I treated them like we had won the last test. And in many ways, we had won. Just not on the scoreboard.'

And on the Thursday night before the test, Lowe tugged at the cultural side of the Kiwis by putting on an old-school 'boil-up' — a traditional 'pork and pūhā' feast, in which Sir Peter Leitch, the Mad Butcher, supplied the pork bones and Dean Bell's proud Māori father Cameron brought the pūhā, the traditional Māori green vegetable.

* * * * *

In contrast to the Kiwis' blissful unity, Australian rugby league had entered a state of civil war, with relations poisoned between its two key stakeholders. After the second test 'great escape', Kangaroos coach Terry Fearnley was spooked into making some drastic changes to a winning team, dropping four Queenslanders (Greg Conescu, Mark Murray, Chris Close and Greg Dowling) and replacing them with New South Welshmen from his State of Origin team (Des Hasler, Mark Ella, Peter Tunks and Ben Elias).

The chairman of the Queensland Rugby League, Ron McAuliffe, blasted Fearnley with a touch of poetic licence for blaming the poor performance on his Queensland contingent. 'What has been happening in Beirut is nothing compared to what happened to the Queensland players in Auckland,' said McAuliffe in *Rugby League Week*. 'It was football assassination. Fearnley is guilty of a diplomatic blunder and a selection disaster. The biggest mess since King Alfred burnt the cakes.'

The *Courier-Mail* reporter Lawrie Kavanagh called it 'an interstate slur'. And Des Morris, the coach of Queensland, declared that the selections 'are the result of the frustrations NSW have felt over the drubbings Queensland have handed them over the past five years'.

Not all of Fearnley's NSW players approved of the controversial move. In his autobiography, freshly capped Kangaroos prop and New South Welshman Steve Roach questioned Fearnley's judgement and the message it sent: 'Suicidal. Wrong, completely and utterly wrong to change a winning side.'

So even though Australia led New Zealand in the series two tests to none, the Kiwis entered the third test in a lather of national pride and adulation while the Kangaroos were a house divided.

Far from being a dead rubber, the third test of each series played between 1985 and 1988 was to be played for points — culminating in the 1988 World Cup. So, in effect, this was the opening round of Australia's World Cup defence.

At breakfast on match day, Lowe went through the game plan with his team and gave them clear, simple instructions. He expected Olsen to run over Wally and break the line. He told Kurt Sorensen to be debutant Des Hasler's worst nightmare and 'scare the shit out of him'. Clayton Friend was to run the ball, Kevin Tamati was to sort out the Aussie prop forwards as usual.

Lowe remembers being convinced more than ever they could win in the centre of the ground through Olsen: 'Olsen was so dominant over Wally, but it was no shock to me. I've got a pretty good view — I coached both of them, I coached against both of them,' says Lowe.

'They're mates of mine and I love them both. But only Olsen had the mix of size and skills to give Wally trouble. Olsen had a great bag of tricks and I remember telling him before that second test — playing at club level you open up your full bag of tricks but at test level you open the zip a little, show a trick and see if it works and if not, open the bag a little bit at a time.'

* * * * *

For Kiwis team trainer Graeme Coutts, the bus trip from the team hotel in Takapuna to Carlaw Park was one he will never forget. 'The players were so wound up they were shivering,' remembers Coutts. 'When the bus driver turned the music on, Lowey got up and yelled "Shut that rubbish off" and the team travelled in silence.'

By chance the Australian team bus pulled up beside the Kiwis' bus at the last traffic lights before the turnoff into Carlaw Park. The Kiwis stared at their opponents and one player broke the silence with the words: 'We're going to kill those bastards. Everyone dies here today.'

Olsen remembers the moment: 'No one said a word once the bus took off.'

The players elected to follow their new protocol and only perform the haka if they won. Mark Elia, who was playing in England, suggested they borrow the English tradition of applauding fans on both sides of the ground before the game.

'We fanned out and ran over to the fans in a line,' says Howie Tamati. 'We felt a wave of emotion hit us that was so powerful it shook the rickety old stands. You could feel it. We knew we had them.'

Before kick-off Olsen looked towards his mother and he could hear her screeching her support, fortifying him with pride and love. He remembers thinking to himself: 'Right now, I have a chance to make her happy.'

* * * * *

The third test began at a furious pace with both sides throwing the ball around and focusing on attacking football. Australia tried to take control through the forwards, but the Kiwis were having none of it. Their defence was impenetrable.

By the half-hour mark, New Zealand led 2–0 thanks to an Olsen penalty kick. A piece of X-factor genius was required to break an Aussie defensive line manned by battle-hardened players and fresh faces whose international future was on the line.

Cometh the hour, cometh the man. With five minutes to go in the first half, Olsen received the ball on the halfway line on the second tackle, four tackles remaining in the count. As the suffocating Australian defence moved in for the kill, Olsen put in a delicate and precise grubber kick behind the Kangaroos' defensive line. He then kicked the ball off the ground and regathered, making a 20-metre inroad and forcing the Aussies onto the back foot.

On the fourth tackle Olsen was again given the ball. This time, he chipped over the top of the Kangaroos' defence before brilliantly collecting the ball on the bounce, right off his toes and propelling him deep in the Australians' half.

On the next tackle, a disoriented Australian defence succumbed to a Mark Graham charging run that was finished off by Clayton Friend. The Carlaw faithful went berserk, led by a beaming Prime Minister David Lange.

It was rugby league to make the gods weep with pleasure. To kick twice in the same set of six tackles was the kind of flair that the Kangaroos were not used to — a high-risk manoeuvre that was discouraged and would be punished in the Winfield Cup. Olsen's brilliance had split the Australians apart and the Kiwis went into the halftime break with a precious eight-point lead.

Richard Becht was at Carlaw Park working as a journalist and will never forget that passage of play: 'Its seared into my memory. When Olsen kicked and regathered twice in the same set, it may have seemed audacious, but it absolutely typified the Kiwis' approach.'

It was the mandate from Graham Lowe to play exciting rugby

league that electrified Carlaw Park according to Becht: 'The players were encouraged to let the ball talk. Watch that test and you'll be astounded to see the ball movement and the support play. It was truly breathtaking, compulsory viewing.'

Lowe was thrilled that his players were expressing themselves with his beloved Kiwi style. His team played in symphony but with improvisations: 'The idea was to be creative with the ball. If we were going to make mistakes, I wanted them to make them trying creative things, not just in running up the ball. Olsen had a licence to thrill and entertain. The Aussies had no defence to what he was able to conjure.'

When the Kiwis came into the change rooms at halftime they were happy with their effort but not overconfident. Olsen recalls the players took ownership of leading the team: 'It was amazing. Lowey hardly said anything and the players took turns talking. "This is war." "Don't give them a point." "Remember Queen Street." "If you get hurt, get up." "We are going to die here before we lose." "Tackle your arses off."'

The team gained additional motivation from fans listening outside the wooden change rooms. Olsen remembers the '14th player' that day. 'The fans were listening outside the change rooms and they were going crazy. Our final words were 'Let's go out and finish them for our fans, let's pay them back for what they've done for us.'

The Kiwis came out with fury in the second half, tackling ferociously and supporting each other in unison. The battle continued to rage in the key playmaker positions with Olsen and Clayton Friend dominating Wally Lewis and Des Hasler.

The Kiwis halves could do no wrong. At one stage, Friend comically crawled through a scrum, emerged on the other side with ball in hand, and made a long break. One of the commentators noted that Olsen was now being marked three on one, stifling his output but creating space opportunities for his teammates to exploit.

Before long, Friend crossed over for his second try of the match, pushing the score to 14–0 after Olsen's successful conversion. It was an afternoon to remember for Friend, the little mullet-haired halfback from Manukau, who rose from amateur football to a man-of-the-match performance.

By year's end, he would agree to join the North Sydney Bears in the Winfield Cup. He would always remember partnering Olsen in the halves during the series. 'Just remember, the Aussies had Wally and we had Olly,' Friend says.

With the halves in complete control, the Kiwis forwards took their intensity to another level. Kevin Tamati drove forward with bull charges, challenging and questioning the Australian forwards. Kurt Sorensen harassed debutant Des Hasler at every opportunity.

The Carlaw Park faithful rose up as one behind their team, roaring 'Kiwi, Kiwi' in unison, a baritone birdcall of working-class emancipation, of beating off the bully, of belonging, of the voiceless gaining their voice, of collective passion and purpose.

Olsen will never forget the sound, and for him it was like a connection to something higher: 'It was so loud, it rumbled the stands. We had not beaten the Aussies at home for 14 years, and the fans' disappointment and frustration was all released through that tribal chanting. It gives me chills thinking about it — "Kiwi, Kiwi".'

Mark Graham and Hugh McGahan rallied the defence, plugging holes and screaming at their teammates, 'No points, no points, don't let them in.'

By the time James Leuluai sidestepped Mal Meninga to cross over for a third try to take the score to 18–0, both Kiwi and Aussie commentators were united in their summary: New Zealand had outplayed Australia in every facet of the game.

At the fulltime whistle, the crowd rushed on the field and surrounded their heroes while Graham Lowe looked on, fists raised with tears in his eyes, having guided the Kiwis from toothless to ruthless.

An exhausted Wally Lewis lay down on the Carlaw Park turf, beaten and exhausted. For the first time in 67 years, the Kangaroos had been held scoreless and the Kiwis had drawn first blood in the World Cup-qualifying pool games.

Graham Lowe waved all of his players towards the victory haka in front of the main grandstand. Hooker Howie Tamati assembled his players and, surrounded by a circle of thousands of hooting fans, they savoured one of Carlaw Park's greatest moments.

Kevin Tamati stepped up to lead the haka still wearing an Australian Kangaroos jersey he had exchanged. After the first few stomps, he tore it off and led a ferocious and emotional shirtless haka. Directly behind him was a beaming Olsen who would later call it 'a moment I can't think about without getting goosebumps. It was like a curse was broken.'

The haka finished with all of the players leaping in the air and they were then engulfed by their adoring and celebrating fans. Kevin Tamati says, 'I finally got to beat the Australians. Olsen and I finally got their scalp.'

For Olsen, the victory haka had deeper significance: 'This was also for players like Dennis Williams who never got to have a win for the Kiwis over the Aussies in those dark years.'

For the Māori and broader New Zealand community, the haka is soaked in meaning. It summons their tūpuna or ancestors and atua — gods from the earth, sky and sea — to connect directly with living souls and help them with their challenges.

This Kiwi team did not use the haka for help, however. Their haka was a thank you to the New Zealand public and those that came before them.

'To see the New Zealand supporters gather on the field in total adoration as the players did the haka was a moving moment even for a green and gold Aussie,' wrote Tony Durkin in *Rugby League Week*.

Lowe remembers that haka as one of the great moments of his career and one of great cultural significance. 'It was spine tingling. There had been a lot of talk about the haka and how it had lost its impact — that the Aussies saw it as a bit of a dance, some entertainment. That's why this one was so meaningful; it was earned in battle and it was on our turf, in our place. It's a life highlight for anybody that was there.'

Olsen's little buddy and halves partner Clayton Friend won the man-of-the-match award and Olsen says: 'I couldn't have been happier for Clayton. He tore them up that day.'

Olsen remembers the sheer jubilation in the dressing room and captain Mark Graham calming them down to say a few words to the team that included: 'We are walking tall and will always remember this moment. It will go down in history.'

And he was right. In 2015, *New Zealand Herald* rugby league writer Michael Burgess wrote a feature on the team celebrating the 30th anniversary of the team of 1985 and described their legacy: 'A special Kiwis team full of names that have endured across decades and captured the imagination of the sporting public.'

* * * * *

Despite New Zealand losing two out of three games in the 1985 test series, Olsen was named man of the series. In one of rugby league's great Cinderella stories, a reserve-grade garbage collector had for a magical one-year stretch become the dominant figure among the very best British and Australian rugby league players.

John Ribot feels that Olsen was the right selection: 'Not one Kangaroo questioned him getting man of the match twice and man of the series. I'm a trivia buff and I've never heard of that happening before for a losing team.'

Ribot recalls a post-match dressing-room scene that best encapsulates the Kangaroos' state of mind. 'In the dressing room after the game, Terry Fearnley gave us a bake for our performance and Wally stood up and challenged him, saying he should acknowledge the Kiwis who were a team of champions. And they were — a bunch of warriors who wanted to do something special for their country.'

During the post-match function, Olsen, the prodigal son returned, was joined on stage by his mother, Sissie.

Together they allowed the tears to flow in a wonderful moment of shared humanity and redemption.

'All Olsen ever wanted to do was the best for all the coaches he had, his family, friends and Samoan, Māori and New Zealand people,' says Graham Lowe. 'And he did it. They both had been through so much and let it all out. There wasn't a dry eye in the house.'

For Lowe, Olsen's dominance was no surprise: 'Wally is the best, but when Olsen produced his best form he was one of the most devastating players in the world and he showed that against Wally,' says Lowe. 'I've spoken to Wally about that series and he said that everywhere he looked, there was just the big figure of Olsen Filipaina pounding through and he just inspired everybody.

'One other thing Wally mentioned is that Olsen smiled at him through all of the matches, even in the toughest of conditions and it used to piss him off.'

For Lowe, the 1985 test series starts and ends with Olsen. 'He had the toughest role, marking the best player in the world, and he outskilled him — was too nimble for him,' says Lowe. '1985 was like the last link to the beautiful and entertaining New Zealand amateur game, filled with characters before the robots took over — Olsen was the last of the era.'

The impact of Olsen's performance was felt right across New Zealand. Future All Black Eroni Clarke watched on in wonderment: 'He tamed the Aussies, and that was a pivotal thing, one of our greatest sporting moments,' remembers Clarke.

'Olsen disarming and schooling King Wally Lewis, their great man, before my eyes had a huge influence. It lit a flame and kept my dream alive because if Olsen could make it, so could I. He played like us, looked like us and it was the first time we had seen a Pacific man completely dominate in rugby league.'

Clarke says there was a new hero in the playground: 'We couldn't get enough of rugby league after that and when the kids were playing bullrush, there was always one kid saying, "I'm Olsen, I'm the bump!"'

Olsen's childhood hero, Pacific pioneer All Black Sir Bryan Williams, enjoyed Olsen's breakthrough performance immensely:

'There were so many parallels in our style and journey,' Williams says. 'Australian rugby league always looked down on New Zealand league and he ended up making Wally Lewis look second rate. We were very proud of Olsen and he broke through the ceiling.'

While Olsen's Eastern Suburbs coaches and teammates looked on in bewilderment, there were exceptions, including Kiwis and Roosters teammate Dean Bell: 'Olsen is one of those players who you can't fully appreciate unless you play with or against him,' says Bell.

'You can't fluke three matches in a row against the dominant icon of the game. If Wally has a good game, Australia wins, but not this time. Olsen got in Wally's face and gave it to him. The Aussies were shocked but none of us were.'

Some Australian reporters and ex-players were in awe of Olsen's performances, openly wondering why club coaches in Sydney hadn't got the best out of him.

Bob McCarthy, a former Kangaroo, virtually demanded in his column in *Rugby League Week* that Arthur Beetson reinstate him to first grade at Easts.

And the Australian hooker Ben Elias, who had played alongside Olsen at Balmain, sang his praises. 'Five-eighth Olsen Filipaina had one of those days where he ran riot,' said Elias in his autobiography *Balmain Benny*. 'No side could have beaten them today. The game was a kick in the teeth for all of us and they smashed us. We had the Trans Tasman cup but after that disaster we had our heads down and our tails between our legs when we limped back into Sydney.'

Kangaroos coach Terry Fearnley concurred with Elias: 'I don't think any side I could have chosen would have beaten New Zealand today.'

When Kangaroos captain Wally Lewis reflects on the 1985 series he feels that there were two keys to the Kiwis' transformation to world-beaters:

'Perhaps the biggest obstacle in those ANZAC battles was that Olsen hated losing as much as I did — and many of the Kiwi teams Olsen played in were in my opinion, the best New Zealand teams ever fielded.

'Guided by Graham Lowe, they had special talents, abilities and were the best of friends. And that made them tough to play against.'

For Graham Lowe, the win had broader ramifications: 'We woke up New Zealand. We stood up to the bully and proved that we could tear apart a team which so often does just that to others.'

It was all about playing to your strengths, according to Lowe: 'With our tiny population, across the board New Zealanders have had to be tactically astute to win at anything. For the Kiwis that meant being unpredictable and instinctive. The regimented Kangaroos did not expect our surprise tactics and it neutralised their advantages. Surprise was a strategy, much like in boxing where the greatest danger comes from the punch you don't see.'

Olsen appeared as if he played under a spell to the confused Aussies, and according to Lowe, they did not know what hit them. For him it was all about the direct match-up. 'New Zealanders love one on one player rivalries — look at Ben Te'o and Sonny Bill Williams in the British Lions against the All Blacks in 2017.' Lowe explains. 'All people could talk about was the big Polynesian match-up at inside centre.

'And for New Zealanders in 1985 could there have been a better match-up than our Olsen and their Wally, right in the centre of Carlaw Park, with nowhere to hide? They were completely disoriented once Wally was shut down — Olsen cut off the head of the snake.'

Kangaroo Steve Roach wrote about Olsen's performance in 1985 in his autobiography: 'Filipaina was unstoppable and more than gave Wally Lewis a run for his money in the 85 series. He ploughed over the top of Wally Lewis in a way I've never seen anyone do it before or since.'

New Zealand's leading rugby league historian John Coffey summed up the significance of Olsen's performance in the 1985 test series: 'No one disputes that Lewis rates among rugby league's modern greats, that his achievements for Queensland and Australia will always be a part of the game's folklore,' Coffey wrote in the *New Zealand Rugby League Annual*. 'But in the thrilling 1985 trans-Tasman series he was totally overshadowed by the near unstoppable Filipaina.'

For his part, Wally filed the series away and moved on with his career. 'Perhaps the greatest compliment is that Olsen Filipaina was completely ignored by Wally Lewis in two autobiographies written about his career,' wrote Coffey.

'Clearly Lewis did not want to be reminded of how he fared against a player who that season spent much of his time in the Eastern Suburbs reserve grade.'

* * * * *

The question of who really won the 1985 test series can be answered through the differing fates of coaches Graham Lowe and Terry Fearnley. While Lowe was feted as a national hero and recognised around the rugby league world as a genius, Fearnley was coldly sacked.

To soothe interstate tensions, the ARL brought in the so-called 'Terry Fearnley Rule', whereby an incumbent State of Origin coach of Queensland or New South Wales could not also coach the national team at the same time.

The Australian public were merciless in their criticism of the Kangaroos. 'We really fluked the series,' wrote 'Man on the Hill' in his column in *Rugby League Week*. 'What a hiding and pathetic display with some big reputations severely dented. Wally Lewis adopted a traffic cop role, shouting and pointing at his players, but the former king was again eclipsed by Olsen Filipaina. Wally is not one of those destined for the scrapheap but he no longer walks on water and no longer will have an adoring media genuflecting at his every move.'

* * * * *

A new era had dawned.

For the first time, New Zealand began to peg its identity to its rugby league side. According to historian John Coffey, 'almost one million television viewers (or one in three New Zealanders over the age of five years and more than 50% of males 20–39) watched the live coverage of the first test from Lang Park and the numbers were maintained for the next two tests'.

Due to this exposure, the Kiwis team of 1985 became rugby league's first household names to cross over in New Zealand — a legacy for the next generation of Kiwi stars who not only dared to dream of playing in the Winfield Cup but did so without an inferiority complex or the scar tissue of previous generations.

The Kiwis played as if they had a sixth sense. They merged into a telepathic unit instinctively and knew where each other would be, with the forwards hunting like a wolf pack and the backs anticipating each other's moves like wizards.

They played with ferocity and they projected a sense of unity and purpose.

Under Lowe's guidance they were gripped by a contagion to play strong, fast and exciting rugby league. Their third-test win must have seemed like deliverance to the Carlaw Park faithful.

The Kiwis team of 1985 blossomed in the culturally competent hands of Graham Lowe, a man of revolution not evolution, whose simple, loving and targeted approach instilled belief in a group of humble and insecure men and grew them into world-beaters.

Lowe says: 'I brought love to those boys, brought in concepts that were previously taboo in rugby league. Love — aroha, shared emotions, the power of vulnerability as a strength, not a weakness. They opened up about their fears and dreams and we were able to build their confidence together and overcome the inferiority complex the Aussies had over us.'

They broke fresh ground in sport and used mutual disclosure as a binding element for disparate groups of men unable to express themselves under the hyper-masculine social conditions of the times.

His techniques and philosophy were revolutionary and transcended rugby league, and it is little wonder that after his coaching career Graham Lowe was in high demand on the New Zealand corporate speaking circuit.

As Lowe had conspired, the 1985 Kiwis team exposed a faultline in Australian rugby league — the gaping feudal chasm between NSW and Queensland. Put under pressure by the Kiwis, the division created dysfunction and chaos. And having endured such a barren spell in rugby league, the Kiwis pounced and Carlaw Park became a Kangaroos' slaughter ground.

* * * * *

The next Pacific playmaker to follow Olsen in the Winfield Cup was Tony Kemp, who watched the 1985 games as a 17-year-old in Auckland. In time, he would play 25 tests for New Zealand, many of them in Olsen's No. 6 jumper.

'Watching Olsen play in my position, and we had the same bottom-heavy physique, he directly gave me the belief we could beat the Aussies,' Kemp later explained. 'That was a huge mental leap for us and we were the first generation to come through not fearing the Aussies. We could now beat them in both league and union. I remember talking to Kevin Iro in my teens and both of us saying, "Let me at these Aussies — if Olsen can do it so can we!"'

Sir Michael Jones, who played 55 matches for the All Blacks in rugby union from 1987 to 1998, was also inspired by Olsen and his 1985 teammates. 'The diversity of that team was thrilling for us and it was our first elite team to feature a real mix of Māori, Pacific and European players,' he once explained.

'It was hugely uplifting for our community and there were powerful forces at play that could have discouraged the team. But they gave us a lot of hope and belief and were a great picture of the unified Kiwi nation.'

Likewise, Stacey Jones, who in the 1990s and 2000s would become one of the greatest Kiwi rugby league players of all time, was enthralled by the 1985 matches: 'That was the first clear picture of what rugby league meant,' he says. 'Everyone was raving about Olsen, how he was back from Australia and there he was in front of me, larger than life.'

The legacy of the 1985 team resonated with other members of the next generation. When exciting Māori playmaker Robbie Paul made his Kiwis debut in 1997 there was only one hero to be spoken of. The 27-test Kiwi, known for his instinctive style, says that watching Olsen in 1985 had a profound effect on him: 'When I was a kid I thought I was Olsen Filipaina, doing little chip kicks and bumping people off.'

* * * * *

The impact of that 1985 team went beyond rugby league and spoke to the cultural revolution that had taken place in New Zealand society. For Samoan actor Oscar Kightley, the 'new' New Zealand was on display in those test matches.

'We loved that Kiwi team,' remembers Kightley. 'It was full of brown faces and I remember my ma and pa watching the TV with such pride and saying, "He's Samoan" and us all feeling good about it.

'I've never forgotten it. I was 15 and these were real heroes. We'd watch TV and go to school, play games at lunchtime and suddenly we wanted to be Olsen. And then you get to admire hard dudes like Mark Graham and you've got Pākehā and Māori heroes as well who are playing alongside our Samoan heroes. It was as easy as that.'

Seeing Pākehā, Māori and Polynesian players embrace each other with such affection had a deep impact on Kightley, whose community had been vilified in popular culture and traumatised by Muldoon's Dawn Raids.

'I saw guys hugging each other after a try and I thought to myself . . . nah — white guys are alright! I've got permission to love them and engage with them,' says Kightley. 'It was more than winning games — it was about the effect it had on our self-esteem, pride and self-belief.'

It is a view shared by writer Gordon McLauchlan. The cultural battle, according to McLauchlan, was 'between the puritan Pākehā and their sense of order and their obsession with imposing it on Polynesian exuberance'.

For McLauchlan it was the first time all New Zealanders could look in the mirror and see themselves reflected: 'In 1985, a new generation of

Pākehā, Māori and Polynesian New Zealanders saw a rugby league side that looked like them, played with spirit and mana, and the toughest of our working-class boys cried tears in defeat and victory. That was something we had never seen before.'

It was a moment of national honesty according to McLauchlan: 'The real and truthful New Zealand was on display that afternoon when those men did the victory haka at Carlaw Park in 1985.

'For New Zealand to grow up and take its rightful place on the global stage, it needed to fully develop its mana. The cultural revolution needed a face and those Kiwis provided it.'

9

ONE OF THE GREAT MYSTERIES OF LIFE

'I looked inside Olsen and found a loveable man.'
— Brian 'Chicka' Norton, North Sydney Bears Coach

When the Kiwi contingent returned to their Winfield Cup clubs after the 1985 test series, Olsen Filipaina attracted the most attention of the confused and bewildered Australian media.

On his return to Australia, Geoff Prenter, a league writer from the *Sun*, assembled questions for Olsen from a team of journalists across the various newspapers. The article was titled 'The Third Degree' and its aim was to unravel the mystery and make sense of what had just taken place.

Among the *Mirror* journalists, Rick Allen quizzed Olsen about his 'amazing form reversal' from playing reserve grade to being the star of the 'World Championships', Tony Megahey wanted to know if he felt unfairly criticised, and Jon Geddes wondered if he had ever been happy playing club football in Sydney.

Roy Masters, from the *Sydney Morning Herald*, asked him about his fear of flying. Gary Lester, from the *Sydney Sun*, put it to Olsen that his performance in the third test against Australia was one of his best, while English journalist Mike Stephenson asked him how he would employ his talents if he were the player-coach of Easts.

It was rugby league's very own version of the Spanish Inquisition.

Geoff Prenter's question was the one they all wanted to hear: 'What's your opinion of Wally Lewis?' Olsen replied: 'I know he is rated the world's best, but I don't take notice of ratings. He doesn't worry me, but I respect his ability and realise he has to be closely watched. My philosophy is to give the opposition something to think about rather than worry about them.'

Olsen flat-batted most of the questions but said he wanted to play five-eighth and concentrate on attack, 'because that's what I like most and so do the paying customers'.

On his return to work on the garbage truck in Sydney, Olsen found his popularity had surged again, especially among the NSW fans whose own five-eighths had been constantly outplayed by Wally in State of Origin. 'When I got back after the series, people were congratulating me saying, "Good on you, Olly — you beat King Wally",' says Olsen.

'They were rushing out of their houses to talk to me and shake my hand during my garbo run. It was amazing.'

On the same Sunday that Olsen had carved up the Kangaroos in the third test, Easts were beaten 22-nil by Manly in Round 18 of the Winfield Cup. With just seven games left to play, Arthur Beetson's Eastern Suburbs Roosters were sitting eighth on the ladder, their hopes of finals football fading. 'There's just no flair, that's our problem,' announced Beetson after the match.

Despite the growing calls for Olsen to be reinstated to Easts' first grade, Beetson sounded hesitant. 'He's going to have to earn his first-grade spot,' Beetson said in *Rugby League Week*. 'I've tried very hard to get him firing this year, but he's a different player with the Kiwi jersey on. I don't know what else I can say to him. I guess I'll have to consider Olsen closely after the way he played in the tests. He is one of the great mysteries of life.'

* * * * *

In Round 19, Easts hosted Olsen's former club, Balmain, at the Sydney Sports Ground. The Tigers, still coached by Frank Stanton, were leading the competition after winning 14 of their opening 18 games. Here was a perfect opportunity for Olsen to prove that he could carry his representative form into club football.

Beetson finally relented and selected Olsen at five-eighth in first grade and gave him creative licence, noting that his kicking game had been superb in the test matches.

In his *Sunday Telegraph* column Beetson outlined Olsen's mission: 'Crank up the three-quarter line — that's the job I've got for Olsen Filipaina. There is going to be a lot of pressure on big Olsen to perform up to the standard he produced in New Zealand. And the fact that he is up against his old teammates, who have all played strongly, will centre a lot of attention. I'm confident the big fella can handle it.'

Olsen did as Beetson asked. He outplayed his opposite number, ran the ball powerfully, and kicked all three of his conversion attempts. Despite the one-point loss, Olsen was voted the man-of-the-match award by Ray Chesterton of the *Daily Telegraph*. The *Sydney Morning Herald* noted that he had 'brought back some of his best test form', while *Rugby League Week* declared that he 'should finish the season in first grade'.

* * * * *

When Olsen returned to Eastern Suburbs first grade it was alongside Laurie Spina, the son of Italian cane-cutting parents from Ingham in North Queensland. Spina played 171 first-grade games across four clubs — North Sydney, Eastern Suburbs, Cronulla Sutherland and was captain of the North Queensland Cowboys in their first year.

Spina enjoyed playing alongside Olsen: 'He had so much raw strength on the field and it took so many players to tackle him. I would love to have seen him more aggressive, but he was such a gentle person off the field. Very quiet and humble and a lovely guy — like a big teddy bear.'

Olsen played the final six games of the season at five-eighth, scoring 32 points and earning rave reviews for his 'ferocity and class', his 'explosive bursts' and 'brilliant passing'. After one particularly powerful display, Peter Frilingos, of the *Mirror*, predicted that Olsen 'only has to maintain last Sunday's form to be the lynchpin of the Easts attack in 1986'.

Journalists began to question Beetson about Olsen's future at the club. Beetson knew that Olsen had limited options — he would command a sizeable transfer fee and few clubs could afford to pay the transfer as well as Olsen's sign-on and match fees. Staying with Easts, or returning to New Zealand, appeared to be the most likely outcomes.

In Round 23, Easts returned to the winner's circle with a resounding 24–6 win over Canberra. Filipaina led his 12-man Roosters to victory, setting up two tries and inspiring coach Arthur Beetson to again acknowledge Filipaina's efforts: 'The Big O was truly outstanding today, the best form he has ever shown for the club. He killed Canberra today and gave his opposite number Ivan Henjak nightmares.'

The *Telegraph*'s Grantlee Kieza gave Filipaina the Pye Man of the Match award and his match report was titled: 'Big O leads ambush on Raiders'. Kieza wrote: 'Filipaina's web of destruction constantly embarrassed Canberra's defence and Filipaina showed the kind of inventiveness and power which made him the outstanding player in the test series, mocking the Raiders with explosive bursts and brilliant passing.'

Rugby League Week's Charles Christian spoke rosily of Olsen's future in his match report titled 'Olsen ransacks awful Raiders' and wrote: 'If Olsen Filipaina's future with Easts depended on his performance against Canberra last Sunday, the club should sign him for life. Despite the advantage of an extra player, Filipaina ran hotter than a Rotorua geyser.'

With two 'must win' matches remaining in the season for Easts, the spotlight was on Olsen for their next match against the North Sydney Bears and he didn't disappoint.

Eastern Suburbs crushed the Bears 34–18 and Olsen put on another brilliant display. The *Rugby League Week* match report noted: 'The "Big O" thought he had returned to Carlaw Park last weekend, the way he tore holes in the Bears' defence.'

In the end, not even a revived Olsen could save Easts' season. The club finished seventh, two spots out of the coveted final five, and Beetson commenced a clear-out of his player roster. Although the record of 10 wins and 11 losses was a big improvement on their previous season, it had still been an underwhelming year.

'Olsen never really performed for us, even though he was a tremendous talent,' wrote Arthur Beetson in his autobiography. 'He was the loveliest bloke in the world, but his preparation for games was bloody awful — for example he would go and play tennis on match morning. He didn't like training, just wanted to play games.'

Later, in his autobiography, Olsen's Roosters and Kiwis teammate Dean Bell wrote of the positives and negatives of being coached by Arthur Beetson. 'You have to respect him for what he'd achieved and for his knowledge. I got on with him well, he's a great guy. If he had a problem, though, it was that he couldn't really handle the man-management side of things.'

One of the players who thrived under Beetson was halfback and fellow Queenslander Laurie Spina. Yet even Spina recognised that his boss had a hard time reaching Olsen.

'It was a shame that Arthur couldn't bring out the best in Olsen till late in the season where he played really well,' he later explained. 'He needed a modern coach to do that — to treat him the way he needed to be treated.'

* * * * *

While Olsen sat in limbo, unsigned by Easts and with an $18,000 transfer fee on his head, the *Sydney Morning Herald* profiled him in their weekend magazine, *The Good Weekend*.

The story, by Ginny Dougary, painted the picture of an exotic man still uncomfortable in his surrounds. 'The giant enigma suffered culture shock when he landed here. But neither honesty nor modesty will calm his critics,' wrote Dougary.

'As he talks in his slow, easy drawl, flashing his white teeth, daughter perched on one foot, son on a knee and green budgerigar on a shoulder, Filipaina looks faintly absurd and out of place in his modern Ryde house. It's hardly surprising to discover that Filipaina hates living in Sydney, or any big city, for that matter. For the past five years he's kept much to himself.'

On his playing future, Olsen told Dougary that he would continue collecting garbage, even though he didn't need the money. He floated the possibility of dropping down to amateur football. And he reiterated his mantra that sport was just one part of his life.

The story in the prestigious *Good Weekend* confirmed the public's fascination with Olsen and he was one of only two rugby league players to be profiled that year alongside Parramatta's Ray Price.

His piece in 1985 sat alongside other *Good Weekend* profiles in other editions that included Frank Sinatra, Tina Turner, James Dean, Meryl Streep, Peter Weir, Madonna, Nelson Mandela, Martina Navratilova and Rupert Murdoch.

* * * * *

Olsen's brilliant game against North Sydney two games from the end of the season was to liberate him from his Eastern Suburbs nightmare.

Not only was he trapped with a coach who couldn't manage him, but his 'signing fee' price of $18,000 was a barrier that few clubs could overcome.

'By now,' Olsen later recalled, 'I didn't really care where I played. I had just played a year with my Kiwi mates Hugh McGahan and Dean Bell and I was now used to chopping and changing clubs. It was no hard feelings and keep moving. You had no idea who your next team was.'

By mid-September, as the Winfield Cup finals series was reaching its conclusion, North Sydney swooped in for Olsen's signature. Norths had not qualified for the finals since 1982 and were coming off a terrible season in 1985 in which the club won just four games. Coach

Greg Hawick had courted controversy by sacking popular captain and New Zealander Mark Graham, before he was sacked himself.

His replacement, Brian 'Chicka' Norton, came into the job claiming 'the club is sick'. Several high-profile players walked out. Armed with cash from the gambling revenues of the North Sydney Leagues Club, the committee decided to open the chequebook and buy a fresh team. Eight players were signed, including Queenslanders Les Kiss, Terry Butler, Gavin Jones, Brett French and Martin Bella.

'Norths in their most ambitious attempt yet to buy their way out of the doldrums have invested in some pretty big names starting with the world's most destructive five-eighth, Olsen Filipaina,' wrote George Dunkerley in *Rugby League Week*. 'But in the North Sydney jigsaw, it is perhaps the smallest piece that could prove the most crucial — 168-cm Clayton Friend.'

Norths had put enormous faith in their new Kiwi contingent. They reinstated Mark Graham as captain, while Olsen and Clayton Friend were the halves combination, a reunion of the pairing that had destroyed the Kangaroos in the test series earlier in the year.

Never before in the history of the Sydney competition had Kiwis been placed in such positions of playmaking authority. It was the biggest upheaval in North Sydney's 77-year history and the club and its long-suffering fans had every reason to expect big things from their new-look big-budget squad.

* * * * *

In October 1985, New Zealand went on a tour of Great Britain and France, winning three tests, losing one and drawing another.

Olsen remembers with a laugh when he put his plan to withdraw from the 1985 tour into action: 'I called Lowie and said . . . look, the doctor says I'm too injured to fly up. I thought I could pull it off, but he was ready for me.'

Lowe was prepared for Olsen's pre-flight nerves and recalls taking a hard line: 'He called me and talked about how his doctor had said he can't tour due to a knee operation. And I called him out on it and said I knew it was a slight knee operation and he would be good for the tour. Once I told him I would fly over there to meet with his doctor, he broke. I told him New Zealand needs him and I would carry him onto the plane myself if I had to.'

Lowe had one trick up his sleeve that meant Olsen would strongly consider making the trip. He appointed him the tour vice-captain, an honour that maximised his chances of getting on the plane. Lowe said to the media at the time: 'I appointed Olsen Filipaina in the firm belief he has the right leadership qualities. A senior player of tremendous international experience.'

Despite the appointment, Lowe remembers his discomfort that Olsen would pull out: 'Right up till the plane took off, I was expecting them to announce a missing passenger. But to his credit he kept his word and got on the plane. He had a long, rough flight, the poor guy. He was just terrified.'

* * * * *

New Zealand won a thrillingly close first test 24–22 at Headingley, led by Mark Graham who was a towering warrior in the forward line, throwing himself at the British forwards with controlled fury. The major difference between the teams, Graham was taken out of the game with a fractured cheekbone after some calculated thuggery from Great Britain winger Des Drummond.

The *Observer* newspaper report noted New Zealand's mix of brute force and intelligence had clinched 'the most exciting of victories. The visitors dominated the first half with an irresistible display of running and passing. Britain's defence was often in bemused disarray as captain Mark Graham, stand-off Olsen Filipaina and prop Kurt Sorensen carved gaps through the middle with ominous ease. Filipaina, who makes a brick outhouse look fragile, led the magnificent support play.'

On the tour, Olsen opened up to his teammates in a way that few had experienced before.

Chris Rattue, a New Zealand journalist who accompanied the team, noted that Olsen 'survived on his wits' during the tour and made it through 'without having to dip into his wages'. He showed his full range of street smarts, hustling players on the tennis court and in card games, even buying groceries wholesale and 'selling the goods at a small profit to his less industrious teammates'.

Olsen's teammates were in awe of his energy and hustling abilities. Captain Mark Graham remembers two-on-one tennis games which Olsen would always win. Hooker Howie Tamati recalls Olsen taking great delight in fleecing newspaper reporters of their money.

'He would watch their form like a hawk, make a judgment, give them a huge start, string them along a little bit and then trounce them, taking their money with a big smile. He had copped so much from journalists over the years, it was like therapy.'

Childhood friend and teammate James Leuluai notes that his hustling went beyond the tennis court: 'We all learnt the hard way never to play Olly in anything that requires hand-eye co-ordination. In darts he would miss the triples and let you win a few games to build you up.

'Then he would let the beers kick in and we would get confident and bet for a meal or for the loser to do the winner's washing. Then sure enough he would start nailing triples and win every time.'

Howie Tamati noticed the change in Olsen. 'He was part of our group M.I.A. — Māori Internal Affairs — and we were the lead practical jokers. Olsen was a mastermind behind a lot of pranks, but nobody ever suspected him and everyone else got the blame. Over seven weeks you get to know people and I loved touring with Olsen.'

In the absence of his inspiring and injured captain Mark Graham, Graham Lowe decided to appoint Olsen Filipaina as captain for the second test. Lowe says: 'It doesn't matter whether Olsen was officially captain or not, he'd always been in that leader role. They now call them senior leadership teams and we didn't have any of that sort of stuff. But you know I had main men and that's what Olsen was from day one. A coach's dream.'

In the *Journal of the Polynesian Society*, writer E.G. Schwimmer wrote of 'the Mediator' — a Māori man who leads his people from behind: 'In many Māori communities we may find, apart from the recognised chiefs, another influential person whose exact position is hard to define. He may be a teacher, clergyman, doctor, public servant or social worker or simply a special person to whom the community has become attached. When the community has to make great decisions, he is usually somewhere at the back of them, although often not in any official sort of position.

For Graham Lowe, Olsen was his team's 'Mediator': 'Olsen didn't seek honours at all but part of my role was putting responsibility on him like the vice-captaincy,' says Lowe.

'He wasn't the captain but people followed him and those who were concerned about things, could look to Olsen and see a calmness. And even though he was really worried himself, he would never let it show — like a rock. Panic can be infectious and it's good to have calm people.'

* * * * *

On Saturday, 2 November 1985 Olsen Filipaina ran onto Central Park Stadium in Wigan as the 42nd New Zealand Kiwis captain since 1908 and the sequel to being appointed captain of the New Zealand Schoolboys in 1972, 13 years before. He was the latest in a proud line of Māori and Pacific Islander captains of the Kiwis including Steve Watene, Roy Christian, Dennis Williams and Fred Ah Kuoi.

The Kiwis ran through the tunnel and into a seething cauldron of singing Great Britain fans. The British fans sensed a weakened New Zealand without skipper Mark Graham, and they were right.

Great Britain's centre Garry Schofield, smarting from criticism of his first-test performance, ran riot, scoring four tries to equal winger Billy Boston's record for tries in a test match.

Great Britain won a famous and entertaining victory 25–8 in front of 15,500 screaming fans urging them onwards, as they executed their coach Maurice Bamford's instructions to 'throw it wide'.

For the third and final test match at Leeds, Lowe had captain and guiding spirit Mark Graham back in charge of the Kiwis. Graham scored the only try of the match as the Kiwis went to war with Great Britain in a spiteful and brawl-filled encounter. It was a low-scoring slugfest that ended in a 6–6 draw and a tied series.

After the third test, Mark Graham left the tour to return home for medical treatment. The Kiwis were without a tour captain and Olsen and Hugh McGahan were called into Graham Lowe's room to learn that Hugh McGahan had been appointed the Kiwis tour captain for the seven-game French leg of the tour.

In his autobiography *Hughie*, Hugh McGahan wrote of the moment: 'The best thing about the whole meeting was that Olsen said he agreed with the decision, and that he would be happy to play under me. Those sentiments were very special.'

Olsen remembers the meeting: 'I wasn't disappointed. I was thrilled for Hugh and he was a good Māori man and a great teammate at Easts. He was there for me when I was in the dumps in reserve grade and I could not have been happier that he was captain. It's enough pressure playing five-eighth without worrying about everybody else and doing team talks and media.'

Young Kiwi Darrell Williams sees the tour as a highpoint of his career, especially being accepted by the senior men who carried themselves with authority — as the bearers of knowledge.

'To spend all day and night with guys like Olsen and Mark Graham and the Sorensens was the greatest honour and they were the real thing,' says Williams. 'We played and trained hard, drank, danced, had great meals, played pranks on each other. They were men's men and I was lucky to be part of them.'

* * * * *

Away from the football field, Olsen was a family man devoted to his wife and children. The violence inflicted on him by his father made him determined to be the best man he could for his son John and daughter Louise.

The postcards he sent home while on tour show a sensitive, fearful, almost New Age guy. From England he wrote of his horror of the return flight:

To Miss Leslie Taylor,

Hi Darling,

Nine days left and the four days in London to go. By the time you get this it should be less. I hope you are saying prayers for me to get home safely. I'm getting scared because I look at the photos of you and the kids every night and the closer the tour ends the more scared I get. I'm afraid I won't see my family because of the flying. PLEASE HELP ME my Darling, I'm scared.

Give my love to the kids.
Love always,
Olsen

Days later, before he flew to France, he wrote to Leslie again:

To Miss Leslie Taylor,

Dear Darling,

Hope this lettercard finds you and the kids in good health. I think by the time you read this I will be in France. Things over here are good but I still miss you and the kids. I'm well and looking forward to coming home. I went to see all these places today and decided to get a haircut. Well, getting tired now, can't write much more because I don't think I'm used to writing letters. Never mind the next one I write will be normal like the others. I miss you terribly so give my love to the kids. Give Louise and John a big kiss for me and don't forget to tell them their 'DADDY LOVES THEM'! See you when I get home, I LOVE YOU ALWAYS AND FOREVER,

Bye MY DARLING,
Yours Forever,
Olsen XXXXXXX

Upon his return from the tour, Olsen joined the North Sydney Bears for pre-season training and entered a gentle world of white picket fences, poets and Port Jackson fig trees in Sydney's affluent lower north shore. The Bears were the 'nice guys' of rugby league, a reflection of the upmarket demographics of their catchment.

Their fans were patient, willing to bide their time for their next premiership after their brief moments of glory in 1921 and 1922. 'To follow Norths,' wrote journalist Mike Gibson, 'you have to be a dreamer.'

Intellectuals were over-represented at North Sydney Oval. One prominent Norths fan was Lex Marinos, a softly spoken Greek-Australian actor, playwright and radio personality.

Another was Alex Buzo, an Albanian-Australian playwright and author of 88 books. Andrew Moore, a labour historian and Norths fan, explained why his club was different in the club history book, *The Mighty Bears*:

'In an era when some other teams behaved like barbarians — slapping each other on the face before entering the field in order to build up their adrenalin — the Bears reportedly relaxed to the mellow tones of 2Day FM Radio. This group of modern gladiators apparently trotted onto the paddock with songs like The Eagles' "Take it Easy" running through their heads.'

A Norths promotional brochure in 1986 contained a story titled 'The Tale of the Bears of the North' which summarised the utopian life of the Bears. 'They lived in the best of kingdoms. The air was sweet, the hills were rolling and the sea breeze was an aphrodisiac to the Big Bears' nostrils. In short, they had become complacent because it was too good. They lost their aggressive stance and smelt the flowers.'

When it was announced that Olsen was joining the club, Alex Buzo — who wrote several poems for his favourite club — penned an ode to the incoming five-eighth.

It was titled 'On First Learning that Norths Have Signed Olsen Filipaina' and published by the *Sydney Morning Herald*:

Much have I travelled in the realms of League,
And seen them all from Pearce to McTigue;
Round many verdant ovals have I been
Whose oft-banged fences are blood to our screen.
Of one stout army I hear nought but ill:
A fiefdom where Lucifer would fit the bill.
Yet did I ne'er sup with elongated spoon
Till of Olsen I heard from Mercury's platoon;
Then felt I like some diver of the deep
When a medic reveals with nary a peep
That testosterone levels have been sapped and slowed,
O brave Cortez knew without being specific
To stay above and well clear of the Pacific
And kick the round balls of a different code.
(With apologies to 'On First Looking into
Chapman's Homer' by John Keats)

Olsen was unsure what to make of North Sydney. He had never played football in such an environment and Leslie described the shift as: 'Moving from the snobs in the east to the northern party club.'

Arriving at his first training session, Olsen expected the usual road runs and gruelling fitness tests. Instead coach Chicka Norton handed him a Steeden ball and said, 'You don't play football on highways and roads, you play it on grass. Let's play football.'

It was the first time since he had played under Dennis Tutty in his first year at Balmain that Olsen had enjoyed coming to training. 'At Balmain and Easts we had road runs and I hated them, but at Norths we do all our training with the ball,' Olsen told the *Sydney Morning Herald*.

He started arriving early to practise his goal-kicking — something he had never done before in his life. He was determined to show his gratitude for Norton's more customised approach to coaching.

This new-found joy was tempered by some personal bad news. Back in Auckland, his father, Aloese, had left his mother Sissie to start a new life with another woman.

'It devastated Olsen because his mother was crying every day,' Leslie says. 'It was not a good marriage, but she did it for her boys to make sure they had good values. She was fighting for the relationship to stay together and there was a lot of pain on all sides.'

For his six years' playing stint in Sydney, Olsen's father Aloese and his gambling habit had been a significant drain on his finances and he had blown all of the money Olsen had sent him.

His father's sudden departure, though, meant that the Filipaina household in Māngere East had lost its breadwinner. Olsen was determined to send more money home to ease the transition for Sissie.

* * * * *

On Sunday, 9 March 1986, Olsen ran onto Wollongong Showground for his first Winfield Cup match for the North Sydney Bears. Comfortable alongside Mark Graham and his Kiwis scrum base partner, Clayton Friend, Olsen converted three important goal-kicks and Norths beat Illawarra 16–12.

In his new more supportive environment, Olsen began to socialise with his teammates and enjoy their company. When Kiwi reggae band Herbs played in Sydney, he, Clayton Friend and Dean Bell were invited onto the stage. 'The three showed no signs of stage fright and belted out a boisterous rendition of the classic, "Sweet Chariot",' reported the *Daily Telegraph*.

For the first time, it appeared that all the ducks were in a row for Olsen. He had a coach that seemed to understand him, at a club that appreciated his talents. He was playing alongside his Kiwi teammates who made him feel comfortable in the dressing room. And away from football, he had achieved a sense of financial and emotional security.

'Olsen,' wrote Kiwi journalist Eric Young, is a player 'who the

Sydney critics like to describe as enigmatic. Misunderstood would probably be a better word.'

Olsen continued his fine form in Round 2, scoring a try and kicking five conversions to lead Norths to a 16-point win over Wests. Then, in a 10-point Round 3 loss to Penrith, he strained a hamstring and was forced to the sidelines for a week.

It was a frustrating interlude for Olsen, but Norton kept the faith and reinstated him to five-eighth despite the fact that Norths won the Round 4 match without him.

Moreover, Norton made him the captain of the backline against defending premiers Canterbury; it was a sign, perhaps, that Olsen had finally found a club coach that understood him.

In this new senior role, Olsen was to lead and mentor the untried centre pairing of new signing Queenslander Brett French and rookie teenage prodigy Greg Florimo. Florimo had quickly risen through the ranks of the North Sydney Bears juniors and was the golden boy of the club.

Fans saw him as living proof that the genteel local area of North Sydney could still produce world-class rugby league players. Flame-haired Florimo stood out instantly. He was from humble roots, the son of a motor mechanic, and to supplement his football income he worked as a rigger and scaffolder.

'I was 18 or 19 coming up in reserve grade and I had an international star with so much ability playing inside me,' he later said of his debut alongside Olsen. 'I had a special connection with Olsen. It was awe-inspiring, it really was. Whatever he said, I did. If he said, "Run there," I ran there. If he said, "Tackle this," I tackled that.'

Olsen would take him under his wing, giving young Florimo a nickname — 'Flyspray' — as well as lifts in his car to and from training sessions. Florimo would never forget the experience.

'What attracted me to Olsen was that he was such a joyous person, always happy, smiling and with something to give. He was the leader and when things got tough, we went to him and just followed him around. All the players loved him and what an honour it was to be mentored by him.'

* * * * *

Sitting in the grandstands for Norths' Round 6 match against Canterbury was Graham Lowe, who had come to Sydney to prepare for the upcoming test series against Australia. Nearing 29 years of age, Olsen was ready to retire from international football. He could see a new generation of players rising and ready to take over.

'I didn't want to be in the spotlight any more,' Olsen later explained. 'Whatever happened in 1986 could not have been greater than 1985 and I didn't need to prove anything more to myself. I didn't care about being number one — I just wanted to make Mum and my family proud, to get them some money. And I did that. So I announced my retirement from representative football. Let someone else have a chance.'

If Olsen didn't want to impress Lowe, his performance against Canterbury spoke otherwise. Phil 'Buzz' Rothfield summarised the match in the *Daily Telegraph*: 'New Zealand's reluctant test hero Olsen Filipaina almost single-handedly destroyed premiers Canterbury at Belmore with a blockbusting performance.' Norths had crushed the Bulldogs 19–4, introducing a young Florimo to winning rugby league.

Lowe made it his mission to talk Olsen out of his Kiwis retirement after his virtuoso performance. He cornered Olsen in the change room after the match and told him to forget about the critics in the media. The chat had the desired effect, with Olsen telling the press: 'I've had a chat to Graham Lowe and I'll be playing for the Kiwis.'

* * * * *

In North Sydney, after six seasons of hot-and-cold football, the riddle of Olsen Filipaina seemed to have finally been solved.

'I don't know how people have said Filipaina is hard to coach,' said Chicka Norton to *Rugby League Week*. 'You've got to understand the person and you can't get through to him by yelling, not that I'm accusing other coaches of doing that. I told him he was in charge of a very young backline and it was up to him to look after them and call the shots. I would have to say he's a very easy player to coach.'

Norths started the season well but then slumped, losing five games in a row and plummeting from third to ninth place on the ladder.

Olsen's injury issues were compounding. He handed the long-range goal-kicking duties to Les Kiss as his hamstring could only handle the leg extensions of the shorter goal-kicks. His knee was troubling him and his right elbow had been smashed in the St George game, resulting in '13 pieces of bone floating in your elbow', according to the club doctor.

The Round 12 match against Frank Stanton's Balmain loomed as a fork in the road for both clubs. Balmain were fifth, with five wins and five losses. Norths were ninth, with six losses and four wins. After weeks of playing attractive football and still losing, Norths toughed it out to beat Balmain 16–7.

'It's ironic that we played better in our recent losses than we did today,' mused Mark Graham after the match, 'but football is a lot like life — sometimes the rewards come when you least expect them. Today was just reward for perseverance. And we are back in the hunt for a semi-final spot.'

With the losing streak behind them, Norths demolished Cronulla by 21 points at North Sydney Oval. Olsen was dominant, terrorising the Sharks' five-eighth, Michael Speechley. 'New Zealand's test five-eighth Olsen Filipaina engineered all three tries in a slick and devastating performance,' concluded Tim Prentice in the *Mirror*.

Norths battled hard to stay in contention, and by Round 22 the club had spent eight weeks hovering outside the top five in seventh place. With just five games left to play, a win over league-leaders Parramatta was just the result they needed for the race to the finals. And win they did, beating the Eels by four points and then Manly by six.

But Olsen and Clayton Friend were nowhere to be seen. As both men had committed to New Zealand's test matches against Australia, Norton had been forced to select a new halves combination of Graham Murchie and Mark Cannon.

* * * * *

While Norths were waiting for their star halves to return, the Aussies were waiting to ambush the Kiwis in the first test of the 1986 series at a windblown Carlaw Park. On a rain-soaked and boggy ground, the Kangaroos outdid the Kiwis at their own game, winning 22–8.

Early in the second test at the SCG, the score was locked at 0–0. Taking matters into his own hands, Olsen received the ball 20 metres out from the Kangaroos' tryline, accelerated and brutally steamrolled over the top of hooker Royce Simmons.

He then fed the ball to Mark Graham in support and wrapped around him to receive the return pass and score a brilliant try. Commentator Eastlake bellowed: 'The big man has crashed over.' It was simple, elegant and brutal rugby league.

'His power was awesome when he ran at me and any Kangaroo in the middle that day,' recalls Royce Simmons. 'Olsen was always one of the players we talked about as a group and even though he was marked by the great Wally Lewis we knew he was a strike weapon and had a plan to smother him. Sometimes the plan didn't work.'

As Olsen lined up to take the conversion of his try, Eastlake cooed: 'He's an amazing player. When he puts on a black and white jumper he honestly grows taller, wider and meaner and shows all of the skills we know he possesses and that he very rarely shows in this country.'

It was a close match, but the Kangaroos prevailed 23–12. The test was notable for the Kiwis debut of Gary Freeman who would become the first New Zealander to win a Dally M best player award in the NRL, eight years later in 1994.

Freeman is forever grateful for Olsen's support in his big moment: 'I got myself a corner in the change room and I was shitting myself,' Freeman remembers. 'I was playing with my heroes, but Olsen was nice and calm, no yelling and screaming. Even on field he was great. He never told me what to do and respected that I had got to this level with my own style of game.'

For Freeman it was an honour to play with one of his heroes: 'To play next to him was unbelievable — just a nice simple "Give me the ball when you're ready". Even during the week and on match day on the bus I would try to sit next to him because it was calming. It was going to be okay if Olsen was next to me.'

One standout memory for Freeman from his debut illustrated the difference between New Zealand and Australian league cultures. In the dying minutes of the game, Freeman gave the ball to Olsen: 'We were desperate and Olsen tried to chip over the top of Wayne Pearce,' Freeman says.

'If he pulls it off and regathers, we could have been a chance to win the game. But Wayne Pearce caught it and the Kangaroos scored a try. There is a lot of luck in football and Olsen knew that. He didn't worry about it and that was the thing in New Zealand. We were trained that if you don't have a crack, you'll never win. I loved that about Olsen — that he would try that chip over the top. He had the old Kiwi spirit.'

Freeman also got a taste of Graham Lowe's man-management skills: 'Graham was always personal with his players,' says Freeman. 'He would ask them how they are feeling, what's going on with their life, give them simple plans he would run over with them, always giving bits and pieces of information at training. He would encourage Olsen with positivity and you could see him grow before your eyes. The belief would build and then he would do anything for Lowey.'

* * * * *

In the third test at Lang Park the Australians dominated for a comprehensive 33–12 victory. Order had been restored in the rugby league kingdom.

With five minutes left in the match, Kiwi Gary Prohm made a

break and passed to Gary Freeman who offloaded to a galloping Olsen Filipaina 20 metres out and smelling a try. He stepped two players and surged towards the tryline — bearing a final gift for his Kiwi fans.

With socks down, big thighs pumping and Polynesian eyes flashing, it looked like a certainty. But there are no fairytales in New Zealand rugby league. Out of nowhere swooped his old nemesis Wally Lewis, the Emperor of Lang Park, with a brilliant try-saving tackle around the ankles. The Lang Park faithful roared in approval. The king was back on his throne and would go on to win man of the series.

With the end of the game looming, Darrell Williams scored a consolation try in the corner after a brilliant short ball by Kurt Sorensen.

Ball in hand, Olsen went to the touchline to place the ball on the sand mound and line up the ball for the conversion. He was one of the last exponents of the fading art of the toe-poke goal-kick, which had served rugby league well since its inception but was going out of fashion.

The toe-pokers had been disrupted by 'around the corner' kickers like Kangaroos rugby union convert Michael O'Connor and it was now the normal kicking style in England.

Olsen's goal-kicking attempt was to become a historical footnote as the last ever toe-poke conversion attempt in Kiwis colours. The next wave of Kiwis kickers — Kevin Iro and front-rower Peter Brown — both used the new 'around the corner' style, which was standardised after that.

Professional till the end, Olsen stepped up one last time for his dying artform, like a ghost from another time.

Darrell Eastlake described the kick on the Channel Nine commentary: 'Filipaina now three metres in from touch, right on the twenty-two line, not an easy angle, he's only taken two paces back, certainly got the height, and got the two points.'

It was to be his last touch of the ball in international rugby league.

* * * * *

It was also Graham Lowe's last test in Australia as Kiwis coach. Soon after, the NZRL fired Lowe and he moved to England to coach Wigan, vowing to never coach New Zealand again under the current management.

The Kiwis players were confused and unhappy and the *Sydney Morning Herald* jumped on the story: 'Kiwi revolt looming — resentment is growing among the Sydney-based New Zealand rugby league test players over the alleged sacking of coach Graham Lowe.'

Four of the Sydney-based Kiwis players called a press conference in Sydney and both Mark Graham and Olsen Filipaina announced their retirements in protest at Lowe's treatment, stating they would never pull on the Kiwis jersey again.

Kiwis players Gary Prohm and Clayton Friend also attended and spoke to journalists in solidarity with Lowe, who for them was more than just a coach. He was the father figure of the modern, commercial and respectable New Zealand rugby league.

The players were damning in their assessment of the unexpected move with now ex-captain Mark Graham saying the NZRL had a 'death wish'.

Graham says: 'I have officially finished with the NZRL. Lowe made the Kiwis a world-class side and without him the game will go downhill fast in New Zealand. With Lowe in charge, New Zealand were capable of matching it with any opposition. I'm afraid the game will be in trouble without him.'

Olsen spoke at the press conference adding: 'I don't want to have anything to do with the NZRL — I'll give it a miss altogether. Graham Lowe took the game in New Zealand to unbelievable heights and now he's finished.'

And like that, it was over.

* * * * *

Back at North Sydney, the Bears needed to win two of their final three games to make the semi-finals, and with his Kiwi test pairing returned,

Norton mysteriously stuck with his replacement trio of Graham Murchie, John McArthur and Mark Cannon.

Olsen and Friend, who had begun the season so positively, had sacrificed their first-grade spots to play for New Zealand, and they couldn't break back into a winning side. It was dreadfully unlucky for both men.

Clayton Friend was rated the best halfback in the world by rugby league magazine *Open Rugby* that year, and Olsen was rated the world's number four five-eighth. Additionally, Olsen had wanted to retire from international football at the start of the season to concentrate on the Bears and his loyalty to Graham Lowe had led to him losing his spot with his club.

Norths fans faced the surreal situation of some of the cream of world rugby league talent withering on the vine on their reserve-grade team. To make matters worse, in the 100-player poll conducted by *Rugby League Week*, Olsen came fourth with 11 per cent of the votes for the hardest man to tackle. His opponents still remembered him.

The winner out of the curious situation was delighted Norths reserve-grade coach Denis Constantine who could smell the Bears' best opportunity to snare a Sydney grade premiership since 1959.

Unleashing his angst, Olsen became a one-man wrecking ball against Balmain in the reserve-grade Minor Preliminary semi-final at the SCG in which Norths crushed the Balmain Tigers 26–0.

Rugby League Week's match report was titled: 'Olsen Engineers Sweet Revenge' and journalist Darren Hadland wrote: 'Olsen Filipaina produced his destructive best against Balmain, unleashing the bumping runs which have been his trademark since he hit the Winfield Cup. He was the catalyst for most of Norths' attacking raids and he was the central figure in most of Norths' five tries.'

Waiting for Norths in the reserve-grade Minor semi-final was Manly Warringah who again suffered Filipaina's wrath as he led Norths to a 22–8 win. *Rugby League Week* reported: 'New Zealand test star Olsen Filipaina had a great game, the chunky pivot scoring 14 points from a try and five goals and created havoc with his powerhouse charges.'

Norths' reserve-grade team were now only two wins away from their first premiership since 1959 and again *Rugby League Week*'s Darren Hadland had no doubt as to who underpinned the Bears' unlikely tilt at glory. 'And it's Olsen Filipaina, one of rugby league's great enigmas, who is leading the charge along with Greg Florimo.'

The teenaged Greg Florimo was still moving between first and reserve grade in his debut season, but he was thrilled to play alongside Olsen regardless of grade: 'In reserve grade, any time he touched the ball and involved himself, you held your breath,' Florimo says.

'Olsen had this presence about him. On a bus trip he'd be there, if he had a spare seat next to him, I'd want to be next to him and hear stories about his life. I was desperate to learn about him and from him.'

Awaiting Florimo and Olsen in the Preliminary final was a determined Eastern Suburbs Roosters reserve-grade side, stacked with first graders, and crafting a game plan with the specific aim of neutralising Olsen. They succeeded and Easts dashed Norths' premiership dreams.

John Blanch's match report in the *Daily Mirror* was titled 'Big O bottled up by Easts' and went into great detail on the tactical moves used: 'to stifle North Sydney's blockbusting five-eighth Olsen Filipaina, Easts switched their halves, Laurie Spina and David Trewhella when on the defensive scrums. Filipaina still proved a handful playing directly opposite the nugget Trewhella.'

Easts coach Jim Morgan said: 'David Trewhella helped slow Olsen up and it gave our lock Mike McLean a better chance to get him.'

Olsen had been Norths' best player, but the extra attention placed on him could not be exploited elsewhere and they were defeated, five tries to three.

* * * * *

With the reserve-grade season over, the focus returned to Norths' first grade and despite his form, Olsen remained on the reserves bench.

Olsen's first-grade replacement, Mark Cannon, provided *Rugby League Week* with some unusual feedback on the man whose position he had taken. 'I watch him in action whenever I can,' he told reporters. 'I'm lucky to have a brilliant player like Olsen to teach me. The man is a genius the way he reads a game, positions himself in defence and sets up play.'

With Norton adhering to a long-held rugby league coaching adage of 'not making changes to a winning team', Olsen and Clayton Friend were again on the first-grade bench for the final match of the season against Cronulla. In a must-win game the Bears downed the Cronulla Sharks 17–10 to finish the season on 30 points. They had ended up equal fifth with Balmain with a dreaded playoff awaiting.

By the time Olsen and Friend returned to first grade, it was too late. They started on the bench for Norths in the midweek finals playoff match against Balmain and came on in the second half. Despite leading by three points at halftime, Norths succumbed to a resurgent Tigers, coached by Frank Stanton. Balmain progressed to the finals series. Norths' season was over.

'Norths was a social club and a respectful club,' recalls Leslie. 'There were a lot of positive things and they really made an effort to make sure the wives and partners were happy. There were lower stress levels and I had Mark Graham's and Clayton Friend's partners as my close friends. It really was a classy club to be part of. We felt truly welcome.'

Yet Brian 'Chicka' Norton, the coach who had fostered that inclusive culture, was already on his way out. And his replacement for the 1987 season was the man who had succeeded in making Olsen's life hell for four seasons — 'Cranky' Frank Stanton.

* * * * *

On the first Saturday of June 1987, Olsen Filipaina and his reserve-grade teammates walked off North Sydney Oval caked in mud. Torrential rain had fallen all day, soaking the field and the reserve-grade players who sloshed around and fumbled the ball in trying conditions.

After his reserve-grade game, Olsen headed straight for the reserves bench for first grade, put on his jacket and waited for the players to run out for Norths' first-grade match against Canterbury.

Olsen says: 'I was going through the motions at Norths; I would rather have been somewhere else.'

For 12 consecutive weeks, this had been Olsen's life at North Sydney. At the first training session of the 1987 season, he walked up to Frank Stanton and said, 'Don't worry, I know where I'm playing. Reserve grade.' According to Olsen, Frank just smiled in response.

It was turning out to be Olsen's worst year. Instead of playing Olsen, Frank Stanton picked a range of rookies, out-of-position players and journeymen at centre and five-eighth. It was death by a thousand paper cuts as Olsen turned up to training, only to hear his name read out in reserve grade regardless of form.

'Frank brought in more discipline and liked intensity at all times,' says halfback Paul McCaffery, who played alongside Olsen in the reserves. 'But for Olsen the intensity came in games, and on that paddock he was dynamic and spectacular. We all knew Olsen and Frank had clashed at Balmain and they weren't cosy.'

McCaffery, now a schoolteacher on the NSW North Coast, got to know Olsen's on-field game the more they played together: 'The contact he generated was unbelievable,' says McCaffery. 'He would bump blokes like a human pinball — it was unusual for us and fun to watch. One run from Olsen could create momentum for our team — usually it was the forwards supposed to create the forward momentum, but he would come in and drive and make valuable metres and pump us up. He was way better than reserve grade and created havoc down there.'

Stanton's team was 'over-trained', according to North Sydney historian Andrew Moore who wrote that they were 'equipped to perform effectively as marathon runners but less so as footballers'.

The freedom that players enjoyed under Chicka Norton in 1986 had been eliminated by Stanton's rigid regime.

It wasn't all bad for Norths' Kiwi contingent — Mark Graham

remained as captain, while Clayton Friend played every game in the season and would be awarded Norths' club player of the year.

Friend saw first hand that Australian coaches did not have the man-management tools to get the best out of Olsen: 'I played next to him and know he was a great player. He didn't get on with the coach, but Norths suffered that year from not having him in first grade.'

Yet Olsen's supporters had watched Norths' season unfold with a growing sense of dread. The club was in a terrible slump, sitting second last on the competition ladder after six consecutive losses. And still Stanton had not turned to his big Kiwi five-eighth.

'The Aussie way is someone has to be dropped, someone has to pay, a head has to roll if they lose,' contends Sir Peter Leitch. 'Always dropping and promoting. You cannot do that with confidence players and you definitely can't do that with Polynesians. You stop caring about them long enough and they'll eventually stop caring about you — and then everyone loses.

'Olsen wasn't the type to argue. He would play where they wanted him to play, take his cheque and keep moving and do other things in life. It wasn't life and death to him. To not start Olsen at all in a season that Norths were losing so badly was just ridiculous and petty.'

From Frank Stanton's vantage point, Olsen mostly dealt with reserve-grade coach Denis Constantine: 'I don't recall much going on with me and Olsen that year,' Frank says: 'He didn't play a lot of first grade so I wouldn't have had a lot to do with him.'

* * * * *

With halftime approaching in the rainy Round 14 first-grade match against Canterbury at North Sydney Oval, Olsen was sitting on the bench with his reserve-grade teammates when he received an unlikely 'Hail Mary' call from Stanton to warm up. Five-eighth Greg Florimo had suffered a corked thigh and Stanton needed a replacement.

Olsen obliged. He took off his rain jacket and charged on to the sodden field alongside his Kiwi mate, Clayton Friend. 'I've never felt more comfortable and at home than when I saw Olsen stomping on to the field through the mud that day with a big smile on his face,' Friend later remembered.

With the scores locked at 2-all, Olsen decided to make his first first-grade appearance of the season count. He churned through the mud, broke Canterbury's defensive line to set up the only try of the match, and even completed two spectacular chases through the mud to ankle-tap breakaway opponents, both times saving certain tries.

Frank Stanton remembers the day clearly: 'Norths won that game when Olsen came on at halftime. I knew Olsen could handle the wet ball and he controlled the game and we ended up winning it.'

The report in the *Daily Telegraph* read: 'On came mud-runner Olsen Filipaina who motored through the quagmire with ease, to break tackles and set up a series of attacking raids including the try.'

Reporters gushed over Olsen's performance and lauded Stanton's decision to bring him on for the second half. 'The decision to replace Florimo with Filipaina may have proved a match winner,' reported the *Daily Mirror*.

'He showed all of them that they were wrong,' says Clayton Friend. 'He's all class and he won us the game, no doubt about it. Straight off the bench out of reserves and he breaks a six-game losing streak for us! Really, what a waste of an amazing talent.'

Olsen's match-winning performance to personally airlift Frank Stanton and the Bears out of a terrible losing streak was his final act as a first-grade player in Sydney, his 107th game across three clubs. He was dropped back to reserves the following week and cut from the club by the end of the season.

Clayton Friend notes a lot of turbulence for Olsen and other teammates that year: 'I was honoured to play with Olsen for his last game in first grade. Olsen played good football in reserves and it was frustrating for him that his form wasn't considered because of a personal battle with Frank who was good at tactics but not good at managing individuals.'

For Friend, Olsen didn't need to communicate his problems: 'He didn't need to confide in me because it was common knowledge, mate, that with Stanton, Olly couldn't play for him.

* * * * *

Olsen knew the guillotine was coming and it was officially announced in the *Daily Telegraph* in a story by Peter Frilingos headlined "Bears Chop Filipaina'.

Frilingos interviewed Olsen on the Norths' situation and Olsen replied coldly and pragmatically: 'Frank Stanton is now the coach of North Sydney. He doesn't like me and I don't like him so it was time to look for another club.'

When asked why Olsen had only one opportunity in first grade that year, Frank Stanton recalls: 'Olsen's performances weren't better than the people playing ahead of him in first grade. It's not all about Olsen, it's about the 13 blokes who are in the first team and them being rewarded for their extra efforts at training.'

* * * * *

Yet Olsen's legacy, both for his club and his country, was already starting to materialise. His replacement at five-eighth, Greg Florimo, would go on to play 285 first-grade games for the Bears — a club record — and in retirement he became the chief executive of the club.

Florimo has never forgotten the role Olsen played in his formative years as a Winfield Cup player: 'Olsen was a real leader for me as a young fella coming through, and I was a centre running off him at five-eighth.

'I watched him and the way that he played his game. I'd obviously seen him on television, and I thought, well, that's the way you play as a five-eighth. So that's how I started being very direct in my running, just go straight at the line, based on what I saw Olsen doing.'

That year, as Norths finished ninth, Manly's fullback Darrell Williams became the first New Zealand player to win a premiership in Sydney when Manly defeated Canberra 18–8 at the SCG in front of over 50,000 fans.

As a young man in Auckland, Williams had stayed up late to watch Olsen carve up the Sydney competition.

'I was absolutely inspired by Olsen growing up in New Zealand,' says Williams. 'Here he was — one of our brown faces, a magical Polynesian on television showing them what we could do!'

Williams was not the first New Zealander to be inspired by Olsen, nor would he be the last. Although Olsen was on the way out, a new generation of Pasifika talent was rising. Over the next two decades, as Olsen receded from the spotlight, they would fundamentally reshape the sport of rugby league.

10

THE GALLOPING GARBO

> '"O" for Olsen.'
> — David Tua, 1992

In 1988, Australia's bicentenary year, rugby league entered a new phase of growth. The introduction of the Newcastle Knights, Gold Coast Seagulls and Brisbane Broncos saw the game commit to a national footprint for the first time.

A brand-new and gleaming Sydney Football Stadium opened its doors to the public. And the best players in the world converged upon the newly formed National Rugby League (NRL) with Wally Lewis captaining the Brisbane Broncos and British superstar Ellery Hanley joining the Balmain Tigers.

Olsen had spent the summer training like a man possessed. Newspapers published shots of him looking fit and lean, and they reported that he had dropped below 90 kilograms — 'his lightest weight in six years,' according to *The Sun*.

After being cut from North Sydney, Olsen told journalist John Bilic of his 'road to Damascus' conversion to fitness fanatic: 'I started training hard in frustration at what happened and I really started enjoying it. . . . I really got into it over summer — tennis every morning and competitions on Saturday plus beach runs, squash and light weights. All that plus four hours on the bins every morning. It starts to add up.'

He set his sights on rejoining his old club Balmain, now led by two-time premiership coach Warren Ryan. Olsen knew that Ryan, like Frank Stanton, was a strict disciplinarian who appreciated structured football and fitness.

When Olsen arrived at Leichhardt Oval for training, his old teammates were shocked at his weight loss. 'I had to look twice to make sure it was Olsen,' Wayne Pearce told one reporter.

Ryan gave Olsen his chance in trial matches against Easts and New South Wales Country, where Olsen scored a try and enjoyed playing alongside Kiwis teammate, newly signed halfback Gary Freeman. Freeman, fresh off a premiership in Auckland with the Northcote Tigers, was in the early stages of adjusting to Sydney life.

Freeman remembers the shock and sadness when Olsen did not get offered an incentive contract by the Tigers' player recruiting committee.

For Freeman there was a silver lining: 'Olsen was by my side when I made my test debut against Australia in 1986 and I was there alongside him for his last game for a Winfield Cup side. He still played well in the trials, but it wasn't the same Olsen, he was too light. We shook hands and he just passed the torch to me.'

Although it was disappointing for Freeman not to have Olsen by his side, he was glad to be playing in Sydney and part of a Winfield Cup team on the rise. Coach Warren Ryan put Freeman through a lengthy apprenticeship, preferring others in the first half of the season before he staked his claim as a first-grade regular.

Freeman learnt the hard way that Ryan was a stickler for discipline: 'You had to buy in to Warren's system or you were out in the cold,' Freeman says. 'I was dropped from the Tigers for being late to training. It wasn't my fault, but it didn't matter as no one cared about my excuse. I always made allowances for Sydney traffic after that.'

It also took Freeman some time to work out the structures: 'Whilst I was disappointed not to be playing first grade straight away, I realised that it was an inescapable fact that the game wasn't going to change for me; I had to change for the Aussie style. The coaches would knock the edges off your game and weren't interested really in individual flair which they tried to stamp out in favour of mistake-free footy.'

The stifling of individual creativity was puzzling for Freeman, because Aussie talent scouts in New Zealand were interested in the special players, who then had to fit into a pattern and adjust in Australia.

'In New Zealand we were given a free hand to try things out,' Freeman recalls. 'Under Warren Ryan you stuck to the plan and were not allowed to do anything spontaneous. He made it clear to me that it was his way or the highway in a match against Cronulla where I tried a chip kick in my own half. He dragged me straight off the field.'

And that was Olsen's main issue according to Freeman — he never really accepted the straitjacket that Sydney coaches put on him: 'Olsen and I were the last of a cultural era who played for fun and a case of beer for man of the match. We wanted to win badly but it wasn't the only thing. We tried to entertain.'

For Freeman, the real respect for Olsen came from the players: 'Amongst us players, away from fans and media, Olsen was an absolute legend on and off the park,' he explains.

'He had so much power and his bump was legendary, crashing into players and powering through. He had great skills and wherever he played there was always excitement that every time he had the ball, he would crash through defences or give a great pass.'

* * * * *

Olsen's gruelling off-season training schedule had made him lean for the first time in his life but marooned without his customary weight-based power. Line breaks, once a feature of his game, were harder to achieve. 'I was just another fit guy running around,' says Olsen. 'I lost my game and couldn't play my way — I got down to around 85 kg and was a shadow of myself.'

Warren Ryan ended his season before it got started, cutting him from the 36-man squad. His first-grade career was officially over and perhaps fittingly he did not get to play a match in the new reality of the

NRL era with its scientific intense training, fulltime professional focus and data reliance.

In 1988, his Kiwis teammate Gary Freeman made 15 appearances for the Balmain Tigers as the club surged to the grand final only to lose 24–12 to the Canterbury Bulldogs. Along the way, he heard stories from his Tigers teammates about Olsen: how he avoided the road runs and his aversion to the heat. 'The Big O' had already begun his ascent into rugby league mythology.

'You have to realise that the players just loved playing with him,' says Freeman. 'He was the last of his kind. For them it didn't matter if you were a shit trainer. If they loved playing with you, you got respect across the board and all of the players thought he was a legendary talent.'

* * * * *

With no options left in Sydney, Olsen headed to the bush. He signed with Bowral Blues, a Group 6 club from the rural Southern Highlands of New South Wales. Olsen, wrote Peter Kogoy in *The Australian*, 'is understood to have signed a record contract for a Group 6 club and Filipaina is under tremendous pressure to produce the goods for the Blues'.

Olsen followed in the footsteps of other Māori and Pasifika Sydney NSWRL pioneers who 'went bush' after completing their Sydney careers. The alumni include Samoan Oscar Danielson with the Corrimal Cougars, Māori Henry Tatana with the Cessnock Goannas and Olsen's old Māori Balmain teammate Lloyd Martin who was able to deliver two premierships for the Bega Roosters on the South Coast of NSW.

When Olsen ran onto Loseby Park in Bowral for his first home match in March 1988 he was carrying the hopes of a proud rugby league town. The Blues were established in 1914 — just six years after the foundation clubs in Sydney — and over their history they had won a record 13 premierships.

The blue jersey which Olsen wore was the same Bowral rugby league colours and badge that a young Donald Bradman once wore, before 'the Don' became the greatest Australian cricketer of all time.

Olsen played all but two games for Bowral in 1988, combining well with an old Norths teammate, Graham Murchie, and leading the club to the grand final. A gutting one-point loss to arch-rivals Mittagong meant the season finished on an anti-climactic note, but for Olsen it was an enjoyable year nonetheless.

'The drive down there took forever but I was glad to get out of Sydney. There were a lot of good people there as well, and it was the first time I had played with farmers. I remember I was super fit, but it was no good for my style of football. I couldn't break tackles or handle the knocks as easily.'

There was one downside: cheap-shot merchants looking to make their name against the old fading gunfighter. 'That's how you earn half your money in the bush,' Olsen says. 'People pay money to see you cop one from a kid and it happened almost every match — someone had it in for you to belt you. I would pass the ball, which would go well across the field and you would cop a whack. Nothing hard or tough about it when it's from behind.'

* * * * *

Olsen had one final piece of personal business to complete in rugby league. At the end of the 1988 season he received an invitation to captain the Western Samoa team in the newly minted Pacific Rugby League Cup to be held in his father's birth city, the Western Samoan capital of Apia.

In addition to Western Samoa, the other five participating teams were: Cook Islands, Tonga, New Zealand Māori, Tokelau and American Samoa.

The convenor of the tournament, New Zealander Peter Donnelly, told *Rugby League Week* that the enthusiasm and passion for league in the Islands was 'feverish'.

Olsen was joining a long tradition of both Kiwis and All Blacks returning at the end of their careers to coach, captain or play for Samoa, their ancestral homeland. The group included Kiwis Nigel Vagana, Frank Pritchard and Oscar Danielson and All Blacks Sir Bryan Williams, John Schuster, Va'aiga Tuigamala and Sir Michael Jones.

For Olsen, an on-field reconnection to Polynesia was a joyous chapter in his life: 'I'd been to Western Samoa five times in my life so I had some good relationships but it was amazing how they took me in, especially Dad's sister and aunties in Upolo. After everything that had happened with Dad and Mum it was a very emotional reunion.'

Olsen's only condition of participating was that the Samoan team was not to be picked just from players in Auckland. He insisted at least half of the team had to be homegrown Samoan players from the local competition that had kickstarted the year before.

'It was no good for Samoan rugby league if we just selected players from overseas,' says Olsen. 'They really seemed to appreciate the gesture and the locals lifted alongside the Kiwi Samoans that were picked. We had a wonderful 'ava ceremony and went to the coconut milk factory together. That was a real highlight, to see where it comes from.'

His cultural immersion included eating raw palolo worms at 2 am out on the reefs: 'What a night. My teammates did everything they could to give me a great Samoan experience.'

The players also took him to meet Samoan storytellers where he would learn about the stories of the great men in Samoan history. How the Polynesian people had conquered the Pacific, one third of the world's surface, seeking out, locating and colonising every habitable island in the ocean as far away as Hawaii, and Rapa Nui (Easter Island), thousands of kilometres away on the outer edge of 'The Polynesian Triangle'.

He learnt how his Polynesian ancestors could sail into the wind in their double-hulled canoes and would explore the Pacific Ocean like a highway using their ancient knowledge of the environment.

Environmental knowledge was life and death for Olsen's ancestors who had to understand the seasonal changing of wind directions, different types of birds and their flying range from land, how to treat different currents like river systems, how to read cloud shades and navigate by the stars, the sun and the moon. All the stars had names and featured in songs.

When explorer Captain Cook arrived at Tahiti, he was shocked to find a people who had mastered open ocean navigation without compass or instruments, millennia before his European navigators were brave enough to break away from the shorelines of Europe, Asia and Africa.

Cook marvelled at how his Tahitian navigator Tupaia could at any time know the precise direction of Tahiti without a compass. It was Tupaia who taught Cook how to use the prevailing winds to his advantage.

'They never taught us any of that in school in New Zealand,' Olsen says. 'It was mind blowing.'

* * * * *

The Pacific Cup tournament kicked off in October 1988 and Olsen found some slight cultural adjustments had to be made.

Olsen hadn't learnt the Samoan language growing up in South Auckland and his insistence on the inclusion of local-based players meant there were communication hurdles that he had to overcome. 'I had a crash course in Samoan and learnt phrases like "Pasi palu" which means "Pass the ball".'

Western Samoa defeated Cook Islands and Tokelau in the pool games leading to a semi-final against a strong Tonga team including ex-Kiwi international Duane Mann and ex-St George pioneer, rampaging John Fifita.

In a preview of fiery future Pacific tests, the ancient Polynesian rivals had a titanic back-and-forth clash, with Western Samoa prevailing 40–30. Olsen recalls: 'We were bruised after that one.'

Awaiting them in the final was fellow undefeated pool leaders,

New Zealand Māori, a strong team that had played together often and included future Kiwi test stars Tawera Nikau and Kelly Shelford.

In the official match report, New Zealand rugby league statesman Ron McGregor wrote of a seesawing battle between the Polynesian cousins: 'The New Zealand Māori played good running football, tackled hard, handled well and their support play was outstanding. It needed to be, to survive the second half drive by Western Samoa, but they were able to defend desperately.'

The final score was a win to New Zealand Māori 26–16 in what was a joyous day for Olsen. Like many modern Pasifika people, he had multiple cultural identities and his came together on a field in Apia: 'It was my first time going up against the haka at international level and responding with a true Samoan war dance that the locals taught us,' explains Olsen. 'I received great love from both teams and nobody made me feel bad. It's amazing how Pacific people understand the cultural mix.'

Although Olsen was forced off the field in the second half of the final with an injury, he still won the award for sportsman of the tournament.

Reflecting on the experience, Olsen feels it was great to acknowledge his father's side of the family: 'There are a lot of players these days who have mixed ancestries and have to choose. I was lucky to have represented my Māori side playing for New Zealand and it felt great to acknowledge my Samoan side. I loved giving back and it felt like home, but I must admit I didn't know the words to the Samoan anthem.'

* * * * *

Meanwhile, in the 1988 Winfield Cup, the Kiwis kept coming as 10 fresh New Zealanders joined the competition. Sam 'Rambo' Stewart, a Wellington police officer, had joined the Newcastle Knights and was named captain of their inaugural Winfield Cup side.

'Playing in the Winfield Cup has become a lifeline for the Kiwis,' wrote Darren Hadland in *Rugby League Week*. 'Like the West Indian cricketers . . . their sport has become their escape.'

For Olsen, it all felt a million miles away. In 1989, a season in which two Kiwi players, Gary Freeman and Brent Todd, lined up against each other for Balmain and Canberra in the grand final, Olsen took a year off rugby league altogether.

The break allowed him time to watch his son John play junior league and for him to play competitive tennis and squash, the lack of physical contact giving his body a rest. It was family time.

'There's Olsen Filipaina the football player and Olsen Filipaina the dad, who are both very different,' says his daughter, Louise. 'Dad wasn't around much in the early years due to work and that was the first year we had a fulltime dad. He was quite hard on us growing up, I suppose trying to do the best he could to teach us to be the humans we are today. He was always trying to steer us in the right direction.'

By 1990, though, Olsen was ready to return to rugby league. When he was approached by Ryde Eastwood Hawks to captain the side in the inaugural year of Sydney's Metropolitan Cup, he jumped at the opportunity.

'I had a few options,' says Olsen. 'Having the year off helped me think about things. Instead of going to a club I don't know, like a gun for hire, I thought, why don't I give something back. I couldn't have thought of a better place to finish up serious footy.'

Ryde Eastwood was a family club to Olsen. It maintained a sister-club relationship with his junior club, Māngere East, and was the club of the Dries family who had adopted him during his early years at Balmain. They had always had an open offer for Olsen to join them.

Joining Olsen at semi-professional Ryde Eastwood was his ex-Norths and Kiwis teammate, Clayton Friend, who had some time to kill before taking up an offer in England with Carlisle. Together, they set out on Olsen's final professional rugby league adventure, a year that he enjoyed more than any other in his 15-year pro career.

From the outset, he appeared more comfortable with the media — even playful at times. And the reporters seemed gentler and more reflective of his contribution. 'While he may be a bit older and slower than when he ripped international sides apart, Olsen Filipaina can still cause opposition players plenty of headaches,' wrote Jon Geddes of the *Mirror*.

'The big Kiwi is making his presence felt this season as lock and captain of Ryde Eastwood. The "Big O" had a varied career in Sydney, but on his day there was no more damaging back in the competition. Sometimes it appeared that the highly disciplined atmosphere of the Winfield Cup stifled his talents.'

In an interview with the *Sydney Morning Herald*, Olsen was in fine form, telling John McDonald about his appointment as captain: 'Coach Ken Wilson said he wanted me to lead from the front. I think he only made me captain because I was the oldest bloke in the team. I only came back because my cabinet is full of tennis trophies!'

After his comeback match for Ryde Eastwood, Olsen told McDonald that he was a physical wreck: 'I was very sore. The guys asked me to come back to the club for a few beers and I said I'm going straight home to the bath and wait for Meals On Wheels.'

McDonald, who obviously enjoyed interviewing a more relaxed version of Olsen, attempted to summarise the 'enigma': 'Those few comments reflect the man: unaffected, honest, humorous and with a detached perspective about it all,' McDonald wrote.

'He is all the good things which are at odds with all the bad reviews he has received. Filipaina is that figure most beloved of sports journalists, the genuine character. He might well hold the world record for being referred to as a sporting "enigma" or the world record for being described as standing in tackles like a colossus, making blockbusting tackles and exhibiting bone-jarring defence.'

In return Olsen offered some street-wise philosophy to *Herald* readers' sharing some insights from his time in Sydney: 'In Sydney I'd tense up, get scared to make a mistake. The coach would blow you up at halftime and replace you. Basically I couldn't play my own game. You had to play how the coach said. In Sydney it's just business, cut-throat. The battle over positions is that fierce. You make false friends. They'd say to you "Good game, Olsen" and then "How come he's playing first grade again?" to others.'

* * * * *

Ryde Eastwood's coach, Ken Wilson, was the Newtown Jets captain for their final two years before the Jets were expelled from the Winfield Cup at the end of 1983. He had played against Olsen and was one of the few Australian coaches to understand what made Olsen tick. 'Olsen is a free spirit,' he told *Rugby League Week*, 'and if you try and shackle him you don't get the best out of him. I couldn't be happier and at this level in a good side he contributes plenty, he has a lot of skills. When Olsen tackles a bloke they stay tackled, there are quite a few players that can vouch for that.'

Wilson recalls a funny story from his final playing days for Newtown when they lined up against Olsen's Balmain: 'I clearly remember Newtown coach Warren Ryan's team talk before we ran onto the field. He was only worried about Olsen and gave us instructions not to say anything or do anything dirty to Olsen. Ryan told all of us: "It's like poking a bear, leave him alone!"'

At 34 years of age, Olsen's big-match experience proved invaluable for Wilson. During the semi-final against Wests, he single-handedly turned a 10-point halftime deficit into a 13-point victory.

There were shades of his 1985 magic when he chip-kicked the ball to break the defensive line, kicked it off the ground into the in-goal area, and then dived over to score what one reporter called 'a spectacular and inspirational try'.

The following week, he led Ryde Eastwood to a 19–6 win over Hills in a grand final that was attended by a big crowd and beamed live throughout the nation. A decade after he had arrived in Sydney, Olsen was finally able to lift a premiership trophy.

'What the books don't show,' says Wilson, 'is how Olsen spent endless hours mentoring and coaching our young guys. Olsen was a bit of a cult figure so they listened to his every word. He was humble and just one of the blokes. The young ones couldn't believe their luck and he was good for everyone involved. I was so proud when he held up that trophy.'

The next year, the *Weekly Times* reported Olsen had moved down to Balmain A-Grade to play with West Ryde Denistone who appointed Olsen as their captain-coach in 1991. 'The Stones' were seeking their first A-grade title and finally Olsen got to put the players through the torment of training.

Olsen says: 'After all those years I couldn't bring myself to run hard training sessions so they brought a cop in to do the tough stuff.'

And he duly delivered 'The Stones' their first-ever premiership trophy.

* * * * *

'When Olsen looks back on his career, I hope he doesn't just think about the game and the scores,' says Oscar Kightley. 'I hope he looks back and thinks about how he was the right man at the right time and what he did was so much more than numbers and 80 minutes of a game of footy. He was an ambassador for us.'

Olsen was an ambassador indeed, but instead of opening borders, he had opened up a pipeline. By 1993, as a record 26 New Zealanders were plying their trade in the National Rugby League, Olsen was 38 years old and playing for a local Māori team in the Parramatta A-Reserve competition.

The team was called MACS — an acronym for Māori Aroha Co-op Society — and played at Redbank Oval in Sydney's west. He played for free, despite an offer from the club sponsor to pay him for his efforts. In one match, a reporter from the *Daily Telegraph-Mirror* was there to witness Olsen create six tries and score one himself in a 48-point demolition of Greystanes.

'Seeing Filipaina use the ball with MACS was like watching a master craftsman ply his trade surrounded by a group of eager apprentices,' wrote the reporter. 'And throughout the game "the Big O" didn't take the broad smile from his face.'

It was, perhaps, the most fitting way for Olsen to begin to wind down his rugby league career — surrounded by his own people, playing park football with carefree abandon. He was, right to the end, a man of the people; the galloping garbo of Sydney rugby league.

With his life at a crossroads, and serious rugby league behind him, Olsen had a decision to make on whether he should return to live in New Zealand. With the addition of his new son Quin, he now had three children with Leslie who were deeply entrenched in the Australian way of life.

'My family had always been there to support me, so it was time for me to support them,' Olsen explains. 'I would love to have pulled up stumps and gone back to Auckland, but the kids' home was here in Australia and they would have had to leave their school friends.'

After a series of family discussions, Olsen decided to stay in Sydney: 'My life was simple now. I had the garbo run, Leslie was working and the kids were happy, with John in particular settling in to rugby league. If he wanted to get serious about his league, he would have to come over here anyway so we decided to stay.'

For Olsen it was time to enjoy his life and he played league well into his forties, becoming a cult hero on Sydney's northern beaches playing for Manly Cove. For the lucky residents of Ryde, a rugby league legend would sometimes run around with them and play touch footy in the afternoons after he had finished his garbage run.

His two boys John and Quin would play representative rugby league in Sydney and give him great joy as a father and mentor. And he would become a grandfather to Louise's and John's kids.

His continued absence from Auckland due to his 'aviophobia' only enhanced his mythical status across the Tasman Sea.

* * * * *

Perhaps the most enduring and unlikely legacy of Olsen originated in 1992, when Samoan heavyweight boxer David Tua, from Māngere, was invited to appear on the celebrity version of New Zealand game show *Wheel of Fortune*.

After spinning the wheel, the softly spoken Tua was asked to select a letter of the alphabet. 'O for Olsen,' he replied. With his strong Samoan accent, the words, somewhat indistinct, to some Anglo-Celtic ears sounded closer to 'O for Awesome'. Tua soon became a subject of national ridicule and the phrase entered New Zealand's lexicon.

Tua, a close friend of the Filipaina family, tried to explain that for South Aucklanders, 'O for Olsen' was a common saying. Olsen had become their vowel of choice. But the phrase 'O for Awesome' stuck fast in the cultural memory of a nation. A brand of beer and a line of T-shirts were produced with the words 'O for Awesome', while Tua himself surrendered and reclaimed it for himself, changing his number plate to 'O4OSUM'.

'They gave me a hard time about saying "O for Awesome", but any Samoan that listens to it will clearly tell you I'm saying "O for Olsen",' Tua says. 'I've made peace with it now and I'm happy that I'm linked in with the great Olsen Filipaina. He inspired us all to be better.'

For Tua, Olsen was a crucial South Auckland prototype: 'Olsen showed us a Polynesian power style, straight over the top with your hips and shoulders. Fast and powerful. We recognised that warrior style and look . . . it's gone on to transform the game.'

* * * * *

Perhaps the greatest descendant of Olsen's hip-and-shoulder Polynesian power game was All Black Jonah Lomu, who in 1994 shot to international stardom after his performance for New Zealand at the Hong Kong Rugby Sevens tournament.

Within 12 months, Lomu would become a bona fide star of the All Blacks, scoring seven tries at the 1995 Rugby World Cup and becoming the first global superstar of rugby's freshly minted professional era.

What few people realised, though, was that Lomu had grown up playing rugby league. He had personally witnessed Olsen dominate

Wally Lewis at Carlaw Park in 1985 and, according to his brother, John, Jonah would imitate Olsen running around the backyards and fields of South Auckland.

'I pretended to be Manukau man Clayton Friend,' John says. 'But Jonah always played as Olsen because he loved his physical style. He also liked that Olsen was unforgiving to the other team.'

During the 1990s, Lomu would emerge as one of the most fearsome rugby union players of all time. He became synonymous with the resurgent All Blacks. After he retired, New Zealand's TV One organised a *This Is Your Life* tribute special for Lomu in 2007. Olsen was one of his invited guests, flown in from Australia for the event.

The guests providing tributes and stories were mostly All Blacks royalty including former coaches John Hart and Laurie Mains and former All Blacks teammates Eric Rush, Frank Bunce and Glen Osborne.

When Olsen appeared on stage, Lomu looked overjoyed. Olsen revealed that he had received great support from Jonah in dealing with the kidney disease that they both suffered from and would end Lomu's life prematurely at the age of 40 in 2015.

Jonah's brother John Lomu remembers the night well and says Olsen was Lomu's hero and he always played as 'Olsen' in bullrush and in their backyard games. But Olsen was not just Lomu's hero for his rugby league skills but also for his resilience:

'Jonah was always able to use Olsen for inspiration when he got dropped from the team and he would sit back and say, "Hey, look, my hometown hero has gone through this and he came out the other side",' says John Lomu. 'Olsen didn't give in and kept plugging at it and Jonah took a lot from that.'

There were other reasons Lomu would never forget Olsen, including an incident John recalls when Jonah went on a schoolboy rugby union tour to Australia with Wesley College and, through an oversight, the players' accommodation had not been booked.

In desperation, a tour member called Olsen who billetted the players in his house in Ryde without hesitation.

Olsen recalls the night vividly: 'It's the Polynesian way and it's unthinkable to say no. I do remember the players took forever to shower but to say thanks they performed a haka in our backyard about 9 o'clock one night that shook the whole neighbourhood.'

Olsen's impact lives on in mainstream New Zealand. Ngāpuhi comedian Mike King wrote a story for the Māngere Easts Hawks' 40th jubilee commemorative book that showed how deeply Olsen touched lives.

'My oldest boy Nathan was born in 1986 with congenital heart disease. He had transposed greater arteries and a narrowed aorta. We were told a week after his birth that his chances of living were very slim and he told us to prepare for the worst. So when it came to picking his middle name my wife Rose said to me we should name him after Olsen Filipaina (she knew I was a huge fan of the Big-O) as he was a fighter and the toughest bastard we knew. It worked a treat. He had open heart surgery four times and despite the odds he pulled through. Nathan Olsen King is now your average 17-year-old know it all prick. True story.'

* * * * *

In 1995, as rugby union continued to reassert its dominance, New Zealand rugby league counter-attacked with the birth of the Auckland Warriors. In front of more than 30,000 fans and Tina Turner at Auckland's Mt Smart Stadium, the Warriors became the nation's first professional sporting team and the NRL's newest expansion club.

Many of the players who ran onto the field, including halves Stacey Jones and Gene Ngamu, were of Māori or Polynesian descent. Jones, who eventually became the first life member of the rebadged New Zealand Warriors, was an Olsen devotee.

'By playing in the Winfield Cup,' Stacey Jones later explained, 'players like Olsen — alongside Mark Graham, the Sorensens, Clayton Friend, Gary Freeman, Dean Bell and Hugh McGahan — delivered the base respect for Kiwi rugby league that led to the establishment of the Auckland Warriors in the NRL. That's where it started.'

It's a view shared by master-coach Graham Lowe, who was a part-owner of the Warriors in the late 1990s. To Lowe, players like Jones and Ngamu were following in the footsteps of a giant.

'Olsen was the first great Polynesian playmaker,' says Lowe. 'Before him, the Polynesians in Australia were mostly in the forwards, not the thinking man's spots in the halves. He played under duress on many occasions, was disrespected in reserve grade and he coped, providing hope to thousands that followed. Without him and a few others setting everything rolling, there would be no New Zealand Warriors.'

From his home in North Ryde, Olsen watched the rise of the Auckland Warriors with interest. More than once, as he watched their games in front of the television, he wondered how his career might have panned out had an Auckland-based club existed during the 1980s. All that homesickness and cultural displacement might have been avoided.

As Olsen watched rugby league transform from a working man's game into a commercial juggernaut, his sense of loss became acute. Almost all the institutions that he had been part of had begun their decline.

In 1999, following a civil war in Australian rugby league, his first club the Balmain Tigers merged with rivals Western Suburbs Magpies to become the Wests Tigers. Another of his former clubs, North Sydney, merged for a time with Manly before exiting the first-grade competition in 2002. Even his bush team the Bowral Blues closed their doors.

Dwindling player numbers and finances forced the Ryde Eastwood Hawks, the club where he won his first premiership, into a merger with Balmain in 2005. And his favourite football ground, Auckland's Carlaw Park, was closed to the public in 2007 to be redeveloped as student accommodation.

* * * * *

Recognition for Olsen's services to rugby league trickled in. In 2007 in Wellington, he was inducted into the New Zealand Rugby League Hall of Fame, the 'Legends of League', alongside his friend Gary Freeman and Roy Christian, a Norfolk Island descendant of Fletcher Christian and the first Pacific Islander captain of the Kiwis.

Olsen Filipaina, Kiwis test player no. 529, who scored 108 points in his 29 tests for New Zealand, the eighth highest points-scorer in the Kiwis' history, was inducted and sits alongside 51 all-time legends of the game.

Richard Becht, author, journalist and Kiwis media manager, has no higher praise for Olsen's legacy: 'I was on the "Legends of League" judging committee and I pushed hard for Olsen to be inducted,' says Becht: 'He sits among the top echelon for his contribution — for his character, his skills and he undeniably had an impact on the game. In judging a legend — it's always about what memories they leave behind — I'll never forget what he did and what he was.'

The 2007 NZRL 'Legends of League' induction ceremony was an auspicious occasion hosted at Wellington Stadium by Helen Clark, the New Zealand Prime Minister who was also the patron of New Zealand Rugby League. As the officials, guests and players settled in at their tables, a security guard approached Olsen and asked him to come outside to settle a disturbance at the stadium entrance.

Olsen went outside to be joyfully greeted by his Uncle Mane and 15 of his Ngāpuhi relatives who had driven for four hours from Hastings to Wellington to pay tribute to Olsen's induction. Stadium security would not let them in due to the Prime Minister's office security requirement to vet all attendees in advance.

Uncle Mane was resplendent in a Māori cloak and had come to perform a traditional pōwhiri welcome to represent the family and honour Olsen's induction. After greeting Olsen, security explained that they could not let Mane and his family in.

Olsen told the head of security that if his relatives were not let in, he would leave with them to celebrate at a pub: 'I said to them that if they don't let my whānau in, then I'm out of here and I left it up to them. They've come so far to pay their respect and I can't leave them out here.

When your whānau comes to support you it's powerful.'

After a 20-minute stand-off, security relented and his relatives were invited inside and performed an emotional haka to mark his induction.

Olsen says: 'Their performance was the highlight of the ceremony; it was the best thing ever. I was really proud of them and the New Zealand Rugby League came good and gave them all tickets to the test match. They'd never been before and were over the moon.'

Olsen says when he got back to his table after receiving the award and family tribute, there wasn't a dry eye: 'Legends like Phil Orchard and others were very emotional and they could not believe what my whānau had done. I felt a lot of emotion myself. The whole journey sank in that night. To think about going from walking barefoot in the ice to training as a kid to being in the Hall of Fame with all those legends. And with such aroha. The love of your own people, the people who know you and don't judge you, who make you feel comfortable — it was the most beautiful thing and I got to share my achievement with my mother.'

* * * * *

The following year in 2008 Olsen's mother passed away and he and his family were devastated. 'My biggest regret,' says Olsen, 'is that I wasn't able to protect my mother from my father. She was our heartbeat, our everything and there were hundreds of people who also considered her a mother.'

Her obituary in the *Manukau Courier* read: 'Sissie Filipaina (nee Lemon) has passed away. She is the much-loved mother of my mates Kiwi great Olsen and his long-serving police officer and Manukau city councillor brother Alf Filipaina.

'She lay in state at the Māngere East Rugby League Club and travelled home to Te Huruhi Marae at Awarua in the Hokianga this week for burial. She must have been a terrific woman because her boys are a credit to her.'

* * * * *

In 2009, at an event in Auckland, Olsen was inducted into the Samoan Sports Hall of Fame alongside his childhood hero All Black Pasifika pioneer Sir Bryan Williams.

Olsen was interviewed and quoted in the commemorative brochure: 'It's a great honour because I am very proud of my Māori and Samoan heritage. Being Samoan to me is being respectful, humble, proud, fearless and disciplined. As an 'aiga we looked after each other.'

* * * * *

Some people, though, considered that his pioneering role should have brought even greater reward than inductions into various halls of fame. Tony Kemp, who played 25 tests for the Kiwis between 1989 and 1995, feels that Olsen was on par with great Polynesian rugby union pioneers Sir Bryan Williams and Sir Michael Jones.

'If Sir Bryan Williams and Sir Michael Jones have knighthoods for being pioneers, then so should Olsen,' says Kemp.

It's a difficult situation to change because, according to Kemp, the league community in New Zealand is not a group given to sentimental gestures.

'Sadly, rugby league people are humble and never push their own barrow. It's not right and we are selling ourselves short as a country, that lack of parity in acknowledgment is holding back rugby league. Look at Australia — Wally has his own bronze statue and Olsen has nothing. When it really matters, rugby league is still a second-class citizen in New Zealand.'

Kemp says it is New Zealand as a collective that is at fault: 'We don't recognise our working-class heroes like Olsen who put us on the map, a man who suffered abuse from cowards and did so much for us. But despite it all, when he was wearing the number 6, all of New Zealand believed we could win.'

Olsen's teammate James 'The Finisher' Leuluai feels there may never be another Olsen: 'A man of his size with his fundamental skills was amazing,' Leuluai says. 'He could command the game, was hard to handle, was good on his feet and had brutal defence. Don't ask the media about Olsen. They were interested in labelling him and then not having to think about him again. Ask the Aussie players, they will tell you.'

Leuluai remembers Olsen's impact on his peers in New Zealand: 'He gave us a pathway to follow. We forget now, but back then, Australia was a great unknown for us. Players would go over and never come back. He paved the way for us and made it easier for all of us to get away.

'And when I played alongside him, I always remember how good I felt having Olly there next to me, always teaching me to be better. He would happily attract the defence, giving me the freedom and space to score tries. There were always gaps and opportunities hanging off Olly. He cared about me off the field as well. That's a man.'

For a quiet man, Olsen had enormous influence according to tough Kiwis enforcer prop Kevin Tamati: 'Olsen didn't talk a lot about how he was going to play, what he was going to do. But in the change room all of the players respected Olly for his kōrero — the direction he would give us through his talk. When he had anything to say everybody listened, end of story. What he said he was going to do, he did it and his mana was respected by one and all. Even in banter he had cheeky comebacks — they were rare, but they always got you.'

Tamati also has great sympathy and empathy for Olsen's endurance of racism during both his Sydney club career and his Kiwis career: 'We copped a lot of racism and it was sad,' says Tamati.

'We would work our butts off to get selected and represent our whānau — all of our extended family would watch the TV with their families. And five minutes in someone is calling you a "black cunt" or a "good for nothing nigger". They felt it was their divine right to bring colour into a professional game, the highest level of the game. It was disgraceful and cowardly.'

For author Richard Becht, an often unspoken element of Olsen's career was his unselfishness: 'Olsen was always positive about everyone and didn't need the glory at all.'

For Becht, Olsen's key to living was giving: 'We always used to say that if you were a player you would be mad if you weren't up his arse, following him around. He laid on opportunities with a silver platter. Players would sniff around and support him or he could do it himself. He created so much for others but unlike basketball there is no assists statistic in rugby league. Olsen would have owned the assists wherever he played.'

* * * * *

Whilst Olsen's legacy lives on with players and media, it is with the fans of rugby league that his legend resonates most deeply, transported through the mists of time by those he inspired or entertained.

On social media and television he is brought up frequently, if a player has big thighs or if a big-bodied five-eighth is being blooded or if the Kiwis pick a reserve-grade NRL player or a player runs straight over the top of a defender. The 'Big O' myth lives on.

Facebook is filled with fan tributes to Olsen and they ooze reverence and nostalgia:

'Man, when we have debates about certain players with my grandfather, dad, bros and all my uncles they always put Olsen on the highest of pedestals.'

'My favourite Kiwi player. For him to play as he did against the King is something I get told in hushed reverent voices every time I talk to the older followers of the sport. Was lucky enough to get on the juice with him and Kurt Sorensen one night and the war stories they spoke of will live with me forever . . .'

'Lovely bloke. I grew up in West Ryde and he did our garbage run. Loved to have a chat and throw a footy around with us kids.'

'The Big O bullied and intimidated an Immortal . . .'

'In a test jumper, Olsen is the most consistent player of all time.'

'Me old mate Olsen. Used to always turn up at our club after match functions to have a beer & a laugh & we were a rugby club that was full of Kiwis. Good bloke.'

'Olsen used to be our garbage truck driver and every time he came past the horn was blared because he knew we were Tigers supporters; lovely man and tough as.'

'You paved the way and opened the door for other Polynesians and Kiwis to follow your footsteps and show we are just as good as any other country and for that we'll be forever grateful and respectful, thank you Olsen.'

'I'll never forget the flogging he gave Wally Lewis in that test series. Will take the memories of him playing with me up to the big footy field in the sky.'

'Ran like Hurrell, hit like Matai (bullied and intimidated an Immortal every single time they played) . . . unlike every other great Kiwi who had brilliant tests and not so good tests.'

'Wally Lewis in his time outshone and dominated every stand-off he faced . . . when he played Olsen . . . he would disappear completely in tests. No player, not even Stacey Jones or any name you care to pick, has been able to do that to say any player of the quality of an Andrew Johns, Allan Langer, Darren Lockyer, Jonathan Thurston or a Cameron Smith.'

'They all know who Polynesians are now thanks to you, legend!'

'Who will ever forget the power and skill of this man. A pleasure to watch.'

'u da Man Mr O wit da meanest bump off eva!'

'Without a doubt, my all time, life-long favourite player. The way he ripped the club comp to threads in Auckland was something to behold.'

'Olsen and the like are held in great reverence by past generations because he tamed the supposedly untameable. And made Wally lose his shit.'

'You would struggle to find a better bloke in the game. Even when he played he used to spend his spare afternoons playing touch at West

Ryde with all the local kids. I guess he never forgot where he came from.'

'The Big O, the real mayor of Māngere.'

* * * * *

Sir Graham Lowe sees a great injustice in the lack of recognition for Olsen: 'There's got to be some sort of recognition before too long, not just about his impact as a player but the impact on the Kiwi mentality and our hope,' Lowe says.

'He was disrespected and put in reserve grade and he coped, providing hope to thousands that followed.'

Olsen himself never worried about prizes or accolades. For him, it was enough to have earned a living from the game and to know that he had entertained the crowds. And even though his own chapter of rugby league history was coming to a close, a new one was just starting to be written.

Year on year, Māori and Polynesian players streamed into the top clubs of the National Rugby League . . . household names like Ruben Wiki, Israel Folau, Stacey Jones, Stephen Kearney, Sonny Bill Williams, Nigel Vagana and Benji Marshall delighted fans with their innovation.

They were all heirs of the Pacific Revolution and week in, week out showcased hard-hitting defence, brilliant skills, brute strength and game smarts; as a group they electrified and regenerated the NRL playing style.

'I always get excited to see a Polynesian player make his debut or score a try,' says Olsen. 'To have so many in the league is a dream, to see that talent blossoming. I always said in my time — to those smart-arses who said I was a one-off — "you don't know who Polynesians are now, but you will soon".'

EPILOGUE

THE PACIFIC REVOLUTION

'If Olsen can do it, I can do it.'
— Tawera Nikau, 2017

Ignoring the rain that fell miserably all day, thousands of happy Samoans crammed into Auckland's Mt Smart Stadium, turning the arena into a kind of open-air church.

They were there to see Samoa take on co-host nation New Zealand in the opening match of the 15th Rugby League World Cup on 28 October 2017. Bearing up against the inclement weather, the blue army of Samoan supporters sang hymns, beat their drums, and easily outnumbered the Kiwis fans.

As kick-off approached, the rain miraculously cleared to reveal a beautiful spring night and excited fans sang along to 1984 Māori pop song 'Poi E', the official Rugby League World Cup song in New Zealand.

A man familiar to both sets of fans was escorted onto the pitch, official match ball tucked under his arm, selected as the match-day 'International Legend' to launch the World Cup in New Zealand.

The roar of recognition went up as Olsen Filipaina limped across the turf, placed the match ball on the stand, said a few words, hugged his family, and wandered back over to join the crowd.

'People were calling out "The Big O" and "Legend",' says Daniel

Fraser, the New Zealand media manager of the tournament. 'I remember one big Māori guy with beers and lots of hot dogs charge down to ground level to give Olsen a hongi. It had a real "welcome home" feel.'

It was the second time in two months that Olsen had been introduced to a thankful rugby league crowd. On 3 September 2017, he was welcomed back to Leichhardt Oval as part of the 'Tigers Legends' series, for a speech and halftime acknowledgement at the Wests Tigers' final game of the NRL season.

Now, he was back in his hometown, ready to watch his father's country take on his mother's. Olsen could not separate the two sides: after all, he had played 29 tests and 50 overall matches for New Zealand before playing four matches for Western Samoa in 1988. He had captained both countries and was the perfect choice to walk on the match ball.

At a corporate function hosted by his old friend Sir Peter Leitch, 'the Mad Butcher' and the patron of the Kiwis rugby league side, he was introduced to celebrities and politicians. He shook hands with Prime Minister Jacinda Ardern, New Zealand's newest and youngest prime minister at 37, having been freshly sworn in to the role two days earlier.

'She knew who I was and knew about my career,' Olsen said later, still amazed that she recognised him. 'I've been away from New Zealand so long . . . I thought it was only the oldies who remembered.'

Waiting patiently for Olsen was the imposing figure of Loau Solamalemalo Keneti Sio, Western Samoa's Minister of Education, Sports and Culture. Handsome and square-jawed, Minister Sio took the microphone to make an official speech and praised Olsen for his achievements, his humility, and the pride he brought to the Samoan nation. He then draped a 'Legends of Samoa' medal around Olsen's neck. Olsen remembers 'shaking like a leaf'.

After the presentation, rugby league and union legends lined up to greet Olsen and have their photo taken. Sir Michael Jones gave Olsen a big bearhug and asked about various family members. To Jones, also of Samoan heritage, Olsen was a founding hero for an emerging Pasifika people.

'Just hearing the name Olsen Filipaina lifted you up when you were out on the streets pretending to be your favourite star,' said Jones later. 'He was distinctly Polynesian and stood out and resonated with us in a powerful way. Most important was that Olsen was true to who he was and where he came from. He spoke directly to us that we can make it and we don't need to change.'

Tawera Nikau, a former Kiwis star and NRL legend, congratulated Olsen on the match ball honour.

Nikau was one of many of the next generation of Kiwis who were inspired by Olsen's ability to tough it out in Australia. The big Māori enforcer, who made his NRL debut with the Cronulla Sharks in 1995 and won a premiership with the Melbourne Storm in 1998, can identify with both Olsen's success and his struggle.

After a stellar career including 19 Kiwis appearances, 114 NRL matches and 59 Super League appearances, Nikau lost his wife to suicide and a leg to a motor vehicle accident. He hugged Olsen and told him about life as a selector for the New Zealand Kiwis and his son's progress through the ranks at the Newcastle Knights.

'How great it was to see him with a big grin on his face,' Nikau later recalled. 'Sydney was a rough and tough place and Olsen had to be resilient. I remember thinking, if Olsen can do it, I can do it. Without role models like him it would have been so much harder. He was magical.'

There was a buzz in the room. Change was brewing in rugby league, but in that opening round of the 15th Rugby League World Cup, nobody quite knew its velocity or heat. The Pacific Revolution — the growth of Polynesian and Melanesian dominance at grassroots and NRL level — was about to go global.

* * * * *

Prior to the 2017 Rugby League World Cup, a Pacific nation had never beaten a Tier-1 country — Australia, New Zealand or Great Britain — in a World Cup match. Through the lure of big match payments and, in Australia's case, dangling eligibility for the State of Origin series, the Kangaroos and Kiwis had systematically plundered and stockpiled the best Pasifika talent for years.

New Zealand and Australia had dramatically increased the quality of their own teams through hothousing talent, and drained of their best players, the Island nations were underperforming at international level.

In the lead-up to the tournament, Olsen had unleashed on what he saw as an 'unfair draw' that pitted the physical nations of Tonga, Samoa and New Zealand in one 'Group of Death'.

The Pacific teams, Olsen told Stuff.co.nz, 'aren't going to hold back against each other, while Australia gets a dream run. It's a joke as far as I am concerned.'

But he also predicted that one of the Pacific nations — Tonga, Samoa or Fiji — would break through at this tournament. In 2017, for the first time, the Rugby League International Federation had relaxed its eligibility rules.

Previously, Tier-1 nations Australia and New Zealand had first pick of the best Australia and New Zealand-based Polynesian and Melanesian NRL star players. Once they had committed to play for the Kangaroos and Kiwis, they were not allowed to return to play for their ancestral country.

For the 2017 Rugby League World Cup a rule change had unleashed havoc and heartache. Polynesian and Melanesian players now were able to nominate to play in either a Tier-1 or Tier-2 nation and effectively choose between their country of citizenship and their country of ancestry.

The first two high-profile 'defectors' were Jason Taumalolo, of the North Queensland Cowboys, and Kangaroo Andrew Fifita, of the Cronulla Sharks.

Taumalolo, a 10-test Kiwis player who is Tongan from South

Auckland, turned down the Kiwis jumper to play for Tonga, while Fifita, born to an Aboriginal mother and Tongan father, turned his back on the green and gold of the Kangaroos.

It caused a media storm and shot a bolt of white-hot energy through the entire tournament.

Olsen had been busy in the build-up to the opening game between Samoa and New Zealand, dividing his time between the teams representing his joint ancestral heritage. He joined the Samoan team for their 'packed to the rafters' official appearance at Māngere Town Centre shopping mall.

He was then invited by the Kiwis team to join them for a feast at the residence of the Māori King, Kiingi Tūheitia, at Tūrongo House, at Tūrangawaewae marae in Waikato. Olsen learned about the long history of Māori royalty supporting rugby league, including the first Māori Queen, Te Arikinui Dame Te Atairangikaahu who reigned for 40 years until her death in 2006 and proudly served as the patron of New Zealand Māori Rugby League.

* * * * *

Running onto the field at Mt Smart Stadium was a weakened New Zealand Kiwis side, rocked by the defection of several of its best players, and they were joined by a hungry Samoan side looking to create an upset.

Of the Pacific nations, Toa Samoa had been the pre-tournament favourite to cause an upset, based on the number of eligible NRL players of Samoan background. After a lengthy apprenticeship it was supposed to be their time.

The Samoans featured high-quality players including Herman Ese'ese, an Auckland-born prop whose uncle had played for New Zealand; Josh Papalii, who had played State of Origin for Queensland; and captain Frank Pritchard, who had previously played 27 games for the Kiwis and enjoyed a stellar career including 256 NRL games.

Olsen was thrilled for Pritchard's decision to 'come home'. 'One of my proudest days was pulling on the Samoa jersey in Apia after my

Kiwis days were over,' he explains. 'Being half Samoan, half Māori and to play for New Zealand was a great honour. But when I was asked to play for Samoa, it connected me back in there and made me feel great. I get why Frank did it.'

On field the traditional Māori karanga welcome call was completed, and the excitement bubbled into high-pitched screams as both sides faced off for the pre-match cultural exchange — the Māori haka versus the Samoan Siva Tau. It was challenge and response: Polynesian brotherhood, love, passion, respect and war.

The Samoans went first and as their players bent down in a circle, their shrieks and whistles punctured the night sky. Leading the war cry was Parramatta Eels prop Junior Paulo, who stood like a colossus in the middle of his fast-clapping teammates until they turned to face the Kiwis.

Paulo called them into battle as they marched forward towards their enemy. Ferocious thigh slapping, air punching and baritone war cries culminated in the team launching onto one knee with a growled threat of impending violence.

The haka response was equally fearsome as the Kiwis surrounded their leader, Ngāpuhi captain Adam Blair who was brandishing a Māori taiaha, a traditional long wooden weapon. The men in black marched forward towards the Samoans with a ferocious haka featuring body slapping, pūkana (bulging eyes), whētero (stretched tongues) and tūwaewae takahia (foot stomping).

War cries representing two of the great Polynesian nations, separated by a millennia of migration history, brought together again on the rugby league field in Auckland, the capital of Polynesia.

Yet despite the best efforts of the Toa Samoan fans — that blue wall of love, colour, noise and prayer — Samoa were overwhelmed by New Zealand 38–8 in a physically brutal match. Olsen just smiled and shrugged his shoulders as he left Mt Smart Stadium — it was a match he could not lose.

* * * * *

The tournament headlines would instead be written about the Tongans, who over the next three weeks smashed Scotland, overwhelmed Samoa and famously beat New Zealand in a thrilling encounter.

Mate Ma'a Tonga had broken through in the 15th World Cup — a Tier-2 nation had finally beaten a Tier-1 nation. After edging past Lebanon in the quarter-final, Tonga was unluckily defeated by England 20–18 in their first-ever semi-final.

Although the Kangaroos won the tournament, even Australian journalists acknowledged that the tournament belonged to the Pacific. Some blasphemously suggested that games involving Pacific nations were better than State of Origin.

It was a coming-out party for the Pacific nations led by colourful and passionate culture: the Siva Tau and the Sipi Tau, the haka and the Fijian 'Noqu Masu' pre-match hymn.

The Pacific Revolution, which had been building quietly for years in the NRL, finally had an international outlet. The revolution has brought with it radical cultural change and rugby league would never be the same again.

'Let me tell you some things you may have missed,' wrote Steve Mascord in the *Sydney Morning Herald* after Tonga beat New Zealand. 'The grandstand actually shook, as in an earthquake, several times in the final 20 minutes. The hymns that broke out when Tonga snatched the lead were otherworldly and beguiling. Tonga, you made it worth it.'

* * * * *

A year after the 2017 Rugby League World Cup, I sought some perspective on the Pacific Revolution from Professor Tony Collins, the Director of the International Centre for Sports History and Culture at the De Montfort University in Leicester, England.

Collins has written the definitive social histories on rugby league and rugby union and has studied deeply all the key moments that have brought great change in rugby league.

He admits he didn't see the Pacific Revolution coming so soon: 'If

I knew what was about to happen, I would have gone down to New Zealand. A good friend of mine went to the Tonga games and he said the crowds and atmosphere were unprecedented and he'd never seen anything like it. He was emotionally drained.'

For Collins, it was another example of momentous rugby league change caused by one man's decision to stand on principle: 'Jason Taumalolo will have a medal struck in his name one day,' explains Collins.

'By deciding to play for Tonga, he made potentially one of the most important and far-reaching decisions any player has made in the international game since 1934, when Jean Galia took the first French team on a tour of the United Kingdom, adding France to the pool of rugby league nations. Before that there was Dally Messenger in Australia, Albert Asher in New Zealand and the brave men of the 22 clubs in Northern England who broke away from rugby union.

'Rugby league has always been about standing up for principles. Standing up against injustice and the right to play was ingrained in the culture of how the game was founded and the way it is still played.'

The growth of the Māori, Polynesian and Melanesian player base is the essence of rugby league according to Collins: 'Unlike other sports, rugby league is a game that was founded on a principle. That everyone should have the right to play football regardless of background or income, and no other sport has that history. It has always been the game of people who are outside the established order or ignored. The Pacific players fit that bill perfectly.'

* * * * *

On 28 September 2018, I sat beside Olsen in the passenger seat of his clean, green garbage truck on his morning bin run around Ryde for 'recycling day'. The singlet and shorts of his younger years have been replaced by a standard uniform of fluorescent orange and dark blue work shirt and long pants.

He wore a big grin on his face as he guided the truck through the streets. 'Back in the day driving was the cushy job,' he chuckled. 'It was better for my weight to be out the back running.'

At 61, Olsen is one of Sydney's longest-serving 'garbos', and in 2020 he will clock up 40 years of service. Unlike the old days, he rarely leaves the cabin. He now sits high in the driver's seat, fiddling with buttons like a DJ and checking the mirror to make sure the robotic arms latch on to each bin.

Once powered by human biceps, the robot arm now does the heavy lifting, dispatching the rubbish from kerbside via the side of the truck. 'You've got to keep your wits about you,' explains Olsen happily, as the arms hoisted yet another bin into the air. 'It's just like footy, all about timing!'

Technology has been kind to Olsen. His dodgy knees and broken rugby league body would have rendered him out of a job if garbos still ran at the back of the truck. Now, he twiddles a knob to auto-pick up the rubbish. He notes with a grin — 'just like playing Space Invaders'.

'I rarely get out of the truck now and talk to people because they say a computer measures how long you are taking,' Olsen says.

But older residents still wave at the 'galloping garbo', recognising a hero from an earlier time. Olsen still gets a kick out of it, and always returns the favour with a smile or a nod.

'Everywhere I go, I still get noticed,' he says, shaking his head. 'It's amazing the places where people stop me to talk. Just yesterday I went to the TAB to have a bet on the horses and a guy approached me and we had a good chat and a laugh for an hour. I was sure I would just fade away, but for some reason people are still interested.'

In the uncertain modern world in which automation is decimating entire industries, Olsen feels that his job is safe, as it will still need humans for the foreseeable future.

He doesn't know when he'll retire. Apart from football, for four decades this is the only work he has known. He works on his own now, occasionally with the radio as company but mostly lost in the focus of the job and his own thoughts.

Leslie has returned to New Zealand to take care of her ailing parents but through the miracle of the internet, they talk via video every day.

Leslie patiently waits for Olsen to return to New Zealand: 'I just want him back here in New Zealand, where he should be, where he is loved by all.'

He is hoping to join her in South Auckland but must stay in Sydney for regular visits to his son John who he hopes will be freed from Silverwater Jail in September 2020. On a jail visit in late 2019 John spoke about the pride he has in his father's career. 'A lot of the older inmates in here seek me out and ask if am I related to Olsen. They all think he is an absolute legend and it's a big name to carry around.'

John was foiled robbing an armoured cash transit van in 2012, succumbing to 'greed' and the lure of quick cash to 'keep up with the Joneses.' He is in great shape and hopes to play some rugby league when he gets out of jail.

John says Olsen has been a role model for his sons and he has been preparing for life on the outside by reading voraciously, including *The Barefoot Investor* and Jordan Peterson's *12 Rules of Life*.

'I'm ready to take on responsibility now.' John adds in reflection. 'My dad never babied me and he taught me to be fearless but I channelled it in a negative direction. I can't blame anybody for my situation. I just want to get out and be one of the good stories."

Olsen reflects sombrely, to the sounds of clanging plastic bins: "I just want to see him free for one day!"

* * * * *

Leslie looks back in awe at his journey: 'He wouldn't harm a fly, yet people were cruel to him just because he played the game he loved. He copped rabid racism, coaches who scapegoated him, his health suffered, he played with injuries and came through depression to make life better for us and others. Olsen will always be the quiet, reserved proud Samoan/Māori with a wide grin who caused disruption and havoc on the rugby league field, his happy space.'

Olsen's happy space these days is playing with his grandchildren.

His daughter Louise discovered a new side of him when she became a mother. 'When my son Kaimana came along I noticed how emotional and loving Dad was,' says Louise. 'I was living on the Gold Coast and he would ring me five to six times a day to make sure we were okay and sometimes he would be crying because he missed us all. He's a great grandad.'

* * * * *

As the garbage truck lurched around the streets of Ryde, it gave me great pleasure to see that Olsen's rebel spirit lives on. He pointed to a dashboard camera covered in sticky tape. 'I never liked the camera on me,' he laughed, remembering the nosy reporters of his early career at Balmain.

From the outside, Olsen appears fit and healthy for his age, with the same hair and flashing white teeth. When he walks, though, the ravages are evident. His hobble is an unholy collaboration of hip, knee and ankle injuries. But he still gets out on the tennis court whenever possible.

He has been learning about his Māori side and one of his favourite recent trips was going back to New Zealand to tend his mother's grave at Te Huruhi Marae in Awarua, 15 minutes out of Kaikohe. As part of the trip he spent time with Ngāpuhi storyteller Hone Mihaka who educated him about Ngāpuhi history.

'I can't believe the history of my people up there. They were brilliant in war or peace,' Olsen says.

On the same trip to Kaikohe, one of the proudest moments of his life was being presented with a Kaikohe Lions rugby league jersey and being made a life member of the club. 'It was a great honour,' Olsen recalls: 'That would have been my club if we hadn't moved to the city.'

Ken Edwards, Ngāpuhi President of the Kaikohe Lions, remembers the night fondly: 'I told Olsen that we are honoured to have him, a Hall of Famer, as a returning son of Kaikohe and our waka are now moored together.'

For Edwards, Olsen is the epitome of a Ngāpuhi man: 'We loved Olsen up here because he behaved like one of us, always humble and never bragged about himself,' says Edwards.

'The Aussies may think that being quiet and humble is weak, but we think it's strength. Anyone can lose their temper and lash out or brag about themselves. Humility is valued by Māori. We have a saying up here: Kāore te kūmara e kōrero mō tōna ake reka — The kūmara doesn't have to tell you how sweet it is!'

* * * * *

Olsen remains all smiles on the outside, but on the inside he is fighting a raging battle for his health. For years, he has been taking 14 tablets a day — oral chemotherapy for lupus nephritis, an autoimmune disease affecting the kidneys that he has been having treatment for since 2002.

Its impact includes sapping his energy and occasionally defying doctor's orders to not fly, as he did to attend the Rugby League World Cup opening match in Auckland.

There is one person Olsen believes is responsible for keeping him alive: 'I owe it all to Professor Carol Pollock, my doctor who cares so much about me and my condition. Another amazing person who has really taken me under her wing and never allowed me to give in.

'I really can't complain,' shrugged Olsen. 'Every footy reunion I go to someone has passed on. I go to more funerals than parties these days. I'm glad to be alive and spend time with my family.'

* * * * *

When I ask Olsen what he savours most from his playing memories, his response is unequivocal. 'Entertaining the Kiwi crowds was my job and my dream and my way of giving back to them for investing their money in us. A lot of them worked hard in crap jobs and the smiles and cheers of the crowd was my highlight. I can still hear them and see them now.

'I loved playing for New Zealand and even today when I see the boys in black and white run out on the field I feel an emotion that's hard to describe. Seeing that green and gold jumper was like a red rag to a bull for me. It's impossible to shake.'

* * * * *

'Ye shall know them by their fruits.' (Matthew 7:16–20, King James Bible).

Where does Olsen sit in the Pacific Revolution? For Sir Graham Lowe it is at the apex: 'I think his legacy is the number of Polynesians playing in Australia, that's a start. He was the first Polynesian playmaker in Australia and he had a great footballing brain and saw things other players didn't see. He could scheme through defences, see holes and knew where to run.'

Olsen's story has contemporary relevance according to Lowe: 'Olsen forged the way that said to us all: "We've got the right to do this."'

'History has to reflect who actually made it, who actually made the difference. Olsen is the man they hold up because of who he is.'

For Lowe, Olsen's love of playing the game set him apart and for that alone he treated him as a 'special one, like my own son. Olsen didn't play league for money but for enjoyment. He didn't come through the robot system in Australia and I've never seen a less understood player. He hated that system and I knew it, so I deliberately went the other way with him.'

Making Olsen feel comfortable was the end goal for Lowe: 'The key to Olsen wasn't what you told him on the day of the game, it was how you treated him during the week. He hated 200-metre sprints so I used to keep him away from them and encourage him to play a bit of tennis, a game he loved, instead.'

Removing the clutter was key for Lowe in getting the best out of Olsen: 'It's obviously clear to me that when he picks up any ball he's a natural that can play any sport. There is no magic wand needed to access that talent. Just give him the freedom to be himself.'

For Lowe, Olsen was no enigma: 'What a nonsense, cop-out label. If you see genius, even just once, it's there. It's your job as a coach to find it again. I simply filled him with confidence and made him feel wanted. He probably had more kicks in the teeth than anyone playing football in Sydney, yet he never complained. He just wanted to be loved and I loved him like a second son whenever I got my hands on him.'

And if there is blame to be apportioned for any of Olsen's underperformance, for Lowe it is the coach that is guilty: 'Olsen was a gifted footballer — an asset who had explosive power, size and mobility including good speed off the mark. I've seen them all and he had it all. He had remarkable ball skills and brutal defence, which was a rare combination. Any coach that can't bring that out — it's their fault, not the player's. It's as simple as that.'

For Lowe and many New Zealanders, Olsen's journey was their journey and he was the embryo of the Pacific Revolution: 'A lot of us saw ourselves in Olsen. He walked straight into an intense competition at 23 and matched a level that took the Aussies 20 years to get to. He walked in, unlocked the door and showed people in. Bravo to the Big "O".'

* * * * *

In the years since Olsen retired from football, Australian rugby league has slowly become accustomed to an influx of Māori, Polynesian and Melanesian players. Some have passively integrated into the system and others have stepped up to further the cause.

For NRL journalist Brad Walter, ex-NRL and Kiwis star Nigel Vagana is a breakthrough pioneer for the Pacific players in the NRL. He recalls a watershed moment for Pacific player leadership when Vagana was playing for the South Sydney Rabbitohs. Vagana took a stand and refused to talk to coach Jason Taylor until he pronounced his name correctly.

Vagana's stance broke the ancient Samoan tradition of not questioning elders, but Vagana feels that it had to evolve: 'The first pioneers like Olsen had to deal with racists and they got us accepted and now it's our job to take it to new heights and not take any crap,' says Vagana.

'We have to assert ourselves now and let those early players know their persistence was worth it. We have to get into commentary and coaching. And people have to get our names right. It's about respect.'

* * * * *

A controversial cultural flashpoint of the Pacific Revolution has been commentators and fans who have painfully and often unsuccessfully tried to wrap their tongues around names like Petero Civoniceva, Nigel Vagana and Sam Tagataese.

Consistently pronouncing player names incorrectly inflames the Pacific community, who are gravely insulted by the mispronunciations and mocking by various commentators and league television programmes. For Pacific communities, the family name is everything: parents, grandparents — an extension of ancestry all the way back to ancient and mythical Hawaiki.

Olsen remembers his mother's constant anger at the inability of Australian commentators to get the pronunciation of 'Filipaina' correct. Olsen says: 'She would call me very angry that they couldn't get it right. That it seemed almost a joke.'

Change is coming slowly but surely: 'I have been guilty of stumbling over the names of Polynesian and Melanesian players and then laughing goofily on air,' wrote journalist Steve Mascord. But, he added, 'I will work harder.'

* * * * *

For NRL and Kiwis star Nigel Vagana the impact on players and coaches of the hardwired Māori and Pasifika culture has been a shock to process: 'Polynesians have an inbuilt code to respect elders and it is a sign of disrespect to challenge them. I've seen Pacific players come to Australia and because they won't challenge a coach or trainer, three weeks later they're gone.'

The cultural miscommunication is something Australian NRL and grassroots coaches have had to address, and cultural competence is now a key tool in any coach's suite of skills. 'When a Pacific player won't look a white coach in the eye, the white coach sometimes thinks he's daydreaming or not concentrating,' explains Vagana. 'Then the player gets abused and doesn't perform because the coach simply does not understand the cultural differences.'

Vagana played for four NRL clubs and has witnessed real progress unfold since his debut in 1996 for the Auckland Warriors. 'One positive has been that clubs have in many ways given up trying to change Polynesian culture and adopted a healthier approach of trying to respond to the player's specific needs.'

The NRL is still challenged by the cultural differences but has a growing number of programmes to counter the cross-cultural issues that when not addressed, in extreme cases, have led to suicides.

* * * * *

For Olsen, the awareness of depression and suicide in the Polynesian rugby league community went to the next level in 2013 when 20-year-old Wests Tigers Pasifika player Mosese Fotuaika took his own life after a weightlifting injury.

'I have learnt over time that it's not just a Polynesian problem nor does it go away. We lost Mosese which put the spotlight on Pacific players and before him we lost Steve Rogers, an unbelieveable player and bloke and no one wanted to talk about it.'

Fotuaika's depression was masked by an external façade of happiness according to teammate Sauaso Sue who told the *Daily Telegraph*: 'He was the last person we thought would do that. We didn't see any signs, he was always happy.'

Like Olsen before him, Fotuaika had taken on the role of family breadwinner and was living on a small allowance after sending most of his earnings home to family. He had also bottled up his emotions and according to close friend and teammate Ben Murdoch-Masila, he did not want to be seen as 'weak or soft'.

Dual Kangaroos/Wallabies international Israel Folau explained to

Players Voice the cultural background behind Fotuaika's state of mind: 'A lot of people in the Polynesian community understood how he arrived at such a dark place and felt empathy for him. When Mosese tore his pec lifting weights, he immediately burst out crying. Not because of the pain of the injury but because of the pressure he was feeling – to make his parents proud, to give back to his community, to support his pregnant partner and the fear that his career might be over.'

Manly Warringah's Kiwi-Samoan star Darrell Williams followed Olsen into the Winfield Cup and felt the pressure first hand without any of today's support structures: 'Olsen and I had nothing or no one to help us back then. Today there is still an inability to meet parents' demands. There's still pressure when a player gets dropped or injured. The loss of face can be so heavy that some commit suicide.'

Nigel Vagana explains both sides of the phenomenon. 'We have a communal mentality. What's mine is yours. If I have a pair of shoes and you don't, I will give mine to you. Family is above everything else. It's been the key to our survival and you have to give back to your family that supported you. It's the greatest thing for a Pacific community player to give back to his community and sometimes it's tragic if he can't.'

Being part of a cultural operating system that has survived 3000 years means there is no way to avoid your obligations says Vagana: 'You hear a lot of talk about family in the Pacific community and it's hard to explain it, other than to buck the system means you are an outcast. This makes family a lot stronger. It's taken the Aussies a long time to realise that we look for different things in life. We define our lives in different ways.'

* * * * *

Pasifika academic David Lakisa, whose Master's dissertation was titled 'The Pacific Revolution: Pasifika and Māori players in Australian Rugby League', makes the point that the collectivism of Island culture means footballers don't just share dollars with their kin but the honour of belonging to the NRL.

'When I debut, it's not my debut,' says Lakisa. 'It's my mother's, my father's, my grandparents', my great-great-grandparents', who are watching over me now. It's their debut too and these boys are living their elders' unlived dreams right in front of them on the television.'

As part of research for his dissertation, Lakisa surveyed 47 Pacific NRL players and his data reported three influential pillars — family, faith and culture. Every respondent attributed their success to both family support and the wider extended family and friend kinship network.

The extended family focus is reflected in the high level of money remittances from players back to families in the Pacific and New Zealand. Players also acknowledged the expectation and pressure to improve the family's socioeconomic position and 'pay back' their parents' sacrifice.

The survey notes the rise of Polynesian and Melanesian religious faith and its role in the re-entry of Christianity into rugby league, which cannot be underestimated. Christianity is now central to the game, from players making a sign of the cross or pointing to the sky after a try, to after-match prayer circles including players from opposing teams. Players acknowledge their religion in after-match interviews and sport religious tattoos of crosses and scripture verses.

The third pillar covered in the survey was the importance of respecting culture in getting the best out of Pasifika and Māori players. Respect for elders and protocols, traditional food, prayer, dance, language and music are all important for Pacific athletes.

NRL club staff have been forced to develop cultural competence including Pacific advisors on staff to navigate the cultural, family and religious nuances and provide a strong off-field foundation for on-field success.

Olsen can remember facing ongoing trauma without support — from financial pressure, abusive coaches, racism, unsupportive teammates, the cultural clashes and his surname being mispronounced.

'Looking back, it's bizarre to think what I went through, like it was a dream. They just had no idea about us, and they didn't care,' Olsen says.

* * * * *

The next two 'spine' playmaker Pacific players to follow Olsen into the Winfield Cup were Manly's fullback Darrell Williams and Newcastle's five-eighth Tony Kemp.

For Williams, Olsen's struggle was personal: 'We all knew the Aussies couldn't figure him out and at the age of 23, jumping from the freewheeling New Zealand amateur system into the rigid Aussie game took its toll.'

Williams lauds Olsen's role as an intergenerational bridging figure: 'Olsen was an inspiration for my sacrifices and sure enough through the different generations, a trickle has become an avalanche.'

For Tony Kemp, Olsen's crowning achievement was to dominate Wally Lewis in front of one third of his countrymen watching on television: 'Olsen has to be in the New Zealand team of the century,' Kemp explains: 'No other Kiwi has ever dominated an Australian Immortal like Olsen did, to the greatest player ever. He got over Wally, ran over the top of him and that wasn't meant to happen. You know as a player when someone's got your number and Wally knew. There was no way he couldn't know. When Olsen appeared opposite, Wally could never play the game he was renowned for.'

For Kemp, the attempts by Australians to cleanse Olsen and the next generation of Polynesian players of their culture was futile: 'Olsen stayed true to himself and we don't care what the Aussies think. Our Poly culture is driven through our whakapapa and down to our kids automatically. It's unbreakable.'

* * * * *

As the garbage truck jolts around a tricky cul-de-sac, I ask Olsen to elaborate on his own legacy. He waves the question away and says that is up to others to decide.

I share a few facts with him hot off the press: in 2018, according to the NRL some 48 per cent of the NRL players were of Pacific and Māori descent, as opposed to just four lonely men or just over one per cent of the NSWRL competition when he joined Balmain in 1980. He is not shocked and feels it's just the start.

* * * * *

Two days earlier, Roger Tuivasa-Sheck, a Samoan-born Kiwi, had just been named the NRL's 2018 Dally M player of the year — the first New Zealand Warrior to receive the honour.

Tuivasa-Sheck was the latest in a long line of rugby league talent out of South Auckland, a conveyor belt of rugby league excellence anchored by Olsen.

In front of a live television audience and led by Māori and New Zealand Warriors star Issac Luke, an impromptu four-player haka tribute was performed for their captain that reverberated around social media.

Olsen says: 'Back in the day I never went to the Rothmans Medal Awards. That was for the Aussies. Now it's changed. I was watching on TV and was so proud of Roger, the first Warrior to receive the award after all these years and a South Auckland boy to top it off.'

For Olsen, the honour also needed acknowledgement in Māori style: 'I thought to myself — Issac, you're the leader there. You know what to do, you gotta get up. You know how much of an honour this is, you know how much it means in New Zealand. Then he got up and I got goose bumps. I said "thank you" out loud and it was emotional. I remembered when my whānau did a haka when I was inducted into the Hall of Fame. It's the highest honour of all.'

Olsen last performed a haka at the funeral of his friend, mentor and 'Aussie father' Phil Dries: 'It was a solo one with Leslie singing in support. Words were not enough for what that man did for me.'

Olsen has remained staunchly loyal to the Dries family, visiting his 'Aussie mum' Margaret whenever he can and turning up every year to

Ryde Eastwood junior trophy presentation nights.

Margaret's son Mick Dries lived with Olsen for two years and raves about Olsen's resilience and loyalty: 'We all knew what he was going through, but he came through it and is still the same man I was friends with all those years ago. He has never missed a birthday or family milestone and Olsen has hit a lot of hearts over here.'

* * * * *

I told Olsen, it could be argued that following on from the World Cup, the year 2018 had been the coming-out year of the Pacific people in rugby league. The tipping point. Olsen just smiled mischievously and continued lifting the bins from the kerb.

After almost 40 years of living in Australia I wondered if he had softened on the Aussies: 'I loved playing for New Zealand and I'm black and white forever but with one weakness, funnily enough, in swimming. I loved Ian Thorpe. The "Thorpedo", he was something else, a little bit different, and an outsider doing it his own way. I somehow related to him,' Olsen explains with a smile.

Olsen says he felt the purest love from the New Zealand fans: 'The crowd in Auckland especially used to lift me. They brought out the best in me and if you enjoy your football it shows in your game, you can't fake it. I couldn't wait to entertain them, and I tried to represent the Māori and Polynesian and New Zealand people's way of playing rugby league. Why not if it's more exciting? There are a lot of other games people can play if rugby league is not exciting!'

I had to ask — that after his turbulent journey, does he bear any grudges? Olsen says: 'I saw Frank Stanton a few months ago and his son is sick and he is at home caring for him. I felt sorry for him and all the hate went out of me. We shook hands and I wish him nothing but the best.'

And as for King Wally? Olsen smiles: 'We've never talked once at ANZAC reunions since he brushed me, but I'd love to catch up with him. He was a hero of mine and I only ever wanted to meet him and shake his hand. On the field I got him a few times and he got me a few times. But what good is sport without rivalries? We've got some great memories together and it would be nice to have a beer and a laugh before I go.'

* * * * *

Wally Lewis is looking forward to that beer and has lots of memories to share. Lewis says he wonders how Olsen would have been remembered if he had gone to a club other than Balmain. And having also suffered continual criticism from Sydney's insular media, he took the criticism of Olsen as headline-grabbing ignorance.

Stories criticising Olsen's club form or labelling him enigmatic were not welcomed by Lewis: 'Every time I was coming up against Olsen in a test match there were two or three days of criticism about his ability to perform at club level, and I used to say, "I wish to Christ they wouldn't write that crap." That would only motivate him more!'

Olsen agrees with Wally's assessment: 'By the time I got around to playing the Aussies, I was fed up with the media's jabs, the racism and teammates being cruel,' says Olsen: 'I would take it all out on the Aussies and Wally walked into it a few times.'

The ultimate proof according to Lewis is actually facing Olsen on the field: 'There may have been some people critical of his performances at club level, a lot of unfair judgement, but if they ever wanted true proof of the bloke's ability, they had to line up against him at test level. He was fantastic and demanded his opponents be at their best because he was 100 per cent committed every time — the critical media never had to play against him, and if they did they would have understood very quickly.'

Lewis adds: 'With that black and white jumper on he was something else — that was when he had plenty of pride on board, self-belief and the trust of his teammates who never thought that he was anything less than the best. Simply, if you played against him once you knew any of the criticism that came his way was not deserved. I don't know one bloke that played against him that enjoyed it. He was big, strong and raw-boned and made life difficult for every player.'

With the benefit of hindsight and reflection, where did Olsen rank against all the five-eighths Wally Lewis played against in his 15-year professional career?

'Olsen's strength was far greater than anyone else I faced and I would have him at number two just behind Brett Kenny who I had multiple battles with,' says Lewis.

'Olsen didn't have Brett Kenny's speed but he had strength and determination and pride in that black and white jumper which were a challenge every time I faced him.'

For King Wally Lewis, an inducted Immortal of Australian rugby league, all's well that ends well: 'Life after football presents some wonderful opportunities and one of those hopefully will be to sit down and enjoy a beer with Olsen. I know he's a man of few words, but we'll talk about the old days and a bit of footy.'

* * * * *

Rugby league is arguably the hardest of team sports; its legends are forged in the furnace and subject to caustic scrutiny. The myths that survive are the authentic ones and Olsen's story is the type that binds the sport to its fans.

As New Zealand's first genius footballer of the modern era, combined with his humble off-field persona, he provided a richness of experience to all those he touched and he took his place in the historical process.

In the great ones there is an element of the inexplicable, the intangible and the other worldly. They have a different relationship with time and in Olsen's case his spirit, although scalded at times, was indomitable.

Olsen wore his fame lightly and refused to conform and compromise his tough and humble Māori and Pasifika spirit, a spirit that is a very central part of rugby league today.

Howie Tamati, Olsen's former Kiwis teammate and President of

New Zealand Rugby League, has his own metrics for Olsen's legacy which he feels is woven into the arc of memory: 'Olsen absolutely deserved to be a New Zealand Hall of Famer,' Tamati says.

'They say you're a great player if they are talking about you 10 years after you've retired. It's been more than 30 years and we are all still talking about Olsen. That's a clear measure of greatness.'

In the history of rugby league, where does he sit — the luminous pioneer who outplayed the greatest of all time?

Jazz supremo Duke Ellington loved to say his music was 'beyond category'. Maybe that's where we file the 'Big O'.

* * * * *

As we sat in his garbage truck — Olsen the Pasifika and Māori legend, me an Anglo-Celt Australian who idolised him as a child — it struck me that he was a man out of place but a man for all times; the pianist and the piano mover. An emissary from the future who told us what was coming.

While other players of his ilk are now retired, running businesses or in suit and tie, carving out a career in the media or football administration, Olsen is still happily collecting other people's garbage. He is rugby league to the marrow.

He shares some parting words from the garbage truck before dropping it off and heading to the gym and a punt on the racehorses: 'I suppose it all comes down to me loving playing rugby league, entertaining people and making them happy. And I dedicate it all to my family, my mother Sissie, Leitchy, Lowey, Ces, my teammates, the Dries family, my five children Louise, John, Quin, Alysha and Jazmine and especially my partner Leslie. Without them there is nothing.'

* * * * *

Author Joseph Campbell once wrote: 'The privilege of a lifetime is being who you are.'

Olsen Filipaina enjoyed that privilege. A humble warrior, he embarked on a reluctant hero's journey, crossing the threshold, moving through a strange landscape, facing the road of trials, slaying the dragon and bringing back the magic elixir, living proof to his people that they were worthy.

Throughout his quest he remained true to himself and his people — a transcendental keeper of the flame and an exuberant poem of force.

O for Olsen.

O for Awesome.

ACKNOWLEDGMENTS

Behind every book is a team of friends, family, colleagues, acquaintances and strangers providing advice and tough love to drive the process. Writing this book has been a humbling experience. Nobody can do it alone and thanks to all those who have supported me.

This book is a love letter to the Polynesian and Māori communities. On my journey I've met an array of Pasifika people who have generously shared their time and stories and taught me about an ancient and enduring culture. Thank you all.

I'm in awe of the resilient game of rugby league and have much respect for all the characters who agreed to be interviewed for this book — you have rejuvenated my passion for the 'greatest game of all'.

I am especially grateful to the unwavering support of Olsen's partner Leslie Anne Taylor and his family, in particular younger brother Alf Filipaina and daughter Louise. I hope your trust has been repaid.

To Alexandra Payne, bravo for your belief, bravery and faith in investing in a book on rugby league. It's a shame we couldn't finish what we started, but thanks from the bottom of my heart.

One man that stands out in Olsen's football journey and my writing journey is Sir Peter Leitch. You are a legend with a big heart and deserve all the good things that have happened to you — thanks for your support.

To my family: Divya, Narayan and Priyana. I'm eternally grateful to you for being there when I needed boosting and for delivering me 'quiet time' when I needed to write. I couldn't ask for a better crew!

Thanks to the hard-core leaguies for their input — Ian Heads, Terry Williams, Richard Becht, John Coffey and Tony Collins. Tony, your books could only be written by a man that deeply loves the game of rugby league and they taught me a deeper understanding of 'the only game to be founded on a principle'.

My sincerest appreciation to my business partner and brother-in-law Reg Raghavan whose patience and support I can never repay.

Two people had stand-out roles in helping develop my writing — John Harms from the *Footy Almanac* and Mike Hytner from the *Guardian Australia*. Bless you both for your support.

I give daily gratitude to my late, beautiful mother Patricia for everything she gifted me — a love of reading, writing, books, diversity and life. Bless your soul and I know you would have enjoyed this story.

To Warren Adler and Kevin Chapman from Upstart Press, thanks for backing me and Olsen. It has been a pleasure to work with you.

To the late, great author and my dear friend, John Rowe: thanks for your mentorship.

I am forever indebted to Joe Gorman — mentor, structural editor, soundboard, friend, critic and a man wise beyond his years. Thank you, Joe.

And finally to Olsen Filipaina — thanks for letting me tell your story, albeit reluctantly. You are a humble and wonderful human being who went through so much to take care of your family and entertain your people. And believe it or not, people still want to hear your tale!

I'm honoured to partner with you on this project and to be part of your story.

Ka kite anō au i a koutou!
Patrick Skene

BIBLIOGRAPHY AND RELATED SOURCES

BOOKS

Achor, Shawn, *The Happiness Advantage*, Virgin Books, 2010

Amadio, Nadine, *Pacifica: Myth, Magic and Traditional Wisdom from the South Seas Islands*, Angus & Robertson, 1993

Anastasios, Meaghan Wilson, *The Pacific in the Wake of Captain Cook*, HarperCollins, 2018

Anderson, Atholl, *Tangata Whenua: An Illustrated History*, Bridget Williams Books, 2017

Barlow, Cleve, *Tikanga Whakaaro: Key Concepts in Maori Culture*, Oxford University Press, 1991

Becht, Richard, *Lowe and Behold: The Graham Lowe Story*, David Charles, 1986

Becht, Richard, *Standing Tall: The Tawera Nikau Story*, HarperCollins, 2004

Becht, Richard, *Tiger Tiger Kiwi Rooster: The Gary Freeman Story*, Moa Beckett Publishers, 1992

Beetson, Arthur, *Big Artie: The Autobiography*, ABC Books, 2004

Belcher, Diana, *A Voyage to the South Sea*, HarperCollins, 2012

Belich, James, *The New Zealand Wars and the Victorian Interpretation of Racial Conflict*, Auckland University Press, 2016

Bell, Dean, *The Ultimate Warrior: The Dean Bell Story*, Orion Publishing Co., 1995

Cadigan, Neil, *Out of the Shadows: Wally Lewis*, HarperCollins, 2010
Campbell, Joseph, *Hero with a Thousand Faces*, Pantheon Press, 1949
Chapple, Geoff, *1981: The Tour*, Bridget Williams Books, 2014
Coffey, John, and Wood, Bernie, *100 Years of Auckland Rugby League*, Huia Publishers, 2009
Coffey, John, and Wood, Bernie, *100 Years: Maori Rugby League*, Huia, 2008
Coffey, John, and Wood, Bernie, *The Kiwis: 100 Years of International Rugby League*, Hodder Moa, 2007
Collins, Tony, *Rugby League in Twentieth Century Britain*, Routledge, 2006
Collins, Tony, *Rugby's Great Split*, Frank Cass Publishers, 1998
Deaker, John, *The Converts: Changing Codes*, HarperCollins, 2011
Elias, Ben, *Balmain Benny*, Ironbark Press, 1992
Evans, Will, *Warriors 25: Celebrating 25 Years of the New Zealand Warriors*, Bateman, 2019
Fagan, Sean, *Pioneers of Rugby League: The True History of League's Birth in Australia and its Dramatic First Seasons*, RL1908, 2007
Fagan, Sean, *The Rugby Rebellion: The Divide of League and Union*, RL1908, 2005
Farrell, Joseph, *Robert Louis Stevenson in Samoa*, Maclehose Press, 2017
Ferguson, Alex, *Leading*, Hodder & Stoughton, 2015
Ferguson, Andrew, *The Story of Rugby League*, New Holland Publishing, 2018
Fischer, Steven R., *A History of the Pacific Islands*, Macmillan, 2002
Forster, John, *Social Process in New Zealand*, Longman Paul, 1971
Gagne, Natacha, *Being Maori in the City*, University of Toronto Press, 2013
Gate, Robert, *Billy Boston, Rugby League Footballer*, London League Publications, 2010
Gladwell, Malcolm, *David & Goliath: Underdogs, Misfits and the Art of Battling Giants*, Penguin, 2013
Gladwell, Malcolm, *Outliers, The Story of Success*, Little Brown &

Company, 2015

Golson, Jack, *Polynesian Navigation*, A.H. & A.W. Reed, 1962

Gordon, Rashelle, *Tony Tank Gordon: My Dad, My Legend*, New Holland Publishers, 2012

Graham, Mark, *Mark my Words*, Sporting Press, 1989

Hansby, Bill, *The Hawks: 40 Years of Rugby League*, Suburban Newspapers Publishing, 2003

Hauser, Liam, *The Immortals of Australian Rugby League*, Rockpool Publishing, 2009

Howearth, Bunty, *Mists of Time: Ngāpuhi Myths and Legends*, Reed, 2003

Hunt, Mark, *Born to Fight*, Hachette, 2015

Irwin, Kathie, *Toa Wahine: The Worlds of Maori Women*, Penguin, 1995

Jackson, Glenn, *Benji Marshall: My Game, My Story*, Hachette, 2011

James, Colin, *The Quiet Revolution: Turbulence & Transition in Contemporary New Zealand*, Allen & Unwin, 1986

Kightley, Oscar, *Dawn Raids*, Playmarket, 2017

King, Michael, *The Penguin History of New Zealand*, Penguin, 2012

Krznaric, Roman, *Empathy: Why it Matters and How to Get It*, Random House, 2014

Lange, David, *My Life*, Penguin Viking, 2005

Leitch, Peter, *What a Ride Mate*, Harper Sports, 2008

Lewis, David, *The Voyaging Stars: Secrets of the Pacific Island Navigators*, Fontana/Collins, 1978

Lomu, Jonah, *Jonah Lomu: The Autobiography*, Hodder Moa, 2004

Lowe, Graham, *Graham Lowe: Dreams Die Hard*, Celebrity Books, 1999

Mackenzie Watson, Robert, *History of Samoa*, Forgotten Books, 2018

Maning, F.E., *Old New Zealand: A Tale of the Good Old Times and a History of the War in the North*, Golden Press, 1973

Matheson, John, *Benji Marshall: A Tribute to a Rugby League Genius*, HarperCollins, 2011

Matheson, John, *Monty Betham: Baring My Soul*, HarperCollins, 2008

McGregor, Adrian, *King Wally*, UQP, 1987

McLauchlan, Gordon, *A Short History of New Zealand*, Penguin, 2004

McLauchlan, Gordon, *A Short History of the New Zealand Wars*, Bateman, 2017

McLauchlan, Gordon, *The Passionless People*, Cassell New Zealand, 1976

Mead, Hirini Moko, *Tikanga Maori: Living by Maori Values*, Huia, 2006

Meleisea, Malama, *Lagaga: A Short History of Western Samoa*, University of the South Pacific, 1987

Metge, Joan, *Rautahi: The Maori of New Zealand*, Psychology Press, 2004

Mirams, Chris, *Beleaguered! The Warriors from Dream to Nightmare*, Hodder Moa Beckett, 2001

Moore, Andrew, *The Mighty Bears: A Social History of North Sydney Rugby League*, Macmillan, 1996

Mountford, Ces, *Kiwis, Wigan & The Wire*, London League Publications, 2003

Mourie, Graham, *Captain: An Autobiography*, Wing Tong Co., 1982

Mundle, Rob, *Captain James Cook*, Harper Collins, 2013

Newnham, Thomas Oliver, *By Batons and Barbed Wire*, Real Pictures, 1981

Nicholls, Todd, *Hughie: Hugh McGahan – Kiwi Captain*, Nicholls Publishing, 1992

O'Malley, Vincent, *The New Zealand Wars: Ngā Pakanga o Aotearoa*, Bridget Williams Books, 2019

Oddy, James, *True Professional: The Clive Sullivan Story*, Pitch Publishing, 2017

Pearce, G.L., *The Story of the Maori People*, Collins Bros, 1968

Pearce, Wayne, *Local Hero: The Wayne Pearce Story*, Ironbark Press, 1990

Rampersad, Arnold, *Jackie Robinson: A Biography*, Penguin, 1998

Richards, Trevor, *Dancing on Our Bones: New Zealand, South Africa, Rugby and Racism*, Bridget Williams Books, 1999

Roach, Steve, *Doing My Block: Steve Roach*, Ironbark Press, 1992

Robinson, Sharon, *Promises to Keep: How Jackie Robinson Changed America*, Scholastic Inc., 2004

Rowlands, David, *The House that Jack Built*, New Holland Publishers, 2015

Sadler, Hōne, *Ko Tautoro Te Pito Tōku Ao: A Ngāpuhi Narrative*, Auckland University Press, 2015

Schofield, Garry, *Tries the Limit*, Mainstream Publishing, 2000

Slack, David, *Bullrush: A Celebration of the Great New Zealand Game*, HarperCollins, 2015

Stone, Russell, *From Tamaki-Makaurau-Rau to Auckland: A History of Auckland*, Auckland University Press, 2013

Theunissen, Steve, *The Maori of New Zealand*, Lerner, 2002

Turner, George, *Samoa, A Hundred Years Ago and Long Before*, AMS Press, 2005

Vautin, Paul, *Fatty: The Strife and Times of Paul Vautin*, Ironbark Press, 1992

Webster, Andrew, *Supercoach: The Life and Times of Jack Gibson*, Allen & Unwin, 2012

West, Graeme, *From Hawera to Wigan*, London League Publications, 2012

Wood, Bernie, and Coffey, John, *100 Years of Auckland Rugby League*, Huia Publishers, 2009

Wood, Bernie, and Coffey, John, *100 Years: Maori Rugby League*, Huia, 2008

Wood, Bernie, and Coffey, John, *The Kiwis: 100 Years of International Rugby League*, Hodder Moa, 2007

Wood, Desmond, *New Zealand Rugby Country*, Bateman, 2017

Zavos, Spiro, *The Real Muldoon*, Fourth Estate Books, 1978

NEWSPAPERS, PERIODICALS, WEBSITES

8 O'Clock (NZ)

Auckland Rugby League Gazette (NZ)

Auckland Star (NZ)
Big League Magazine
Brisbane Courier Mail
Daily Mirror
Daily Telegraph
Education Aotearoa website ea.org.nz
ESPN Website
New York Post (USA)
New Zealand Herald (NZ)
New Zealand Listener (NZ)
New Zealand Rugby League Annuals 1972, 1977, 1978, 1979, 1980, 1981, 1982, 1983, 1984, 1985, 1986, 1987
Open Rugby Magazine (UK)
Players Voice website
Rugby League Project website
Rugby League Week
Ryde Weekly Times
Spasifik Magazine (NZ)
Stuff.co.nz (NZ)
Sunday News (NZ)
Sunday Telegraph
The Australian
The Good Weekend
The Guardian (UK)
The Journal of the Polynesian Society (NZ)
The Observer (UK)
The Press (NZ)
The Sun
The Sun Herald
The Sunday Star (NZ)
The Sydney Morning Herald

DOCUMENTARIES/FILMS

Documentary, *1985 Kiwi Australia Third Test*, Close Up Productions, 1985

Documentary, *A Political Game*, TVNZ, 2004

Documentary, *All Blacks for Africa: A Black and White Issue*, Pasta Productions, 1992

Documentary, *Auckland City Centenary: Last, Loneliest, Loveliest*, NZBC, 1971

Documentary, *Auckland City of Sunlight*, NZ National film Unit, 1946

Documentary, *Auckland Rugby League, 100 Year History*, ARL, 2009

Documentary, *Dawn Raids*, Isola Productions, 2005

Documentary, *First Hand: Running the Rubbish*, George Andrews Productions, 1992

Documentary, *In a Different League*, TVNZ, 1990

Documentary, *Men of the Silver Fern: Power, Politics and Professionalism*, Spectrum Communications, 1993

Documentary, *New Streets: Auckland Fa'a-Samoa*, TVNZ, 1982

Documentary, *New Streets: South Auckland, Two Cities*, TVNZ, 1982

Documentary, *Once We're Warriors*, Chas Toogood Productions, 1995

Documentary, *Once Were Warriors, Where are They Now*, 2014

Documentary, *Patu*, Awatea Fims, 1983

Documentary, *Revolution 1: Fortress New Zealand*, Images Inc., 1996

Documentary, *Short Sportz Pt 1: Tana Umaga feature*, TV3, 1991

Documentary, *Tagata Pasifika: Second Migration*, TVNZ, 2015

Documentary, *The Game of Our Lives: Tries and Penalties*, George Andrews Productions, 1996

Documentary, *The New Zealand Wars*, Landmark Productions, 1998

Documentary, *This Auckland*, NZ National Film Unit, 1967

Documentary, *Try Revolution*, Spacific Film, 2006

Film, *Mahana*, The Patriarch Limited, 2016

Film, *Moneyball*, Columbia Pictures, 2011

Film, *Once Were Warriors*, Communicado, 1994

Film, *Sione's Wedding*, South Pacific Pictures, 2006
Film, *The Dead Lands*, General Film Corporation, 2014
Film, *The Jackie Robinson Story*, Jewel Pictures, 1950
Film, *The Orator: O Le Tulafale*, Blueskin Films, 2011
Film, *Three Wise Cousins*, m2s1 Films, 2015
Film, *Utu*, Utu Productions, 1983

TV Programme, *This Is Your Life: Jonah Lomu*, TV One, 2002

REPORTS/STUDIES/PAPERS

Brondolo, Elizabeth, *Dimensions of Perceived Racism and Self-Reported Health: Examination of Racial/Ethnic Differences and Potential Mediators*, St John's University, 2016

Hunn, J.K., *The Hunn Report*, New Zealand Government, 1961

Lakisa, David, *Empowering Voices from the Past: The Playing Experiences of Retired Pasifika Rugby League Athletes in Australia*, Routledge, 2019

Lakisa, David, *Pasifika Diaspora and the Changing Face of Australian Rugby League*, University of Hawai'i Press, 2014

Lakisa, David, '*The Pacific Revolution: Pasifika and Maori players in Australian Rugby League*', University of Technology Master's Dissertation, 2017

Losada, Marcial, *Positive Affect and the Complex Dynamics of Human Flourishing*, American Psychologist, 2005

ABOUT THE AUTHOR

PATRICK SKENE was born and raised in Sydney and writes stories on the intersection of sport, history and culture. His work has appeared in *Guardian Australia*, *The Age*, *Inside Sport*, 'Boxing.com' and *Footy Almanac*. He previously hosted an Aboriginal sports history radio programme on the National Indigenous Radio Service and a boxing programme on SEN Radio Melbourne. *The Big O* is his first book.